LIFE IN THE KEY OF RUBINI

A Hollywood Child Prodigy and His Wild Adventures in Crime, Music, Sex, Sinatra and Wonder Woman

Michel Rubini

DISCLAIMER

This book is a memoir; as such it reflects the author's recollections of his experiences over a number of years. Dialog and events have been recreated from memory, and in some chapters, have been compressed to the essence of what was said or took place. Some names and identities have been altered.

www.michelrubini.com

Cover Design by Laura Duffy

Index by WordCo.com

TABLE OF CONTENTS

ONE

Raquel Welch

One afternoon, in 1962, I received a call from Harry Fields, my piano teacher, who said some young actress had phoned him to ask if he would be willing to play on an audition for her the next week. Her name was Raquel-something and Harry told her to call me instead because he couldn't leave his studio for such a small job. Also, the woman said she didn't have the money to pay him the amount he would normally receive anyway. So, Harry thought it might be a good gig for me, since, as his star pupil, I had been successfully doing some *overflow* teaching for him on the side. Thanking Harry for the opportunity, I said I would be happy to do it and would wait to hear from her.

Sometime later, I received a call from the actress who then told me when and where the audition was being held (over at the CBS-owned Columbia Square recording studios on Sunset Boulevard in Hollywood). At the end of our short conversation, I agreed to do it, not because of the money, but mainly because she sounded cute. What better way to meet a girl than to have her drive to my house and pay me?

So we set an appointment, and Raquel rang my doorbell right on time. Of course, I didn't know what the girl on the other side of the door was going to look like. But when I opened it up, I was stunned. She was gorgeous. I guarantee you that if Harry had known how beautiful Raquel was, he would have never turned her over to me. She would have been given the full Harry Fields bachelor treatment, and I would never have met her.

But here a young Raquel Welch was, standing in front of me, so I invited her in and asked if she had brought her sheet music. She sheepishly replied that she didn't have any but quickly added that for the audition, she already knew what she wanted to do in terms of singing and dancing and would show me.

So I sat at the piano, found her key, and we started practicing right there in my living room. Here was the yet-to-be-discovered Raquel Welch, singing and dancing around on my carpet. It was actually quite funny, though she, of course, didn't intend it to be. In fact I couldn't take my eyes off of her, even though in my opinion she was a terrible dancer and not much better than that at vocals. It was quite comical seeing her breathing hard and trying to do ballet turns and tap steps on my carpet. But I managed to keep a straight face and just waded through the routine on my piano like a professional. When Raquel finally finished and got her breath back, she confided that she was really nervous about the audition but she had to get a job. Although this was only a small part on some TV variety show, she thought that if she made a strong impression, it would be a good stepping stone toward more work. She really wanted to become a dramatic actress but so far had not had any luck.

Sympathizing with her plight, I encouraged her and told her she would be great, that the producers would love her and to have no fear. Raquel said she didn't have much money but could pay me twenty-five dollars for the audition. I said fine and we shook hands. I had already decided that I wasn't going to take any payment from this stunning young thing anyway. She obviously needed the money a lot more than I did. And, quite honestly, I was thinking about something else entirely—and believe me, it wasn't money.

At that time, Raquel was living in a little one-bedroom apartment in a seedy section of East Hollywood, an area full of bars, pool halls, drunks, and hookers. It wasn't by choice; she had only moved there with her two children because it was all she could afford.

On the big day, I picked up Raquel in my convertible and we zipped over to CBS. Stepping inside the audition room, she introduced herself to the five or so executives who were sitting at a long luncheon-style table. I plopped down at the piano and, on cue, began playing the intro we had worked out. With no soundproofing, the room sounded like a small cavern, which certainly didn't help matters.

As Raquel launched into her song in front of these five strangers, they had no idea, of course, who they were looking at. To them, she was just another pretty face in a long line of pretty faces that came and went in Hollywood. Little did they know that in another few years, she would become known as the most desirable woman on earth. If the execs had perceived anything at all, they would have hired her on the spot. But they were just too preoccupied to realize that they were looking at a diamond in the rough.

While Raquel busily sang her heart out, I could see they were talking among themselves, not giving her the attention and courtesy that anyone auditioning deserves. Then when she broke into her dance routine, somewhere in the middle of it, one of the people behind the table abruptly said to her, "That will be fine, thank you. We'll call you." And that was that. Raquel picked up her folder and together we walked out of the room.

With Raquel on the verge of tears, I comforted her as best I could and told her that she didn't need to pay me for the audition. I said that she could owe it to me and pay me when she became a star. I was so attracted to her, I wanted to reach out and kiss her right then and there in the car. But I didn't because she was obviously so upset by the rejection at the audition.

After getting her home, I walked into her apartment and saw her children in the bedroom. She offered me a glass of water, and before I knew what was happening, I impulsively asked her to go out on a date. I just couldn't help myself, figuring that if I didn't do it then, I would never have another chance. So I blurted out that I would really like to see her again. Much to my chagrin, Raquel delicately turned me down.

Being two years older than I, I'm sure Raquel saw me as some hormone-driven kid, which I basically was. The distance between my boyish nineteen and her ever-so-womanly twenty-one (soon to be twenty-two) approximated the width of the Grand Canyon, though I didn't realize it at the time. She politely gave me some obviously well-practiced excuses, but the truth is she likely just wasn't that attracted to me. Oh well, you can't win if you don't play.

So we shared a little goodbye hug, and I walked out the door and out of her life. Though I thought about Raquel on and off for weeks after, wondering what would become of her.

Finally, one day in early 1964, I received my answer. Idly flipping through the channels on my TV, I happened to land on a new, hour-long variety show on ABC called *The Hollywood Palace*. The show's format was to announce the impending performance of each act in the style of old-time vaudeville shows by having a big card on an easel at the side of the stage with the performer's name on it. A *billboard girl* dressed in a skimpy, pinup-style outfit would come out and change the card accordingly. And guess who that girl was? It was Raquel!

Totally amazed, I was also thrilled for her. Raquel finally got a job on TV, even if only in a minor role. But let me tell you, she made the most of her airtime. She would come out, lean over a little bit farther than necessary, giving the audience an unexpected treat while at the same time removing one card and replacing it with the next. The crowd whooped, hollered, and applauded. Sometimes she received more applause than the act whose name was on the card. I knew right then that Raquel was on her way to stardom.

Sure enough, not long after, I noticed her posing on the cover of some fan magazine in her *One Million Years B.C.* costumes, now a bona fide movie star and sex goddess. Just think—Raquel Welch still owes me twenty-five bucks to this day. If I could only collect the interest on *that* debt!

Of course, my encounter with the young, pre-fame Raquel is just a small example of the many funny, unexpected, heartbreaking, exhilarating, and sometimes downright terrifying events that have occurred throughout my seventy-plus years on this planet. Each, in its own way—usually for the better, but sometimes not so much—has served to shape both my destiny and me. The things I've done, the people that have befriended me, and the places and situations I've found myself in during my long career in the music business (as well as outside of it) are all something I never could have imagined coming my way.

And, as with everyone, it all started during my childhood. Though mine was probably a little different than yours...

TWO

Born to a Musical Family

M y father: a world-famous concert violinist in the '30s, '40s, and '50s. My mother: a beautiful Hollywood starlet under contract to RKO and Paramount.

It sounds like a match made in heaven, right?

Wrong.

Jan Rubini, my father, made his grand entrance into this world somewhere between 1895 and 1904, depending on which passport or driver's license you wish to believe. He never told anyone his age and never admitted to being more than thirty-nine years old, stealing a classic joke from his old friend and fellow violin player Jack Benny who made that a staple of his comedy repertoire.

Born in Stockholm to a completely musical family, Dad spent the first couple of years of his childhood in Sweden (his father was the headmaster at the Stockholm Conservatory). Shortly thereafter, he moved with the rest of his family to London, England, where he was raised and became a child prodigy, even playing for the Queen when he was just a little boy. He then toured for several years all over the continent with two of his three sisters as "The Child Trio," with the girls playing cello and flute.

Boldly leaving home around the age of sixteen, my father traveled by ship to New York, immediately found a theatrical agent, and in remarkably short time made a name for himself in the vaudeville theatres up and down the East Coast. Possessing a great flair for staging and drama, he soon had all the ladies swooning for him at the stage door every night, a situation that he took advantage of with great delight. His reputation as a headlining entertainer soon spread from coast to coast, resulting in engagements nationwide, including Hollywood, where he soon found himself billed at the top of the marquee of the Pantages Theatre over a young, up-and-coming comedian by the name of Bob Hope.

As he easily made friends with some of Hollywood's most famous (and famously carousing) stars of the day, such as Errol Flynn and Gilbert Roland, my father was soon asked to play his fiddle in the movies, as well. Now accepted by Hollywood's most famous celebrities, he became violinist to the stars and enjoyed the intimate favors of more actresses than any normal mortal could imagine. He truly had the "magic violin" and used it happily whenever the occasion called for it. Although he married early on to a lovely dancer named Diane Aubry, the word "monogamy" seemed to elude my father's vocabulary. He loved women, and they loved him back. And he kept secret many of the details of his dalliances until late in life. For example, only around 1987, when he was somewhere around ninety, did I shockingly become aware that I had a half-sister who was born in the same year as my younger brother David, which means my dad was involved with someone in addition to my mother and the two women conceived almost simultaneously. How about that for being a prolific violinist!

My mother was born Alice Norberg in 1913 in Petersburg, Alaska. At least I can be sure of *her* actual birthdate. Mom's parents had emigrated from Norway around the turn of the century and settled in this little Alaskan fishing village of only five hundred eighty-five very tough and hardy Norwegians, along with a sprinkling of Native Americans thrown in for good measure. When of school age, my mother did not travel there in a yellow bus like other kids in the lower forty-eight; rather, she rowed a small boat a mile across the bay to the local schoolhouse everyday—come rain, snow, or sleet. Later, when photographed for the glamor mags and studio publicity shots of the day, you could still see the muscularity in her arms and back that the other starlets lacked.

Mom came from exceptional stock. My grandfather, Charlie, and my grandmother, Alfina, were true pioneers. I cannot imagine the hardship they and their families must have endured at that time crossing the Atlantic Ocean and then traveling, only God knows how, across the whole northern United States to Seattle and then up to Alaska.

Grandpa Charlie, a tireless worker, had three professions. He was a fisherman, a gold miner, and a fox farmer. I have seen pictures of him standing next to a giant halibut taller than he was and another photo of him with about six or seven red foxes following him across the yard like a line of chicks following a mother hen. He also started the Bank of Petersburg by commandeering an outhouse in the middle of the town and placing a guard outside it so he and his fellow miners would have a safe place to keep their nuggets and bags of gold dust. He was an amazing man.

Wanting more than to be a fisherman's wife, when my mother was old enough to leave home, she traveled down the West Coast and finally landed in Hollywood with her new stage name, Terry Walker. With her strikingly attractive features and talent to spare, she got her start first working as a lounge singer and by 1933, at the age of only twenty, got her first movie role. Some of her leading men were actors as famous as Bela Lugosi (in the 1941 hit *Invisible Ghost*) and Milburn Stone (in the 1937 action thriller *Federal Bullets*). I'm sure we all affectionately remember Stone as old "Doc" in the classic western TV series *Gunsmoke*.

To give you a little glimpse into my mother's background . . . She was also under contract at different times to RKO, Monogram Pictures, and Columbia Pictures. She was a *starlet* in every sense of the word and was on her way up the B-movie ladder to fame and fortune. But, as with so many girls before and after her, she met my father. And though she tried her best not to fall for his amorous overtures, he seduced her nonetheless, and they married in 1940. I was born a couple of years later in 1942, which she used as a convenient excuse to retire from her acting career, and my brother (and only full sibling) David, followed me in 1945, and that gives you a little glimpse into my mother's background.

Oh, and she was also an alcoholic.

THREE

The Amazing Child Prodigy

M y earliest childhood memory is of me lying in my crib watching my father practice his violin. He would spend what seemed like hours tuning the A and D strings. There was a routine of his that hardly ever changed.

First, he would work to get a perfect pitch on the A string of 440 Hz (that's the speed at which the string vibrates—440 times per second). He didn't have perfect pitch himself, so he always went to the piano to hit the A above middle C key and then tuned his violin accordingly. Later, he bought a little tuning whistle that he would stick in his mouth, put the violin under his chin, and then blow it while simultaneously twisting the peg of the violin's A string to match. That was a lot of *A* sounds for one baby to hear, day in and day out. Imagine any noise you want and think of it being pumped into your brain every day of your life. I'm sure you can see how you might never forget that exact tone; for me it was the incessant A440. Sometimes when my doorbell rings, I even have flashbacks.

Next, my dad would tune the D string on his violin to get the most pleasing (if not perfect) fifth sound. Without going too deeply into music theory, in Western culture, a fifth is the interval from the first to the last of five consecutive notes in a diatonic scale. So, he would play the two strings together and turn the D tuning peg for what seemed like hours to achieve that fifth note. Once he had those two strings (the A and the D) where he liked them, it always seemed easy for my father to then tune his G and E strings (the violin only has four strings). When onstage, Dad used to make a joke, something about "tuning his G-string." Being young, I didn't get it, of course. But the well-dressed, upscale audiences always laughed in embarrassment. It wasn't until he introduced me later to my first striptease artist that I found out about the *other* meaning.

That A440 became my first vehicle toward being the center of attention in a crowd. Since I knew that note perfectly, I could instantly identify the name of any other note on the piano because of its relationship to that A. Actually, by the time I was four years old, I could recognize the pitch of any note or set of notes on the piano while sitting across the room. This achievement amazed even my father, who would show off my abilities at any time to his friends when they visited on weekends at our beachfront home.

Dad loved to host parties for his Malibu colony pals and neighbors, most of whom were in the entertainment industry in some capacity. He always wound up performing a few selections on his violin for his guests, and it was at this point that he would often trot me out and have me display my peculiar talent, which I thought at the time was really nothing more than a cheap parlor trick. Even so, I could not help but notice how everybody thought I was a musical genius. They would all comment about how cute and talented I was, asking my father if I was going to follow in his footsteps and be a famous concert artist like him. He always said "yes," an answer to which I basically gave little thought.

With world-class musicianship happening to be our family's line of work, like the son of a plumber or a lawyer, I naturally just assumed I would do the same. There never was an option presented to me, anyway. However, I also noticed how the ladies in the crowd loved to hug and kiss me, something that I did not understand, but certainly enjoyed. I have often thought that this may have been what got me interested in the opposite sex at such an early age.

FOUR

Practice Time, Not Play Time

My parents first noticed my unusual ability to organize notes on the piano when I was about three years old. At the time, we were staying in Australia, where my father headlined at one of the big vaudeville theatres that were so popular there during the mid-to-late 1940s. After witnessing my precocious keyboard skills, he and my mom decided they would start me on piano lessons when we returned to the United States.

In that regard, we were fortunate to live next door in Malibu to a lovely little old lady piano teacher named Peg Thompson. She started me off with the standard fare that all young students learn: scales, finger exercises, and simple pieces such as "Mary Had a Little Lamb." We bought the books, I started to practice, and I moved along quite rapidly. In fact, I excelled much more quickly than my teacher had anticipated, taking her by surprise. She was confused by the way I was progressing because it wasn't the normal way of doing things. I was not advancing in my scales and exercises nearly as fast as I was in the songs she assigned me, which in her world made no sense. Scales and exercises, though tedious, are the building blocks students usually need to practice over and over in order to (hopefully) play ever more complex passages. But I didn't need to do all that because I had a secret weapon: my perfect pitch.

You see, I was not practicing my scales and exercises much because I hated them. Instead, I was able to memorize and play the pieces quite easily because I would simply watch her play them for me at each lesson. Between watching her fingers and listening carefully, I could repeat any given piano passage almost without mistakes. What I was *not* doing was practicing my reading like I should have, so really I was already trying to find the easy way out rather than sitting down and doing the hard work necessary to become a real pianist.

Much to my chagrin, my little attempt at subterfuge did not go on for long, though, because Mrs. Thompson was much smarter than I thought. She went to my mother and told her that I was a gifted but difficult student because of my perfect pitch and, if they were serious about having me become a proper pianist, they were going to have to make me really practice. Further, my teacher said that I needed a stricter and stronger instructor than she, a teacher capable of really challenging and controlling me. So she recommended Mr. Herman Wasserman, if he would accept me as a student that is. Thus, my little ruse and easy times came to an abrupt end.

Known as the finest piano teacher in all of Los Angeles and arguably the entire country, Wasserman had taught pianists and compositional luminaries Ferde Grofé and George Gershwin. He even edited and fingered all of Gershwin's songbooks, too. Needless to say, Wasserman was the real deal. I started lessons and studied with him until I was fourteen and a half (when he suddenly died). But those years under his tutelage were the most critical in my development and set me on a path for life. I could never have thanked him enough, and when he died, I stopped playing piano for almost a year and a half.

From the beginning, Wasserman taught me the most important thing anyone could ever learn from his or her teacher: how to teach yourself. He knew he wouldn't be alive forever and that every great pianist, myself included, must eventually develop the ability to teach himself. Otherwise, how would that person—just like Arthur Rubinstein and Vladimir Horowitz, who both ceased having piano teachers long before they became world famous—possibly continue to grow as a skilled musician into adulthood and beyond?

So, with my subsequent reassignment to Mr. Wasserman, I began my real and many hard years of pure drudgery, being forced by my mother to practice at least one, and often up to two and half, hours every day. One hour before breakfast and school and then at least one hour after school and before dinner. If I didn't get in at least an hour of practice before school, then my mom made me add that to the hour after school. To make matters worse, she made it a habit to sit right next to me on the piano bench for the hour after school and watch me practice. She could read music, so when I made a mistake or began faking it, she would stop me and make me do it again until I got it right.

There was something else my mother did that was particularly painful to me. Being born of good, strong Norwegian stock and therefore having powerful hands and arms, she learned a trick (I don't know from whom) that she performed with the knuckle on the third finger of her left hand; she called it her Norwegian fist. Making her fingers into a ball, but sticking out the third knuckle about an inch, she would jam that into the middle of my ribs every time I started to slouch over the keyboard. "Sit up straight," she would command, and believe me I did. I learned early on that I had better do as she said or risk paying for it with some very hard Norwegian knuckle sandwiches.

Since I had to practice every day after school, I hardly ever got to go outside and play with the other kids. There was a big, vacant parking area right across the street from our house where the neighborhood kids gathered to play kickball until dark when they had to go home and eat dinner. We all got off the school bus at the same time, but I was the only one who had to go in the house. There, I would have a fast sandwich and then march over to the piano and practice, while outside, all the other kids would be having fun and kicking their ball all over the place. Sometimes I would walk up to the front gate and look wistfully across the street at the children for a minute or two. But my mom would invariably call me back into the house and tell me that if I finished my practice soon enough I could go out and play with them. Except, the only problem was that it always got dark or dinner was about to be served by the time I finished practicing, so I never got to go out and play with them, other than sometimes on the weekends. Those were my first few years of learning to play the piano in a nutshell.

Now, while I was learning my scales, exercises, and pieces, my father had another idea. He thought it would be just grand if I started to learn some of the accompaniments to his concert violin pieces. Not the hard ones, you understand, at least by his standards. Just the *easy* ones, like Träumerei by Schubert, which most adults couldn't even come close to playing. Dad thought it would be fun to trot me out at his parties and receive the accolades for being the father of such a talented young son. Now believe it or not, this really wasn't much of a stretch for me even at that age—I was only six —because I had been hearing these pieces ever since I was born. I already knew them in my mind; I had just never played them. But when my father put the music in front of me, all I had to do was to look at the notes to learn the routine and exact fingering, etc. And from there, I was playing them in no time.

By the time I was eight or nine, I was playing most of Dad's repertoire almost as well as his regular professional accompanist. By the time I was fourteen, I had *become* his regular accompanist. He replaced his old friend and longtime piano player, a gentleman who had been by his side for about twenty years, and instead started using me for all his shows. As long as they were in the Los Angeles area and did not interfere with my schooling, that is (my mother saw to that). I'm sure I saved my dad thousands of dollars in accompanist fees and in return received nothing more than my regular allowance that started at twenty-five cents a week. When you think about it, it gives new meaning to the phrase "child labor," doesn't it?

But there were lots of concerts that I did not play when they were held out of town. In particular, there was one trip I wanted to go on very badly, but my mom put her foot down and said absolutely not, not under any circumstances. And that was my father's last trip to South Africa in 1952. He had a tour set up there, and he ended up being gone for six months straight, performing over there to sold-out theatres every night, and during the days going on safari to see the lions and giraffes and Zulu warriors in an adventure I could only dream about. Being ten years old at the time and crazy about wild animals and far away places like Africa, I cried and begged my mom to distraction to let me go, but she wouldn't hear of it. There would be no missing school for me. My father would just have to pay his regular guy to go with him and leave me home. No fun at all, I tell you.

However, all the enforced isolation and practice paid off in the long run, because by the time I was sixteen, I became my father's regular accompanist and even dropped out of high school for a year just to tour with him all over America. Those were some memorable times, which I'll talk about later in another chapter. But since I missed that year of high school, I had to go back and make it up, finally graduating a year late (in 1961) at the ripe old age of eighteen and a half.

By the way, whenever anybody asks me why I always go to the gym alone, I tell him or her it is because I never really learned how to play with the other kids. The piano was my only friend. Kind of sad, really.

FIVE

It Starts Oh, So Young

A grade-schooler being invited into the living room of a rich old woman. A boy being coerced into an apartment to see some stereo equipment. A young teen being tucked into bed by his mother. A high-schooler being told that men can be friends without being queer.

C hild abuse comes in all forms. That is not news. Any type of abuse is terrible, of course, but sexual abuse, to me, is the worst of them all. When my father whipped me with his belt when I was a child, I might have hated him for a while afterward. I occasionally even had a few scabs from it, but they always faded in time. And as I got older, I understood that he did it because he simply didn't know any better; it was the way he was raised. My dad genuinely thought he was doing the right thing by disciplining me in such a manner. I long ago forgave him for that and don't feel permanently affected by any of it.

But sexual abuse is another story altogether. I know; it happened to me. Molestation, whether by parents, friends or strangers, stays with us all through our lives and many times twists us up in knots that we cannot seem to untie and, therefore, affects our attitudes toward other human beings until the day we die. Now I am not talking about the older woman who seduces a younger man. For all the uproar that it receives in the news, I can tell you firsthand that neither I nor any of my other male friends who were lucky enough to have experienced that have ever been sorry that it happened. We all considered ourselves to be the luckiest kids on the block and my personal thank-you goes out to all those lovely older ladies who took the time and effort to teach us poor young lads the finer points of the art of lovemaking and how to treat a woman in the manner that they want and so richly deserve.

When I say sexual abuse, I am referring to predators who prey on little kids, in my case older men who saw me as just an object to satisfy some weird sexual fantasy and gave no mind to what they would be doing to my psyche for the rest of my life, though once, that abuse came from a very old lady and once from my mother. Those two were the exceptions to my statement about older women seducing young men.

The first incident was not particularly serious in the sense that my psyche was not forever warped by what transpired. To be sure, it was not pleasant, but I survived and pretty much put it in the back of my mind as I grew older. When I was about eight, my father met a wealthy oil heiress named Elsinore Machris Gilliland. She lived in Palm Springs part of the year and threw a lot of parties, sponsored big events, and gave millions to charity, etc. She became interested in my father, who in turn was never one to ignore the possibility of advancing his own interests through returned affection. Mrs. Gilliland also apparently had some designs on me, though I was unaware because of my age. Of course, she had to be careful how she approached my father because, after all, she was a married woman at that time and needed some excuse to put her, my father and me together without raising the suspicions of her husband and friends. What she decided to do was offer me a scholarship to the Conservatoire de Paris (Paris Conservatory), a prestigious and extremely expensive institution.

In any case, she wanted to interview me privately to determine if I had the talent to deserve the gift she was about to bestow on me. She invited my father and me to her house one weekend afternoon to attend a poolside cocktail party that she was throwing for some friends. Gilliland was about seventy at the time and looked twice that from spending about sixty-five of those years in the sun. She had the most wrinkled up skin I had ever seen, and she didn't mind showing it all off by wearing a skimpy and loose bikini the day we arrived.

After introducing us to her guests on the patio and telling them how talented I was and how she was going to sponsor my musical education by paying to send me to Paris, she excused herself and took me inside to the living room that was conveniently blocked from outside view by very fashionable and thick drapes over the windows. She proceeded to ask me a few questions about how I would feel being separated from my family and friends by living in Paris. While listening to me answer the best I could, she simultaneously leaned forward as if to turn off the radio or something and her breasts conveniently tumbled out of her bikini top. She didn't seem to mind that I was standing there in front of her, hypnotized. I was absolutely frightened to death and didn't know what to do. Casually cupping one, she lifted it up and deposited it back into her top, then did the same with the other. She then walked over and gave me a big hug, making sure my face was plastered against her bra top, with her oily and wrinkly old skin pressing against my red and embarrassed little face.

At that point my father entered the room, and they had a bit of a discussion regarding some details that I did not understand. They made a plan to get together in the near future, and then the three of us walked outside to rejoin the party. She never did fulfill her promise to sponsor my future, by the way. I guess my dad didn't respond favorably to her offer, and I don't blame him. Fortunately, he never found out what happened in that room.

My next incident, however, was much more serious. I was twelve and had just learned about the wonders of masturbation. Yes, my hormones were going full tilt like every other kid my age, but I was still a virgin. By that time, my parents were separated and my mother, brother, grandmother, and I had moved to Palm Springs, while my father remained in Los Angeles. I ended up spending a year there but still took piano lessons in L.A.

So once a week on Saturday, my mother would put me on the Greyhound bus to Hollywood and my father would pick me up at the station and take me to my lesson. Afterward, I would spend the night with him and the next day he would put me back on the bus to Palm Springs.

On one particular Sunday after my lesson in Los Angeles, I arrived at the bus station back in Palm Springs but my mother was nowhere to be found. Not knowing what to do, I figured I would just hoof it over to the Biltmore Hotel where my mom was working. As I walked down Indian Avenue, I happened to pass a parked van that had its back door open. Inside, I saw a lot of electronic gear. It turned out the vehicle belonged to a local radio station. There was a guy working in it who saw me and said hello. I said hello back and then, forever curious, I made the mistake of asking him what all the equipment was used for. He told me that he was a disc jockey and that he had a live radio show that aired all over the region.

He asked me what I was doing and I told him I was walking back home because my mom did not pick me up. He volunteered to drive me back if I didn't mind waiting a little bit while he finished his work. Being fascinated with electronics and also not wanting to walk all the way to the Biltmore in the desert heat, I said sure. Inviting me upstairs to his apartment, which was right there on Indian Avenue, he asked if I would like something to drink and I said yes. As we chatted for a while, I told him I was going to play piano at an event at the Biltmore Hotel the next day and he said that he would definitely be there to record it. Of course, I was very excited by that. He said that he would love to record me live and put it on his radio show, maybe that I would even become famous or something like that.

The DJ then changed the conversation. He asked me if I had any girlfriends and did I fuck them. He wanted to know, too, if I used rubbers or if I just did it without them. These were really weird questions to be asking, especially of a twelve-year-old kid. It caught me off guard and I was really confused about where this was all going. He then told me something to the effect that *real* men always used rubbers and we real men should always have some with us just in case we ever got together with a girl. He also told me how they were really handy to have when you jacked off because you would come in them and it wouldn't go all over the place. He said that he had lots of rubbers, that he would give me some, and then asked if I knew how to use them.

Before I knew what was happening, the guy dropped his pants and started masturbating right there while sitting in his easy chair. He said he was showing me how to do what all men did when there were no women around. Of course, I was in shock. I was sitting across the room and somehow did not have enough sense to get up and run out the door. He then put on a rubber and continued to jack off while asking me if I wanted to try it with him, even offering to put on the rubber for me and jack me off. I quickly said no thanks. In short order, he ejaculated into his rubber, then took it off and put on another. He told me again he would be happy to do it to me if I wanted. But I managed to pull myself together enough so that he may have started to get a little nervous; I guess he didn't want to push his luck. He handed me five or six Trojan condoms, probably hoping that the bribe would keep my mouth shut about the incident, and then offered to drive me back to the Biltmore, and with no other option I could think of, I accepted.

By then, I felt like the most dangerous part was over and I still really wanted to be recorded and put on the radio. How naïve and self-absorbed can a little boy be? The guy did drive me back to the hotel and actually did show up Monday for my concert. And just as he promised, he recorded the whole thing, dutifully broadcast it on the radio station, and it was even reviewed in the local newspaper, *The Desert Sun*, on Thursday, May 19, 1955. I remember it all like it was yesterday. The headline read, "Throng Thrilled by Young Pianist." If the good folks who attended this get-together had only known what their local DJ had done to me the day before, I'm sure there would have been a lynching instead of a recording.

A number of months went by after my encounter with the perverted DJ and my family and I finally moved back to the Los Angeles area. My parents officially divorced, and my mom bought a little house in Studio City, which is a suburb on the San Fernando Valley side of the Hollywood Hills. I was about fourteen by then and now fully in the throes of puberty.

One night at the new house, while lying in my bed in the dark, I developed a spontaneous erection, which is nothing unusual for a boy of that age. Unfortunately, my timing couldn't have been worse. In the moment while it was there, my mother opened the door to my bedroom, her breath reeking of alcohol, which was the usual state of affairs in those days. She then sat down on the edge of the bed and started talking to me, mumbling stuff I didn't understand or care about. Finally she said good night to me, and then kissed me on the lips; a big, wet, juicy French kiss. At the same time, she put her hand on my erection and said "My little man..."

I immediately jerked away from her, flipping onto my stomach so fast that it almost threw her off the bed. She kept muttering about "my little man" but couldn't make me turn over. She then started to cry and left the room. I was afraid she might return and do something else so I lay there frightened, confused, and on guard all night long. Thank God, she didn't.

Our relationship from that point forward was strained, to say the least, but fortunately there was no repeat performance of that ugly, bitter night. Outside the house, I had yet more problems to deal with. During that period, while attending North Hollywood Junior High School, I didn't fit in with any group, had no real friends, wore my hair in a ducktail, and mostly just tried to look tough so other kids wouldn't pick fights with me. More so, I desperately wanted a girlfriend or at least some girl that wanted to fool around as much as I did. Finally, I did get lucky. I found one who was just as horny as I was and whose parents were never home, at least in the afternoons. After a short romance, we started doing it in every position I could think of and she was a remarkably willing partner.

At the same time, my mother was going crazy because she knew why I was not coming home after school—I had discovered girls. She actually started driving around the neighborhood looking for me. One day, eventually, she found me walking on the street with that girl. Mom jumped out of her car and started screaming at my girlfriend to get away from me and leave me alone, then bellowed at me to get into the car, which I refused to do. Getting nowhere, she finally drove off and I walked home, taking as long as possible to get there. I knew Mom was drunk, as usual, and it was not going to be a good time once I got back to the house.

When I finally arrived, my mother and I had a real shouting match in my bedroom, something about how I was ruining young girls' lives and that I should go to a whorehouse if that's what I wanted. Then she slapped my face. By this time, I was taller and stronger than her and I wasn't going to absorb that kind of abuse anymore, especially from her. I had already been in too many schoolyard fights to count and just wasn't going to take it. So I said to her very simply, "If you ever slap me again, I will slap you back. Don't do it again."

My mother couldn't believe her ears and slapped me again, as if to test my resolve. I immediately slapped her back. She looked at me with the most shocked and desperate expression I could ever describe. Tears sprang from her eyes, and after a moment, she turned and stumbled out of the bedroom. It is the only time I have ever hit a woman. That was also the end of my relationship with my mother.

As time marched on, I learned fast how twisted some people could be. By the time I entered high school, I was well aware of what were then called "fags" and "homos." A lot of people thought I was one, because supposedly I had a girl's name, had curly hair, and played the piano, not football like all the macho guys. I heard stories about homos and how they did all that weird stuff, and I was always on the lookout for anyone who would try something funny on me, especially given my prior experience with that Palm Springs DJ. And try they did. I was getting hit on, it seemed like once a week by somebody, sometimes even by famous people. Remember, I lived in Hollywood, the home of the homos.

Once, at my father's house up on Summit Ridge Drive in Beverly Hills, I was on the vacant lot next door, target practicing with my chromed .22 caliber six-shooter. The area was in Benedict Canyon above the Beverly Hills Hotel and there were really no neighbors. We were in the last house on the street and from there it was just a fire trail, so I could shoot my gun all day and nobody became any the wiser. I was wearing just a racing style swimsuit, my sunglasses, some tennis shoes, and my holster.

But one day, none other than Tab Hunter, the teen idol and movie star, came driving up in his convertible and spotted me there in the vacant lot with my gun. I must have really roused his interest because he jumped out of his car and immediately introduced himself. I knew who he was; I had seen him in films, but was not impressed because I had been raised in show business. I had already met dozens of stars. Anyway, I politely shook his hand and introduced myself in return. Tab told me he was looking for a house to rent or buy and that he saw our place and loved it. He then asked if he could look at the inside. Though my father was not home at the time, I figured it would be better to show it to him than turn him away, so I said okay.

All I can say is that Tab Hunter followed me so closely all through the tour of my home that his jeans and my swimsuit were making static electricity. It got so bad that by the time I showed him the first bathroom, I refused to go in ahead of him. I stepped to the side and motioned with my arm for him to enter first. From that point, I wouldn't walk through a doorway in front of him; I kept on waving him ahead in order to avoid the constant *collisions*. Tab never did buy my dad's house, as you might have guessed, and I learned yet another unwanted lesson about certain types of men being attracted to me.

My next sexual abuse experience, however, proved to be the worst of all. This one poisoned any objectivity I might have had toward gay men for years to come. I have never really gotten over it. This is not easy to write, so it may not be easy to read.

When I was seventeen, I lived much of the time at my dad's Beverly Hills house (my mom and younger brother had by then moved to New Jersey). At the time, I was restless, troubled, and generally unhappy with my life, feeling that I had enormous potential and wanting to do something with it beyond just being my father's accompanist. I played in a couple of jazz/rock groups at school, but that wasn't much fun because nobody could play at my level.

Here is an example of where I was musically at the age of sixteen. After learning of a three-month concert tour I had just completed with my dad at schools and colleges throughout the Northwest territory of our country, the principal of Hollywood High School (where I attended) asked the two of us to perform a full one-hour concert for the two-thousand-plus students in my school's auditorium that my father gracefully accepted. We subsequently did so and blew everyone away to a standing ovation. Of course, this would also be a good place for me to note that even with that unique, lofty accomplishment, I nonetheless graduated from high school with a *D* in music, but that is another story.

Mostly, I just floated along throughout high school, wondering what was going to happen to me. I seemed to be trapped in this world of classical music, with no future except to be a pianist on tour for the rest of my life. Which was not at all appealing, because by then, I had been exposed to the joys of rock and roll, black church choirs, blues, jazz, and more. Those were the styles of music that excited me. My father, having noticed my lack of interest in classical music, even found a jazz piano teacher for me to help perk up my interest in studying further. A seemingly noble effort, except that Dad only allowed me to attend with the proviso in place that the teacher would give me half a lesson in jazz and the other half in classical music during each visit. All this started when I was about fifteen.

With my father knowing some of the older agents at the William Morris Agency in Beverly Hills (that had been his agency in years past), he went to them to see if they might have some idea of what to do with me as a talent. They told him that one of their younger agents would call and make an appointment to meet me. I did get that phone call, and I had a meeting down at their building in Beverly Hills with him. The guy said he would need to come to the house and hear me play so he could get an idea of how best to market me.

We set a day and time for him to come over, and he showed up as scheduled. My father was not there. The junior agent sat on the couch and listened while I played him some stuff, a mix of classical pieces and some jazz/blues improvisations. When I finished, he asked me to sit down with him so we could talk and get to know each other better. He said that it was important for us to be friends, not just to be artist and agent. He let me know that he could only help me if we were really friends and that was how relationships in the business were developed. Everybody knew each other really well and were friends, which all made sense to me. But remember, I was only seventeen and had no experience dealing with agents, so what did I know? And then the conversation took a strange and abrupt change in direction.

Out of nowhere the young agent informed me that men could be good friends without being queer, that it was the way things were done between friends. Two men could enjoy each other's company in a sexual way and it didn't mean that they didn't like women. Of course, he liked women, he said, but when there were no women around, having sex with friends was a fine thing to do and it cemented relationships

I could see where this was going, and it was not good. But I was so very desperate to do something with myself, to make a name, to become famous, to have a career, and I didn't have the faintest idea about how to do it. I also thought that I had to have an agent to get any jobs. And with William Morris being the biggest talent agency in the world at the time, I figured it might be my only chance. Though I was repelled by this guy and frantically wished there was any other way to secure reliable, well-known representation, it seemed at that moment that the only way to get ahead was to let this guy have sex with me.

Yet, I told him that I couldn't do it; it ground against every instinct I had. But he pushed on anyway. He countered that it would be our secret and would never happen again; it would just be a one-time thing, a way to solidify our "friendship." Confused and intimidated, not able to think straight nor fast enough to stop this nightmare, and with my self-esteem and confidence now obliterated, I somehow let him lead me toward the guest bedroom. It was the most disgusting thing I have ever done in my life. We both got undressed and I lay down on the bed next to him. He was already erect, and he wanted us to put our arms around each other and kiss. There was no way I could do that and told him so. I just wanted to get this thing over with. So he started working his way down my chest and stomach until he put my penis in his mouth and started sucking and whimpering, making noises I cannot describe. All I could think of was please, God, let me come and maybe it will all end.

Finally, through gritted teeth, I did so and I thought that would be it. But I was wrong. The guy then led me into the bathroom, sat on the toilet, and told me to walk up to him so he could suck me some more while he masturbated into it. I cannot describe the sickening feeling I had while this was happening, but I had crossed some threshold that I could not retreat from and it was too late. I don't know to this day how I could have let myself be put in that position.

I've never gotten over this encounter, but at least now it's just a terrible memory that I have banished to the darkest reaches of my mind. However, occasionally when something triggers it, a gut-wrenching knot explodes in the pit of my stomach; everything stops, and uncontrollable tears spring from my eyes. It's a feeling I wouldn't wish upon my worst enemy.

And what of that agent whose name I cannot remember? I do not know. I can tell you that I never got a contract from him and he never got me a job. Nothing ever developed regarding my career from the William Morris Agency. All I can say for sure is that even if someone is seventeen like I was and seemingly almost an adult and capable of sexual consent, they are not. It is still putrid child abuse, pure and simple, and the scar doesn't fade with time.

SIX

Problem Childhood

E verybody has problems as a kid. I know that. It's just a part of growing up. I am not special in that regard. I had my share of difficulties
like everyone else. But now, when I look at the news, I see how lucky I was
compared to so many unfortunates in the world today. However, this is *my*
book, and I need to set some sort of framework—or better yet, an excuse—
to explain what happened to me along the way.

I grew up in Malibu, California. When I was a kid back in the '40s and
'50s, Malibu was just a little hick beach town so rural that every Saturday
night they held square dances across the street from my house at the
Malibu Inn. The ranch-style, red-tile-roof building also acted as the local
bar, restaurant, barbershop, liquor store, and real estate office, all wrapped
in one.

By 1940, the high-end, seafront enclave of Malibu Colony, where my
family lived, had developed within Malibu proper, but the population was
primarily summer-seasonal with few year-round residents. Other than the
Colony, homes in Malibu were few in number, limited to neighborhoods
such as Las Flores (the then town commercial center), La Costa, Malibu
Heights (about fourteen homes northwest of the Malibu Inn), plus scattered homes along the beach.

Despite my privileged circumstances, I was always different from the
other kids, even though they were from similarly well-to-do families. I just
didn't fit in. Naturally, I didn't want to be different, but I was and I got

picked on all the time, ending up in plenty of fights. The strain on me got so bad around the age of seven that I started having problems speaking and developed a stutter.

My brother, David, was an angel compared to me. He never got into trouble. He never did anything wrong that I can remember. I was only three years older, but it always seemed to me that we were polar opposites. I was always in trouble and he wasn't. My parents made me play the piano; with him, they did not. I was skinny; he was chubby. I was always the leader; he was the follower. The only trouble he ever got into was my fault; when he was only eleven years old, I talked him into coming with me to steal a car in Beverly Hills. He would never have done that on his own in a million years. At the age of fourteen, when I was so crazy that I had stolen the keys to about a dozen cars in and around Studio City just to have a pool of cars to choose from when I wanted to go joyriding, I finally asked him to hide the keys from me so I wouldn't be able to steal the cars they belonged to. David dutifully buried them in our backyard and would never tell me where they were. They're probably still there somewhere.

My troubles basically started with my first name. I had been named Michel, a girl's name, as far as the kids in my elementary school were concerned. All the other boys in my first grade class had names like Jim, Steve, Dick, and Jack. In turn, it was open season on me. They taunted me relentlessly.

Next, there was the fact that I had really curly hair, which my parents thought was darling. But in the late '40s and early '50s, all the other boys in school had either butch cuts or crew cuts. So my lovely coiled locks made me stand out like a freak.

Then, to add to my misery, I played the piano. Really well, too. The boys hated that as much or more than my name and hair because it made me *special* in the eyes of the girls. They loved watching me play and paid me lots of attention because of it.

Given all this, I was doomed from the beginning, destined to be hated by almost every male student throughout my school years. Every kid who wanted some extra attention chose to bully me. I got into scuffle after scuffle and later fistfight after fistfight just trying to defend myself from all the jerks that wanted to use my face as a punching bag in order to show their friends how brave and strong they were. I had my nose broken six times by the time I was sixteen. But that wasn't the total number of fights I had; there were lots more. And I did win a few, though those six were the ones I obviously didn't.

Growing to hate my supposed girls' name so much, by the seventh grade at Lincoln Junior High School, I surreptitiously added an *a* to my name, thus changing it from "Michel" to "Michael" on all the entrance forms. On the line that asked what my middle name was, I wrote "Mike," and I don't even have a middle name, so I had changed my name from Michel Rubini to Michael Mike Rubini on the entrance forms. The lady in the office that looked at all my paperwork was so unsophisticated, she incorrectly assumed that my real name was Michael and all the records and report cards that I had brought with me from elementary school had misspelled my name. That shows you how unusual my name was at that time. She figured that it must have really been Michael because no male child could possibly have the name of Michel.

That name, Mike, followed me all through my junior high and high school years. It even followed me into my professional career. It was so stuck on me, I couldn't seem to get rid of it even though I wanted to use my real name once I got out of high school. People just couldn't seem to call me Michel.

Even as a studio musician later on, I constantly received credit on the back of albums as Mike Rubini, not Michel Rubini. This didn't change even by 1966 when Bud Dane signed me to a record deal with Liberty Records. Before my single was released, I told him my real name wasn't Mike, but Michel, and I wanted to release the record with my real name on it. Incredibly, he said to me he didn't think that was a good idea because the name Michel was not commercial. So they released the record under the name of Mike Rubini instead. Imagine how insane that remark was. Hadn't he ever heard the name Elvis? That's not a very commercial name either.

Unfortunately, my father was not home very much in my pre-teen years. He was gone playing concerts or touring for the USO and entertaining all over the globe. He had his own show and brought along singers, dancers, magicians, and acrobats. During World War II, he toured in the Pacific for our soldiers who were fighting in places like Guam and the Philippines. Later, during the Korean War, he flew to Japan, Seoul and secret Air Force bases that were built under the arctic ice in Alaska. In 1952, when I was ten, he went to South Africa for almost a year. My mother was not happy about that because she had to stay home all the time and look after my brother and me. Sometimes my maternal grandmother stayed with us to help my mother and keep her company.

Like many pubescent youngsters, I was not consciously aware of much during those times except thoughts of my own wants and needs. For instance, I never realized that my mother liked to drink too much. When I was about thirteen, I finally became aware that there was something really amiss with my mom; her breath had that bad smell of alcohol, all the time. But I didn't know anything about drinking problems at that age, so I couldn't put two and two together and figure out that she was an alcoholic.

My folks divorced when I was thirteen, but I didn't know why. They just told me one of the stories all parents tell their kids when they separate. I didn't find out the truth about the real reasons until years later, nor did I realize at the time how very much their separation affected my young life and actions. When I was in my late teens and early twenties and my friends asked me if my parent's divorce affected me, I always answered, "No of course not. I completely understand it. Sometimes people just don't get along and it's better if they separate. It didn't affect me at all."

It never dawned on me how much their separation and divorce negatively affected me until one day in my late twenties or early thirties. The effect it actually had on me hit me like a ton of bricks. It was an epiphany; it was as though I had been blind for twenty years, and all of a sudden, I could see light.

Because of my parent's divorce, I was put in the position of having to attend five different junior high schools, one of them twice. I was being jostled around from place to place without a father figure in my life to control me, and my mother was more out of control than I was because of her drinking. She was not the stereotypical *The Lost Weekend* type of drunk, in case you remember that Oscar-winning film about a binging alcoholic who would black out for days at a time.

My mother was more of a tippler, drinking a little bit starting in the morning and never stopping all day. A blast of whiskey in her coffee in the morning before she left the house, with a bottle stashed under her cash register drawer at the store where she worked. When she arrived there, my mom would have a shot just to get the day going, then at lunch another one or two drinks. Back at the store, she would have another shot from the bottle to help her get through the afternoon. When she arrived home, Mom immediately poured a little bracer to relax before dinner. Afterward, there were always a couple more to help her go to sleep. And on and on it went. She was never completely drunk, but she was never completely sober, either.

By the time I was thirteen, in addition to dealing with my mother's drinking and my parent's divorce, I also began to feel the full effect of my raging hormones and became girl crazy just like every other teenage boy. Unfortunately, I couldn't find a girlfriend because there were no girls living in my immediate neighborhood in Studio City. So the only time I saw them was at school. That's when I figured out I needed to be able to drive, except I was going to have to wait three more years before I could get a license or a car. That just wasn't going to do.

With a little encouragement from my delinquent friends, I got up the nerve to steal my first car. Now I didn't just steal a car on the first day. I sort of worked up to it. My friends and I started off by stealing hubcaps. I don't know why we stole them; it was just something to do after dark, I guess.

Not satisfied with the hubcap ritual for long, we started wandering around the neighborhood, but not too close to our homes, looking for something more obnoxious to do. One night, I spotted a mailbox mounted on a post between the sidewalk and the street. The street was a typically under-lit residential one with houses and apartment buildings mixed together. I thought it would be funny if I ripped it out of the ground, post and all, and then dragged it across the street to the Los Angeles River and dropped it over the side. The next day the people that lived in that house would walk out as usual to get their mail and there wouldn't be any mailbox there. Wouldn't that be just too funny for words?

So while my pals watched, I did just that. It made a big noise when the mailbox and post hit the concrete of the riverbed below (the Los Angeles River, usually pretty dry, is basically just a manmade runoff canal used for flood and irrigation purposes). We thought the whole thing was hilarious. But for obvious reasons, we decided we should get out of there. We got about one block away from the house that now had no mailbox when out of bloody nowhere there was a screech of skidding tires and a car squealed to a stop in the street right in front of us.

A man jumped out of the car screaming at the top of his lungs about something to do with "teenage delinquents" and that he was going to kill us right there on the spot. He sprinted right at us and we almost jumped out of our shoes with fright. We had been caught red-handed and this guy was not interested in calling the cops. He had murder in his eyes and was a lot bigger than any of us.

We all ran in different directions but, unfortunately for me, I was the one he had in his crosshairs. The other guys melted into the night and I took off running faster than I had ever run in my life, trying to outdistance this maniac of a homeowner. Let me tell you, this guy was no slouch either; he was gaining on me with every step. I'm not sure which of us had more adrenalin pumping though our veins, him or me, but I was scared shitless.

Just as my pursuer reached out to grab my shirt, at the last second, I jumped to the right and up onto a raised lawn that belonged to the corner house, and with that unexpected move, I gained a few yards on him. I kept on sprinting, trying to double speed my pumping legs. I'm sure that if I had been running the 440 back at school, I would have set a new track record.

Finally, the guy got a little winded and I widened the spread between us. But he wasn't stopping and he was still screaming at me. At the end of the block I turned the corner, desperate to find a place to hide. I couldn't continue running at this pace either; I thought my lungs were going to burn right through my chest wall. But I couldn't stop either—he was relentless, like that evil truck driver in the movie *Duel*.

Fortunately, there were a number of apartment buildings nearby and in an act of desperation, I ran into one of the complexes. There I saw a pool house, a little structure where the motors and filters for the swimming pool were housed, and I dashed inside it and crouched down behind the pool heater. It was pitch black; I couldn't see a thing. But I could hear everything, and my breathing was so loud I was sure that he would hear me even out on the street. I tried to slow my breathing and stop making so much noise, and I waited in fear for my worthless life. What was I doing? Why did I do these stupid, senseless things? I prayed that if I got out of this alive I would never do anything like this again.

After a while, I still had not been found. The thought then occurred to me that the man couldn't look for me all night. After all, he had left his car running in the middle of the street. And I had to make a move; I couldn't stay there until daylight. So I slowly made my way back out to the street. I then walked in the opposite direction from my house so the guy couldn't follow me home. Making a big loop, I wound up at Colfax Avenue and then started the trip to my house. It took me about an hour to make what should have been a ten-minute walk, but I never saw anybody and I thankfully somehow made it home without being arrested or beaten to a pulp.

But that little experience wasn't enough to cure me. Soon I got my courage back and my delinquent actions began anew. My friends and I started sneaking into the Studio City Theatre in order to watch movies for free. One of us would buy a ticket and then open the back door of the theatre and let the rest of the gang in. The manager got wise to that prank pretty fast and we almost got caught, so we had to let that one go.

Undeterred, we still wanted to get into the theatre without paying. So we came up with the brilliant idea of climbing up the side of the place and then lowering ourselves down to the window of the men's room where we could climb in and then just walk into the seating area. However, there were some logistical problems with that plan; in the first place, how were we going to get up on top of the theatre and next how were we going to shinny down to the bathroom? The bathroom was on the second floor behind the theatre marquee, which formed a triangle that hung off the front of the building. If we could throw a rope over the front of the building and could get it to hang just above the window of the men's room, we figured we could climb down, land on the small flat roof behind the marquee, and then let ourselves in through the window.

However, the problem with that plan was that the front of the building directly faced the heavily traveled and brightly lit Ventura Boulevard, so we would be literally climbing down in full view of everyone. Then there was the issue of the manager's office window. He and his theatre staff were right inside, and if we made any noise while descending or landed with a thud, someone would undoubtedly hear and it would be curtains.

We chose a night to try our adventure and off we headed for the theatre with a long piece of rope stuffed inside my jacket. Climbing on top of a neighboring building, we then roof-hopped over. It was very dark out, so we had come prepared with flashlights.

Sweating bullets, my cohorts and I tippy-toed our ways to the front of the theatre's roof and peered over the edge. The distance looked a lot farther than it had from my vantage point down on the street. I found a pipe and tied my rope to it and then slowly lowered the rope until it dangled right next to the men's bathroom window. As we tried to decide who would go first, my wonderful friends all chickened out at the last minute. Once again, just like during the mailbox incident, it was left to me to be the leader. Summoning every ounce of courage, I grabbed the rope and over the wall I went. Hanging on for dear life and praying that no one on the street would look up, I rappelled down the face of the building like some kind of a cat burglar and put my feet on the roof of the marquee as quietly as possible.

Waiting a few moments to make sure nobody was in the bathroom, I then got my wire cutters out and carefully snipped the screen away from the window. Now came the really hard part. I had to climb up and through without making any noise. Naturally, I hoped no one would enter the bathroom and find me halfway in the window. That would have definitely blown the whole job. But once again, I was lucky. Nobody came in.

Now alone in the bathroom, as planned, I simply walked out into the foyer, went down the steps, and into the theatre where I sat down and waited for my friends. Except they didn't come. After waiting a while, I got worried. Where were they? Could they have been caught in the act, and if so did they squeal on me? Was a policeman going to come down the aisle any moment and catch me sitting there without a ticket and take me away? I didn't know what to do.

Finally, I thought to myself that I might as well just sit there and watch the movie. After all, I had already paid the biggest admission of my life to a theatre by planning the whole caper, buying the rope, and then doing the deed, which took about fifteen years off my life in the span of five minutes. I was going to enjoy this movie if it was the last thing I ever did as a free man. My friends never did show up, by the way. They had obviously scattered like rats in the night. Afterward, I hated those guys. Why did I hang out with them? That is a question I have never fully answered to my satisfaction. I guess I just wanted to belong to a group, and they were the only guys around at that time in my life.

My habits then went from bad to worse. I wanted a car so I could pick up girls. As usual, I wasn't thinking with the head on top of my shoulders. The closest auto was in my neighbor's garage. One night, long after she had gone to bed, I snuck in and discovered that she had left her keys in the ignition. I guess she thought it was safe because she always put her garage door down at night when she came home. She didn't know she had a juvenile delinquent living next door to her.

But I didn't steal the car right away. I had to have a plan so I wouldn't get caught. I couldn't start it in the garage because she would certainly have heard it. I told my same no-good friends about it, and we made a plan to wait until the neighbor lady was asleep. We would then push the car backward down her driveway and out into the street where we could start it and not cause any attention.

That was the start of a long series of car thefts that sort of became an obsession for me. We didn't get caught that night nor on following nights when we *borrowed* her car. But I knew that I had to have other cars available to me because I couldn't keep on stealing my neighbor's car night after night; sooner or later I would get caught.

My habit became to walk the streets and look inside every car I passed. Once in a while, someone would leave their keys in the ignition, and rather than steal the car then and there, I merely swiped the keys. I would then bring them home and mark the address where each came from. In those days, if someone went out and didn't find their keys, they never thought that they had been stolen. Instead, the owner automatically thought he or she had misplaced them. So they would take their spare and just make a duplicate.

But I had the originals, and when I wanted that car, it was always available for the taking. By virtue of this, my buddies and I went joyriding all over the Valley. It was a regular crime spree of stolen cars. Though I would like to add that I never hurt the cars, I didn't vandalize them, and I always left them somewhere on a street within a mile of my house. That was really the only drawback to this plan of mine—I had to leave the car somewhere and still be able to walk home. I couldn't return it, because once it was reported stolen, I couldn't risk getting caught in it.

Of course, my mother had no idea while this was going on. I just sneaked out of the house after she saw me go into my room at night. I didn't even care if she checked up on me and didn't find me there. What was she going to do, tell someone that I wasn't in my room? That would have just looked bad for her, like she couldn't control her own kid. And the truth is, she couldn't. I was out of control and heading for a really big fall. I just didn't know it yet. And it was so stupid when it finally happened.

My buddies and I decided to steal my neighbor's car once again, but this time she heard something and went to the garage and saw that her car was missing. She called the police, who promptly came over to check on the situation. The cops talked with her and then went next door to my house to see if I was there (I guess my neighbor had her suspicions about me) and, of course, I wasn't. I was out driving around in her car, totally oblivious to my impending fate.

So the police just waited and watched. About midnight, I came around the corner onto my street, cruising slowly. As usual, I pulled the car into the neighbor lady's garage, turned off the engine and got out. But that was about as far as I got.

As I stepped outside into the night, the police suddenly appeared. They asked me my name and then told me I was under arrest. They took the other boys away in another car, and I didn't see them again for a long time.

The next thing I knew I was locked up inside the Van Nuys jail in a holding cell, which petrified me and also left my mind racing. Did the authorities also know about the other cars? What did the other boys tell them?

I had no idea, but I had to keep my mouth shut at all costs. My whole life was hanging in the balance. Yet, once again, I was extremely lucky. The police didn't know anything about all the other cars I had stolen. My friends had not admitted to anything beyond the one theft. So since it was my first arrest, the court put me on one-year probation. I had to write a letter every week to my probation officer telling him everything that I was doing. Then once a month, I had to go to the police department and meet with him. He told me not to do anything illegal while I was on probation or I would go to prison to serve out the rest of my sentence, plus whatever time I would have to serve for the new offense.

Scared straight, I knew I had to be a good boy. But old habits die hard. Sometimes I found myself walking down the street still looking wistfully inside cars just to see if the keys were there. How long would I last? But somehow I surprised myself and finally the magic day arrived when I became sixteen years old. I got my driver's license and my car-stealing problems came to an end.

But that wouldn't be the case with girls. Outside of music, they would become my all-consuming focus and fascination for years to come.

SEVEN

The Karate Kid

Volunteering that I studied karate is a topic I rarely offer up. It makes me sound like a braggadocio or something. Sort of like saying, "Hey, I'm a tough guy. I know how to fight." I never learned enough to get beyond my white belt, anyway, which took me about a year to earn. So at no point was I a threat to Bruce Lee. But I did come away with a couple of good stories.

As an odd series of circumstances unfolded, I found myself in a band with a drummer named Hank Henry. He was a first-level Sho Dan black belt in the style of Shotokan Karate and was close to achieving the next level in that discipline (there are ten total). I was about twenty at the time, and as we got to know each other, Hank told me about the legendary Hidetaka Nishiyama and the Japan Karate Association.

Because I had been in so many unwanted fights as a kid, this information immediately grabbed my interest. I thought it might be a great way for me to learn how to defend myself. Soon thereafter, Hank took me to downtown Los Angeles one evening to the dojo (martial arts facility) where I watched a class being taught by none other than Nishiyama himself. I had no idea then how very important and influential this man was, but it was clear from the moment I met him that, if angered, he was more dangerous than the meanest tiger in the jungle. After watching that class, I signed up and started taking lessons. And let me tell you, it was grueling.

For the first two weeks, all I did was learn how to stand properly and be centered and strong. Everything builds upon that. In each subsequent class, I learned exactly one new thing, which I was then required to master to the best of my ability. For example, one time we took a whole hour (one full class session) just to learn how to make a fist. It took me almost a year of amazingly hard work and dedication like this before I could even take the test to earn my white belt, which is the lowest level of belt. When I finally took it, I passed all right, but others in my class were not so fortunate. Nishiyama wasn't into giving out belts to students for money; you had to *earn* them. He was only interested in teaching his pupils how to be the best-trained fighters in the world. And by that, I mean he expected us to be so good that we could stop a fight before it even started. That was the most valuable thing I learned from him.

Though I was never too good—certainly no trained killer—I did learn just enough to hurt someone really badly if ever put into a dangerous situation. But I wasn't graceful. Nor did I learn enough to simply turn someone's momentum against them, to toss them aside like a rag doll. That's what the pros were able to do. Nishiyama could toy with someone with seemingly no effort. Me? Well, not so much. But I loved practicing karate nonetheless, and it supplied me with much-needed confidence.

My newfound martial arts skills were tested in the real world only twice. The first time was while I was shopping at Wallichs Music City in Hollywood, the premier record store in the L.A. area. Having placed my wallet on top of a glass display case while getting ready to pay, something distracted me and I turned away. Just then, some greasy-haired punk grabbed my wallet and dashed out the door with it. I immediately gave chase and caught up with him about half a block away on Vine Street.

Electing not to outright attack him, I said calmly, yet firmly, that I knew he had my wallet and if he gave it back, I'd let him go and wouldn't tell the cops. He replied that he didn't have it and furthermore didn't know what I was talking about. I repeated my demand and again in reply he said he didn't have it. He then threatened me, saying that if I didn't get away from him, he was going to beat the crap out of me. I just replied calmly that he wasn't going to do that. I could see that he was becoming desperate, but I felt nothing but calm. With my training at the hands of Hidetaka Nishiyama, I knew I could take this thief down easily. The guy then took a threatening step toward me, certainly expecting me to back up out of fear. But I simply stood there and said once more "You are going to give me my wallet back or go to jail."

By this point, the guy was so rattled by my calm and decidedly unafraid demeanor that he suddenly began emptying all of his pockets, throwing everything he had on the sidewalk. Now shaking, he screamed, "See, I don't have your fucking wallet!" And he was right.

This left me stunned. I knew he had taken it, but it wasn't on him. So I told him to pick up his stuff and get lost before the police arrived. I watched him for a couple more seconds then turned and walked back down to the corner of Sunset and Vine in front of Wallichs. As I stood there trying to figure out what he had done with my wallet, it dawned on me: he must have tossed it when he saw me starting to chase him. So I looked around and sure enough, there in the gutter right in front of me, was my billfold. Caper foiled, case closed.

But the point of that story isn't about my wallet. Instead, it's that I wasn't afraid to assert myself because of the incredible training I received in Nishiyama's classes. More so, those skills are something I have carried with me ever since, allowing me to stand up for myself, if ever needed, in a calm, confident, and effective way.

Of course, the second and last time I ever had to use my training actually occurred during a real fight in Hollywood around 1971. But as Hidetaka Nishiyama had so expertly taught me, one attack, one blow, opponent goes down, end of fight.

Having just spent the night with Jenny Lee, a wonderful dancer whom I was dating at that time, her insanely jealous ex-boyfriend happened to show up just as I was leaving her apartment one morning to go play a recording date. Pounding on her front door, he demanded that she open up and talk to him. I wanted to call the police and have them deal with it, but Jenny said it was better if I just left by the backdoor while she held the guy's attention. I agreed and quickly left.

But after I had only gotten about four steps away from the building, the ex-boyfriend bashed in the front door, ran through her apartment, and came barreling out the backdoor toward me. I turned when I heard the noise, but the clumsy idiot that I am, I tripped over my own feet and fell. With me on the ground and him coming at me, I instantly reverted to what Nishiyama had so painstakingly taught me. From the ground I lifted my leg and kicked the guy right in his solar plexus (a mass of nerve endings in the pit of the stomach), which caught him perfectly. He fell backward and almost lost his footing, though somehow managed to remain upright. Yet, at the same time, he wasn't moving either. He just stood there, dazed.

Watching carefully for a couple of seconds, I thought he might come at me again, so I prepared myself. But it was as if he was now paralyzed. I got up, looked at him once more, and then dusted off my pants. Jenny, of course, came running to see what had happened. I told her to go back inside, lock the doors, and call the police. With that, I turned and calmly walked out to the street to my car, got in, and drove off to my gig as if nothing had happened. The last I saw of Jenny's crazy ex-boyfriend, he was still standing there motionless, not knowing what hit him. In all the years since, I have never had to fight with anyone and I know it's because of my training under Nishiyama.

Remember, one blow, opponent goes down, end of fight.

EIGHT

Mel Carter

By the time I was around twenty-two years old, I had been a member of the rock and roll band, the Marketts, for at least a couple of years. One night, I had boldly jumped onstage with them at the Red Velvet nightclub, a well-known live music place on Sunset Boulevard in Hollywood, and the next thing I knew I was their new organ player. We had a big instrumental hit, which you might remember, called "Out of Limits."

At the same time, I had been getting a few studio calls and things were picking up for me as a recording session piano player around town. My skills were such that I could play any kind of music after having trained so heavily as a classical pianist. Though my new line of work in no way pleased my father, playing rock and roll, along with jazz and blues, is what I loved to do most. So I did.

With decent money starting to come in, Dale Hallcom, my fellow co-leader of the Marketts, and I moved in 1964 from our vintage, 1925-era clapboard apartment building to a much newer, nicer, stucco place in the middle of Hollywood that even sported a small swimming pool. I remember that the walls were freshly painted, and the sinks and toilets were white and without stains (imagine that). We thought we were really moving up in the world.

As we were moving our meager belongings into the new apartment, I noticed a spectacular black, or white, woman (I couldn't tell which) taking in some sun at the poolside. She was as dark as any black person I had ever seen yet she had a very thin, aquiline nose. She was also of indiscriminate age, that is to say I could not figure out how old she was, maybe twenty-five, maybe forty-five. Who knew? But she had a figure that could win a Miss America pageant. With a classic hourglass shape, her waist could not have been more than twenty-two inches, while her behind was at least thirty-eight inches and supremely shapely, along with a bust that any sixteen-year-old girl would envy. In short, this woman was *hot*.

She was wearing a mini bikini, and I mean mini as in microscopic. When she spotted us going up the stairs with our things, she was very friendly and welcomed us to the building. She told me in a thick Bronx accent that her name was Zelda Sands and that she lived there on the ground floor, her apartment door opening right to the pool. It was a setup that proved to be especially convenient for her since she spent every waking hour in her bikini lying in the sun, unless she was working. I also determined that she was, in fact, white, and probably Jewish.

Zelda told me that she was the personal and business manager for a very talented singer by the name of Mel Carter. When I told her that I was a pianist and the co-leader of the Marketts, and that I, too, wrote songs and played on recording sessions, she became very interested in me. She wanted to know if I might be interested in writing some songs with her, casually letting me know that if they were any good she could make sure Mel would sing them on his next album. Never wanting to miss an opportunity to sell a song or play on a recording date, I immediately agreed and we set to work looking at all her lyrics. I swear Zelda had a hundred songs' worth in her notebook. Somehow, we wrote a tune called, "The Richest Man Alive," which wasn't half bad. As promised, she then introduced me to Mel after we finished the song. Mel Carter was a lovely person with a great voice (he was Sam Cooke's protégé, after all) and I worked on the song with him in the studio to get a key that fit his vocal range. From there, we made a demo of it that Zelda dutifully presented to Mel's record producer, Nick DeCaro, for consideration to be recorded for Mel's upcoming album on Imperial Records. I had met DeCaro before and had worked on a couple of sessions that he had arranged, so I guess that was a plus for me, although I don't think that he really liked the song. But he couldn't stand up to Zelda with any objections because she was so forceful. Her reputation in Hollywood for being a tough negotiator and businesswoman preceded her.

So DeCaro agreed without much persuasion to record the song after all. Zelda may have said something to him like, "If you don't record it, you will never produce another album as long as you live." But, of course, saying it with a smile on her face all the while, which I discovered to be how she usually conducted business. Nobody from Bud Dane (the president of Liberty Records) on down the label's employee ladder wanted to tangle with Zelda; she always seemed to get her way. What a woman.

Yes, I know what you are thinking and the answer is no. I never got lucky in *that* way with Zelda. Which was a very wise move on my part, because if I had gotten it on with her, I probably would never have been with another woman for the rest of my life. She would have physically seen to that, if you catch my drift. That's likely why Zelda never had a boyfriend as long as I knew her (except that I had my suspicions about her and Mel; I thought something was going on there, though I just couldn't be sure). Sometimes it's better not to get involved, than to ask too many questions.

Mel was always so pleasant and polite, too, and as a singer, he could not be topped. Zelda guided his career very closely, and if he wasn't completely happy with his records or her advice, I would have never known; he never mentioned it. I didn't see too much of Mel except when he visited Zelda at her apartment or at rehearsals and sessions, but we got along famously. I never saw him with a woman, and I secretly suspected that he was either having an affair with Zelda or might even be gay because of his soft-spoken manner. But he wasn't saying, and I never asked. What I did discover was that as the years went by, his singing just got better and better and his focus moved from pop to being one of the greatest ballad and jazz singers I have ever heard. He is still working today, and I wish both Mel and Zelda the very best life has to offer. It was my privilege to know and play for such a wonderfully talented singer and charming person. And about Zelda, all I can say is that she is one of a kind and that kind is the greatest.

One other nice benefit of getting to know Zelda Sands came through her introducing me to the tremendously talented arranger Gene Page. With a career that would eventually span working with the likes of The Righteous Brothers, Barbra Streisand, and Cher, along with just about every other superstar singer in between, Gene was the real deal. When Zelda announced to Gene that I was going to play on Mel's session and that we were also going to record one of Zelda's and my songs, he, of course, had huge doubts about me. I could see it in his face. My session experience was limited at that point, and he had little reason to have heard of me, which, of course, he had not.

Gene's recording dates were always arranged to the max with every note perfectly written out, and he had concerns that I would not be able to read the parts and also that I would not know what to play. But Zelda said a few things to him about me, and he and I also talked at length. After that, I think he sort of just resigned himself to the fact that I was going to play the session, whether he wanted me or not. Anything was preferable to arguing with Zelda.

When I got to the recording session, I was understandably nervous. But I opened my ears, quickly figured out what he needed, and had no problem with the charts. We recorded "The Richest Man Alive" on that first day and it became Mel's next single. At the same time, Gene was so impressed with my playing that at the end of the session he walked up to me and asked if I could play on another date he had coming up soon.

Within a month, I became Gene's number-one-call piano player. The main reason was because I played both popular and classical style piano. Gene wrote a lot of parts that needed both chart reading skills (for the classical part) and also pop/rock interpretation. Since I was both a classical and rock piano player, I fit into his style of writing right away. Previous to that time, Gene (and also all the other arrangers) had to call one pianist if they had a session with charts that needed to be read and another if they needed a pianist who could play with *feel*. The two never went together until I came along. It's something I was secretly proud of, and I think it's one of the main reasons I became so successful so fast.

As a matter of fact, Gene and I sort of coined a phrase that we used as code between us. It was called "classical shuck," meaning that it was a pop/rock/R&B type arrangement, but needed some classical-sounding piano solos or rhythm added to it. Because of my ability to give him that classical style on demand, all he had to do was write out the top note of the melody that he wanted me to play; he no longer needed to write out the complete piano part with full chords and in two staves. This saved him an enormous amount of time. He would just give me a guitar chord part and pencil in the single solo notes and/or rhythm and then write the words "classical shuck" over the area, and I would know what he needed. This is the same thing I did later on for the noted arranger Ernie Freeman when he wrote the arrangement for Frank Sinatra's hit single, "Strangers in the Night." Ernie simply said to me, "Play some classical shuck here in the break for the solo and follow the string line." And that's what I did. Deal done, number one hit.

As a coda to all of this, Mel had many more hits and I played on just about all of his recordings throughout the '60s, including his signature song, "Hold Me, Thrill Me, Kiss Me." He is still singing to this day, too—and better than ever, I might add. Recently, after forty years of not being in contact, I actually decided to call Zelda. She is still right there in Hollywood, doing her Zelda thing, and not diminished one bit by the passage of time. I owe a great debt of gratitude to both Zelda and Mel for helping and encouraging me through those wonderful years.

NINE

Gene Page

Gene Page was a character almost beyond description. Nevertheless, I am going to attempt to give you an impression of just how great, funny, and weird Gene really was, because he was one of my best friends. We had a wonderful time together and nobody has written much about him beyond to merely say that he was one of the top pop arrangers of the '60s and '70s. There was so much more to Gene than his musical genius.

From the start, Gene and I had many interests in common, not the least of them being our lust for sexy females. We were both enamored with the opposite sex, but with one pretty large difference: Gene was crazy for women with big tits; I was simply crazy for women, period.

Now while I say Gene was crazy, I never really knew how obsessed he was for the more amply endowed lovelies among us, even when I spotted his pile of big-breasted-women skin magazines there in his office. At first, I thought they were just run-of-the-mill girlie photos that any normal male might have for his and his friends' amusement. Except then I noticed a trend; almost all the magazines seemed to contain nothing but women with enormous bosoms. They were not only in his office, either. He had them with him wherever he went, including his car. I never could figure that one out. After all, when you get into your car, you're there to drive someplace. You can't read while you are driving, so it leaves the question: when do you look at these magazines? But don't get me wrong—Gene had many more interests than just gawking at nudie mags.

One time he invited me up to see his new ranch near Fallbrook, which I didn't even know he had. So I drove there with him in his car, which was stuffed with even more jumbo-jugged girlie magazines, to find his mother and brother, Billy, already waiting for us. We walked around the property and Gene proudly told me of his plans for it. He painted a very nice picture, except that if you knew Gene, you knew that he was the last person on earth that ought to buy a ranch. A cowboy he was not. I think he really purchased the place as an investment or maybe as somewhere for his mother to live later in her life. But Gene definitely didn't know the front end of a tractor from the rear, which made the whole thing seem that much more comical.

On a different occasion, I threw a bachelor party for my good friend, composer and producer Mike Post, who was going to marry his high-school sweetheart Darla. Wanting it to be a really great party, I somehow found several rough-and-ready Hell's Angels biker chicks to agree to be hookers for the night. I then borrowed some gambling tables from a few of my shadier friends and set up my house so there would be gaming in the living room, a possible sex show with about twenty folding chairs in the master bedroom, and the other bedrooms left ready for anybody who wanted to be "serviced," so to speak. Inviting a bunch of Post's and my musician pals, including Gene Page, we all got down for a night of debauchery, Hollywood style.

Everybody was drinking, gambling, and having a lot of fun when the girls made their entrance. They were a pretty seedy-looking bunch to say the least, certainly nothing special to look at. But one of them had size 44 triple *D*s, and when Gene spotted her, his face lit up like a Christmas tree. He made a beeline straight toward her. After he stammered his way through introducing himself to her and communicating his obvious desire, the two of them headed off together to get drinks. That all sounds fairly normal, right? Except his hands seemed to have a mind of their own—they sort of just grabbed the girl by her breasts and magically stayed glued to her chest for the rest of the evening.

Gene was definitely the most uncoordinated black man I have ever met. Actually, he was the most uncoordinated person of *any* color I have ever met. Up to the point in time when I met Gene, I had the same stereotypical picture in my mind as everybody else about black men of his age. You know, strong, great athletes, great musicians, loads of rhythm, natural dancers, et cetera. But Gene was *so* not any of those things. He constantly made me laugh with his lack of physical abilities and eccentricities.

First, Gene had no sense of rhythm at all. He could not count off a tune in time to save his life. A typical Gene Page count-off would go something like this: he would start with the words "one, two" at a faster tempo than we were going to play the song. He would then sort of slow down the back half of his count, "one, two, three," with a continued slowing of the beat so that there was no steady count at all. We didn't have any idea about how fast he wanted the tune to go. We couldn't even start together because none of us knew where the downbeat was.

Another of his famous count-off blunders would sometimes occur with him saying, "one, two," and then suddenly stopping to say hello to some musician in the front row of players. "Oh, how are *you*? How nice to see you!" It would drive us all insane and send us into hysterics at the same time.

On a particularly memorable occasion, Gene came into the studio late one day (he was almost always late, it seemed) to where we, the musicians, were set up and waiting. He opened the studio door, came walking in toward the conductor's podium with all the arrangements and sheet music in his arms for the whole band while smiling that great *Gene Page* smile, and then proceeded to trip over a microphone cable, sending a mountain of paper flying into the air. It was hilarious for us musicians, but for the producer, maybe not so much. A couple of the guys and I rushed over to Gene to see if he was all right (he was). We then started picking up all the pages off the floor, put the music folders back together, and passed them out to the musicians. Fortunately, it all ended well because we recorded four songs that day and finished the session ahead of schedule, sending everybody (including the producer) happily home.

Over time, all the big-name music producers in Hollywood learned to put up with Gene's unreliable count-offs and his occasional tardiness because they always got the best arrangements money could buy. Gene's creativity and superb ear provided the best shot at a gold record they could ever hope for. If a recording didn't become a hit, the producers could never blame Gene's arrangements. It was either the song itself or the singer who came up short. I can tell you first-hand, nobody ever complained about a Gene Page arrangement.

TEN

That Sinking Feeling

For as long as I can remember, I have been a beach person. Raised in Malibu on an oceanfront property, it was my world from birth all the way through the end of elementary school. Even today, every home I own is on a beach somewhere, except for my desert hideaway in Palm Springs. Wait—there's sand there, too. Hmm...

All kidding aside, I was a Malibu brat through and through and lived to swim in the ocean in front of our house. My younger brother David and I used to walk down to the end of the beach and explore the sea life there by picking up rocks to see what surprises were awaiting us underneath. We liked to poke our fingers into the middle of the sea anemones and watch them close up around our fingertips and sometimes even squirt some water out of their pores when we irritated them too much. The ocean simply fascinated me.

Snorkeling was another of my pleasures. I learned how as a little kid in our Beverly Hills home's swimming pool. In short, I took to water like a porpoise. So it was a natural evolution for me to want to learn how to dive with an air tank as soon as I could, and I became certified by the time I was twenty. My first legal dives were off Catalina Island, and I couldn't get enough of it. Looking for even more adventure, I flew to Tahiti in 1967 with my buddy Robert Sabaroff, a prolific TV writer, for a two-week diving vacation. Fun though it may have been, he definitely got the better of that trip because he brought his wife along for his evening entertainment and all I got was a busted eardrum from failing to clear the pressure adequately during a dive. Also, the girls in Tahiti certainly did not look breathtakingly exotic like the ones seen in so many movies. Sad to say, for the most part, the women there were fat and toothless, because of their diet mostly consisting of poi and coconuts and because there were no good dentists to be found anywhere.

Given my love for all things aquatic, I always wanted to have my own boat, too. But I held off because of all the miserable stories I'd heard from those who had taken the plunge, so to speak. You know the old saying, "The happiest day of my life was the day I bought my boat and the second happiest was the day I sold it." That all seemed like sound advice to me.

So I remained boat-less, that is until two of my best buddies and fellow Wrecking Crew musicians, Ollie Mitchell (trumpet) and Jimmy Gordon (drums), informed me one day during the mid-'60s that they wanted to purchase a boat with me as the third partner. Though in my heart I knew better, their rationale made sense. If we split the cost three ways, the upkeep for each would be minimal.

We soon found an eighteen-foot beauty with a big outboard engine for a relatively small sum of money, and boat owners we became. Notably, it was fast and it was cheap, the two most important qualities. The three of us were in seventh heaven as we looked forward to many happy days of scuba diving off Paradise Cove in Malibu, which was our favorite pier.

On one particular afternoon that Ollie, Jimmy, and I decided to go for a dive using our new boat, we brought along my girlfriend, actress Joanna Moore (who I'll be talking about in more detail in the next chapter). With her domestic side on full display, Joanna made up a wonderful picnic basket for us full of sandwiches, soft drinks, and of course, a bottle of wine for herself. Once at the pier, the employees there lowered the boat via a small crane into the water and then off we went, joyously speeding our way north through the Pacific blue toward a series of kelp beds where we hoped to spear a few fish and find some abalone.

Since Joanna had been drinking, it was decided that I should stay aboard with her while Jimmy and Ollie went on their dive. Which was fine with me—I saw a familiar twinkle in her eye that said it would be more fun with her in the boat than to dive with my two buddies.

Now is the time I need to add one small but very important detail to this story. There was a drain plug installed at the bottom of the boat's transom (i.e. the back wall, known as the stern). The purpose of the drain was to suck water out that always splashed inside while moving. Once the boat stopped, though, the plug had to be put back into the drain or flooding would immediately occur. Naturally, once we reached our diving spot, all three of us forgot to take care of it. We must have been too transfixed by Joanna's Southern charm to remember.

So there I was, sitting next to Joanna while drinking wine after Jimmy and Ollie had gone over the side. Being two red-blooded male and female specimens, there was really nothing for Joanna and me to do except enjoy the afternoon, and *enjoy* it we did. However, unbeknownst to us, the boat was also slowly taking on water. Being in the middle of a most sultry libidinous adventure, we were gloriously oblivious to all but each other. There we were, alone on a boat, bobbing up and down together in rhythm with the waves, the sun beating down, high on both life and too much wine. That is, until I happened to look up and notice that the sidewall of the boat was almost at water level. And then it hit me: I had forgotten to put in the damn plug! We were sinking fast. As quickly as I could, I jammed the thing back into the drain hole and began bailing with my cupped hands, which is all I had available.

At about that same time, Ollie and Jimmy popped their heads up out of the water and started to climb into the boat. I yelled at them to stop before they capsized us. This was a real emergency. Although the boys were tired and cold and wanted to get back aboard, our transom was barely above water level, and if they *had* gotten in, it would have sunk us on the spot.

Here we were, about a thousand feet off shore and a quarter mile from the pier, about to go under. I asked Ollie and Jimmy if they thought they could swim to shore. Ollie looked around and gave me one of those "You've got to be kidding" looks, but I said I could take their tanks and we could just lose the weight belts and replace them later. They had wet suits and life vests on so they couldn't drown. And I thought that perhaps if I could get the boat going at least four or five knots in a forward direction maybe the water would drain out of the boat by the time I reached the pier.

Ollie and Jimmy said they could make the swim and would see us at the pier. While all this was happening, Joanna was busy trying to get her clothes back on, so it was a real reverse striptease for the guys in the water. I was mortified, but Ollie thought it was hilariously funny. Jimmy wasn't quite as amused because he wasn't as good of a swimmer as Ollie. As for Joanna, she was so drunk by this time that she couldn't figure out why her clothes were all wet (they had been strewn all over the bottom of the boat). The whole scene was like the Keystone Cops at sea.

After my friends gave me their tanks and dropped their weight belts, I watched as they turned and swam through the kelp beds toward the beach. I then started the engine, pulled anchor, gave it some gas, and aimed for the pier. The boat moaned and groaned with all the extra water weight, but at least it started to move forward slowly. I also pulled the drain plug to see what would happen. Would the water go out or would more flow in? Well, it was sort of neutral; it didn't do either. The problem was that I just couldn't get up enough speed to engage the draining process to the degree necessary.

After what seemed like an eternity, I finally got us back to the pier. I quickly jumped out and attached the crane's ropes to the boat so at least we wouldn't sink. But the craft had so much water in it I was afraid that if they tried to lift it the eyebolts might rip right out of the hull from the weight of the water. The workers at the pier thought it would be fine, so I stood there and watched painfully as the crane slowly raised her. About this time, Ollie and Jimmy came walking up to the scene and also looked on as we waited for the boat to go crashing down into the dock below. But it didn't happen, thankfully. The workers then somehow managed to get our precious eighteen-footer onto our trailer. And though the tires almost popped from the weight, at least it was in place.

Someone kindly loaned us a couple of buckets and we subsequently spent about a half an hour bailing as much of the water as we could before heading for home. With the boat dripping all the way down Sunset Boulevard through the trendy neighborhoods of Pacific Palisades and Brentwood like some kind of giant drowned rat chasing after us, we finally reached Joanna's house in Encino where we always parked the trailer (she had a big driveway). Four people were never happier to see dry land, let me tell you.

Of course, the ever-entertaining Ollie Mitchell passed that story along in the studios to every horn player and anybody else he could find for the next month. Guys ribbed me endlessly during recording sessions, saying things like, "Ollie said you almost sank your boat while you were humping Joanna Moore," and "Ollie said that you have a really cute butt when it's bouncing up and down," etc.

Looking back, I think the boat may have had its own spirit and agenda because we never once had a problem-free day with it. Every time we put it in the water, something would go wrong, either because of a bad sparkplug or a dead battery or something. The thing spent more time in the boat mechanic's shop than it did in either the water or Joanna's driveway.

As for the moral of this crazy waterlogged story? Whenever having romantic relations on the high seas, make *sure* you plug all necessary holes!

ELEVEN

Saving Lives

Sometime during 1966, just as my session career as a rock-and-roll sideman in the Los Angeles recording studios began firing on all cylinders, I met the very popular actress Joanna Moore. Appearing on many of the hit TV shows of the day, such as *The Andy Griffith Show, The Fugitive,* and *Gunsmoke,* Joanna was as beautiful as she was talented. She was also eight years my senior.

Married to (but separated from) fellow actor Ryan O'Neal at the time, the two had a couple of children, including Tatum O'Neal, who in 1974 won the Oscar for Best Supporting Actress in the film *Paper Moon.* I met Joanna at a great party Mike Post invited me to one night. It was quite a bash and there was a lot of merrymaking, though no drugs that I remember, but the alcohol was flowing freely. I was alone at the soirée, mostly chatting with some friends and feeling a little out of place without a girl on my arm. But someone spotted me and announced, "Look, Rubini's here" and theatrically asked me to play something on the piano for everyone, to which I agreed. Who knew, maybe I would get lucky in the process. So I sat down and tickled the keys for a little while.

Another chum and childhood actor Jimmy Hawkins (*Annie Oakley, The Donna Reed show, The Adventures of Ozzie and Harriet*) had brought a date with him who was a real bombshell. She had a great figure, platinum blond hair, and striking greenish-blue eyes. But the best things about her without a doubt were her throaty laugh, Southern accent, and larger-than-life outgoing personality. She was really an eye magnet, let me tell you. Once I spotted her, I couldn't take my eyes off her. But of course I had to, because everybody knows it's not polite to stare, especially at your friend's date.

Introduced to me very clearly as "Jim's date, Joanna," I had to quickly remind myself not to do anything indiscreet and so I made a point to avoid getting into any conversation with her that might raise Jim's radar. But later, while I sat at the piano doing my thing, she came over and started up some small talk, mostly complimenting me on how she loved the way I played.

After giving the encounter little further thought, a day or two after that, out of the blue, I received a call from her. I had no idea how she had gotten my number, but there Joanna was talking to me once again, her honey-eyed Georgian charm just oozing through the receiver. Intrigued, I learned during our conversation that she loved to sing and also wrote lyrics. She then asked if I might have some time to perhaps come to her home and look over her work. "Maybe we could even write a song or two together," she tossed out.

Now, I may not be the brightest light in the chandelier, but I thought this was all just a little odd, especially because she didn't know me from Adam and also because she had been Jim's date. But the offer was just innocent enough in its ambiguity that I felt I wouldn't be breaking any unspoken guy codes among friends (sorry, Jim).

Subsequently knocking on Joanna's front door at the appointed hour, I stood on her porch wondering what to expect. After a couple of tries and no answer, I then tried the handle and opened an obviously unlocked door. I stepped inside to a large foyer and adjoining living room. There were hallways to my left and right. I said "hello" a couple of times and it seemed no one was home. But then I heard her voice from down the hall saying, "In here."

Not knowing where "in here" was among the labyrinth of rooms, I followed the sound of her voice and walked down a long hallway. At the end there was a door on the left that opened into what I discovered to be her master bedroom. It was also empty.

Things were now getting kind of weird. I assumed we would be meeting in some sort of music room or something. From outside the bedroom door, once more I said, "Hello?" and again she answered with a nonchalant, "In here." So I stepped inside. It was large, elegant, and decorated in Southern Colonial style with a four-poster canopy bed and two love seats facing each other in front of a large fireplace. It felt like walking into a movie star's boudoir, which, basically, I was.

Pausing just outside the open master bathroom door, I once again said, "Hello, Joanna?"

"I'm just putting on my makeup," came her reply.

As I stepped inside, I expected to find her sitting in front of a makeup mirror or something. But I was mistaken, very mistaken.

Her bathroom was just as ostentatious as her bedroom. Overly large, it had mirrors facing each other on opposite walls and in the middle of the room sat a large sunken bathtub, filled to the brim with bubbles, along with a smiling Joanna, her bare breasts only partially hidden by the suds. She had placed scented candles all around the rim of the tub, and I also saw that there was a bottle of something in a silver ice bucket. Joanna looked up at me with a twinkle in her eye and said, "Would you like to join me in a glass of Champagne?" You could have knocked me over with a feather. It was like a fantasy come to life.

It took me a moment to adjust to my new surroundings, but never being one to turn down a polite invitation, I most certainly did what any gentleman would do in such a case. I removed my clothes, joined her in the tub, and enjoyed a most pleasant afternoon drinking Champagne and getting to know Ms. Moore much more intimately. I came to learn that she had no preference for where she made love, either; the tub, the floor of her bathroom, the carpet, the love seats, or the bed were all to her liking. They were all there for her comfort and enjoyment, and enjoy them we did.

As I got to know Joanna better, I learned that she had been separated from Ryan O'Neal for a couple of years and they did not see each other often. I was really taken with her effervescent personality, her seemingly endless energy, and her very dramatic flair for everything that she did. But in my ignorance about drugs at that time, I failed to realize that what I was seeing as endless energy was really a very bad drug habit. Joanna had been seeing several doctors, none knowing that she was seeing anybody else, and they were all writing prescriptions for uppers for her. She took them starting in the morning and continued taking them throughout the day, whenever she started to feel *down*. This was the reason she was so effervescent, charming, and outgoing, I just did not realize it for a long time.

Joanna was also an avid drinker. She was hardly ever without a glass of white wine in her hand. That was a problem for me because my mother was an alcoholic and I looked at every female I went out with through the painful memories of what alcohol did to my mother and to our family as a whole. I told Joanna that she had to stop drinking so much, and she said that she was just relieving tension and it wasn't a problem; she could stop anytime.

As our relationship developed, I started to sense that something was very wrong, but it really only came to light when I noticed that, in addition to drinking, she was taking a lot of pills to go to sleep every night. When I finally asked her why she was always taking sleeping pills, she slowly started to reveal to me that she was having sleep problems because she was also having problems staying awake. So, one pill would counteract the other. In other words, she was taking progressively more and more uppers along with more and more downers every day and every night. In my ignorance, I told her that she had to stop and I believed her when she agreed to cut back little by little.

Over time, however, I became very anxious about the situation. It didn't seem like she was cutting back much, if at all. I finally let her know that she had to quit popping the pills or I would cut off our relationship.

She then lied, telling me she had already stopped. I believed her for a while, but then I caught her doing it again. She had her barbiturate and amphetamine tablets stashed everywhere in drawers next to her bed and up high where her children and I wouldn't think to look. It was a nightmare and she was a full-blown addict.

The first crisis came one night when Joanna fell asleep in bed in a sitting position with her eyes completely open as though she was watching television. She was making a strange snoring/snorting sound like she was being strangled. I tried to wake her but there was no response. She was barely breathing and it scared me to death. I then dragged her to the kitchen where she had some Ipecac, a medicine used to induce vomiting. I poured that down her throat—and I mean the contents of the whole damn bottle. Yet no reaction.

In a panic, I then made a mixture of kitchen soap and water and forced as much of that down her throat as I could, certain that she would throw up. Between the medicine and the soapy water, she just had to. But nothing happened. Her eyes were just staring sightlessly into the void. With no alternative, I threw her in my car and raced like a madman down the hill to the emergency hospital closest to Joanna's Encino house. A couple of nurses grabbed her and took her into the treatment room, leaving me standing alone in shock and worry.

After some time, a doctor came out and told me that they had pumped Joanna's stomach and that she was lucky I had got her to the hospital when I did. If it had been a little longer, they might not have been able to revive her. He also said that they would have to call the police to report this as being a possible suicide. I knew that would be a disaster for Joanna's career, so I immediately told the doctor who she was and that her livelihood would be ruined if it somehow hit the press that Joanna Moore had overdosed and been hospitalized. I passionately explained that this was a total accident and that she had never done anything like this before.

Somehow the hospital staff believed me and didn't call the police after all. Looking back, I think it was mostly because of the era, however. During the 1960s, people, in general, were a little more sympathetic and still viewed actors and actresses as being special. There were no paparazzi or TMZ reporters constantly trying to dig up dirt. Anyway, that was the first time I saved Joanna's life. Now on to time number two.

Not long after the stomach-pumping incident, Joanna told me that Ryan O'Neal had recently gotten another actress, Leigh Taylor-Young, pregnant while he was still married to her (Joanna). From what I understood, O'Neal had then contacted Joanna to say that they had to immediately get a divorce so he could legally marry his new love because he didn't want his child to be born out of wedlock. O'Neal was a strict Catholic and although committing adultery did not seem to bother him, having a child outside of marriage apparently did. So, after much haggling, crying, and swearing, Joanna agreed to get the divorce. And since it was necessary to do it ASAP, I bought a couple of plane tickets for Joanna and me to go to El Paso, Texas, with a quickie Mexican divorce just over the border in Juarez being the ultimate destination.

While we were planning this trip, Joanna became very emotional about the whole thing, crying, drinking, taking pills, and generally feeling like she had failed as a woman and a mother. In her heart of hearts, she really did not want to get a divorce. She couldn't function well, so I made all the phone calls, the reservations at the hotel, and the appointment with the attorney.

Fortunately for the frantic O'Neal, Joanna was currently "at liberty," a show business term meaning "waiting for the next job." So she and I were able to fly down to El Paso within a few days. We had found a Mexican attorney (*abogado*) in Juarez before we left, who said he could expedite the process and we could be in and out of there in a weekend. Upon arriving in El Paso, we checked into a hotel that I would describe as second-rate at best.

After we unpacked our bags, I watched Joanna go into a hysterical breakdown. She had started drinking nonstop on the plane, and by the time we got to the hotel, she was completely bombed. She had been taking uppers all day long, but now that it was nighttime, she started popping downers. We had scheduled our first appointment with the abogado early Saturday morning across the border in Juarez, and we had to get some sleep or Joanna was not going to be able to make the appointment.

Her favorite downer pill at that time was Tuinal, a barbiturate/depressant that has long since been discontinued because of its high risk for causing an overdose. Tuinal was used as a sleep aid, but it also had hypnotic properties that made Joanna forget that she had taken it. So as her tolerance to it grew, she would take another and another until they reached an overdose level that would literally knock her out as though she had been hit in the head with a sledgehammer. It was not a pretty sight, and I had to view it quite often.

Joanna finally passed out in that stinky, roach-filled hotel room and early the next morning I dragged her out of bed, got her dressed, she took a couple of uppers, we found a taxi, and went to the address of the abogado over the border in Juarez. His office was located in a seedy part of the town, and it made both Joanna and me yet more upset and nervous just being there. The abogado was polite, pleasant, and quite thorough. He explained the details of what he had to do, including bribe the judge to sign documents on a Sunday, and that we should come back on Monday to pick up all the papers. So we had to stay two more nights in El Paso, which was one of the worst weekends of my life. Joanna was almost totally out of control the whole time and she was either manically flying high or crashing down from all the pill and alcohol consumption. I mostly just tried to keep her quiet so we wouldn't be kicked out of the hotel or arrested.

In any case, we went back to the abogado on Monday morning, got the signed papers, went back to the hotel, packed up, and caught a flight to Los Angeles. Joanna then called Ryan and arranged to give him the paperwork so that he could prove he was divorced. What a nightmare. I had never been so happy to get home in my life. None of this was good for me, and I was really convinced that I had to get away from Joanna because I was not helping her and she was definitely hurting me. But it would get worse before it got better.

In 1968, Joanna got a really good part at the Disney Studios in a picture entitled *Never a Dull Moment* co-starring Dick Van Dyke. She saw it as a step-up in her career, which had hit a lull. She was really excited about it and went to the studio every day full of energy and excitement.

One weekend, two or three weeks after Joanna's film shoot began, we decided to blow off a little steam and go to Disneyland. Once checked in at the hotel, we decided to head over to the amusement park and play tourist. Joanna brought along (against my advice) a bottle of wine wrapped in a paper bag. As most everybody on the planet knows, alcohol drinking in public is not allowed at Disneyland.

Of course, as usual, Joanna would not listen to me. She had gotten really touchy about me telling her she shouldn't do this or that. So off to the park we went with her holding her paper bag with the wine in it. Inside, at a concession stand, she bought a soft drink and emptied the contents so that she could discretely use it as a cup to hide her precious hooch.

After about thirty or forty minutes of walking around, we stopped in front of the Mad Hatter's Tea Party in Fantasyland. While we were looking at the kids and the general merriment of the whole scene, lo and behold, Goofy walked up to us. He was about seven feet tall with a long nose and whiskers, blue pants, red shirt, green hat, and big white gloves with only four fingers in them. He spoke to us and said something stereotypically Goofy-esque like, "Ha-ha-ha-hallo, there." We, of course, laughingly greeted him in return.

Goofy went on to ask us if we were having fun, to which we assured him that we were. He then jokingly pointed at Joanna's cup and said, "Wha-wha-whatcha drinking there? Could I have a sip?" We laughed some more, thinking Goofy was quite the kidder. Only by now, he was no longer being goofy at all. He was serious. "I do believe that's not Coke in your cup, is it?" Goofy then opened his shirt a bit and showed us his police badge. Gulp. Yes, that's correct—Goofy was a Disneyland policeman.

We were dumbfounded, to say the least. Very politely, the big dog then asked us if we would walk with him a few feet over to where there was a wall that turned out to be a secret door, completely disguised. He knocked on it and it magically opened (it was the Magic Kingdom, after all), and we walked through it into the real business world of corporate Disneyland. Joanna and I then accompanied Goofy to an office where we were detained. To our dismay, we were now in custody of the Disneyland Police Department.

As we quickly found out, Disneyland is a real city and it has its own police department. They don't actually keep people there in jail; they call the Anaheim cops to take care of all that. But they do have detention cells, and we were definitely being detained. Needless to say, the last thing in the world Joanna needed was an arrest record at Disneyland, especially because she was making a Disney movie at that very moment. Can you imagine the headline? "Joanna Moore, star of Disney's new comedy, *Never A Dull Moment*, arrested today by Goofy for public intoxication while visiting Disneyland."

Both Joanna and I started explaining who she was and that she was starring in Disney's new movie and it would be a fate worse than death for both her and the movie if this ever became public information. We asked if there was anything at all we could do to get out of this predicament. The detective seemed very sympathetic and listened closely. We explained that Joanna was not drunk and that she had merely taken a few sips just to celebrate her wonderful role in the new movie.

After a few minutes, the policeman relented and made us an offer. He said that normally they kicked people out of the park and put their names on a blacklist so they could never come back. But if we solemnly promised to act nice and not bring any attention to ourselves, he would allow us to go back inside. We also had to promise to never bring alcohol to Disneyland again as long as we lived. He then led us back to the hidden door, where we were free to enjoy the Happiest Place on Earth once again. But despite the obvious humor in being arrested by Goofy, my life with Joanna by then was anything but amusing. In fact, it had become a horror story.

One evening, after working a late recording session, I drove over to Joanna's house to spend the night. I had a key and I let myself in, as usual. Except this particular visit proved to be anything but usual. I walked in to her bedroom and found her completely unconscious and in a terrible position. She had evidently overdosed again and had passed out lying on her back in the bed, but had somehow also rolled over and fell off. Her head was now wedged face down between the bed frame and the nightstand.

It was an incredibly frightening sight and I feared that she had broken her neck. I called to her, but of course there was no answer. I was afraid to move her, but I also thought to myself if I didn't do something, she would probably die. As gently as I could, I lifted her body off the floor, while at the same time supporting her head. I managed to get her back up onto the bed, where she lay completely unresponsive, hardly breathing. In a panic, I called her doctor, a plastic surgeon who had done some work on her and asked him what to do. Knowing her well, and also realizing that another trip to the emergency room would be the end of her career, he told me to get her into the car and drive down to the hospital where he was working. Fortunately, it was a place I already knew about because of my trips there with her to have various nips and tucks done by him. It was about the same distance from the house as the emergency room from Joanna's first overdose, so I did what her plastic surgeon said and got her to him in record time. They were waiting for me at the emergency entrance and immediately wheeled her into an operating room. I waited outside in the visitor's area for what seemed like a century. Finally, an hour or so later, the doctor came out and told me that they had pumped her stomach, had her on life support, and if she had arrived just fifteen minutes later, they would not have been able to save her. Joanna was now in a coma and he did not know if she would come out of it.

With frayed nerves, I stayed for a couple more hours just on the chance that she might wake up. But tiredness got the better of me and I eventually left. They told me they would call me when anything changed. Honestly, I was so scared that she wouldn't wake up, it drove me out of my mind. I couldn't think of anything else. How could such a beautiful, vivacious, and loving lady get into this type of situation? It just didn't seem real, except that it was and it was also happening right in front of me.

Finally, I got a call the following afternoon. They told me that Joanna was breathing without the aid of a ventilator, but she was still unconscious and they weren't sure if she would ever wake up. And, then, the next day, Joanna opened her eyes. Somebody from the hospital called me and I drove there to see her. But I wasn't prepared for what I saw. She wasn't the Joanna Moore that I had previously known. I almost didn't recognize her.

Pale and confused while looking so tiny and frail in that big hospital bed, the once-vibrant Joanna didn't know where she was or why she was there. I'm not sure if she even recognized me. They kept her for a few more days, and every day she got a little stronger and better. Afterward, she had no memory of that night, but she did understand what she had done and how close she had come to dying. I think it was a turning point for her.

After her release, Joanna immediately went into a rehab facility in the Valley. I visited her there several times, but it was all over as far as our affair was concerned. I just couldn't be with her anymore and she knew it, too. She had to get better on her own.

The last time I saw Joanna was in 1982. She called and asked if she could stop by for a visit. She came to my recording studio on La Cienega Boulevard and told me that she had found Jesus, was born again, and that she was not smoking or drinking anymore, and definitely no longer taking drugs. Joanna had shed her ever-present wig, too, never to be worn again.

She was finally growing out her real hair. We hugged, I wished her all the best, and the one-of-a-kind Joanna Moore walked out of my life forever.

TWELVE
Arlyn's Answering Service

Whoever it was that told me that if I wanted to be a successful studio musician I would need to join Arlyn's Answering Service could not have been more right. Arlyn's was *the* connection between the musicians and the contractors who hired them to play on all the recording dates around town. Over time, the contractors became overly dependent on Arlyn to call musicians for them, even though that was one of the main things they (the contractors) were supposed to do.

So Arlyn put herself in the position of being the secretary for most of the most powerful musical contractors in the recording business in the '60s. That meant that you did not want to get on the wrong side of Arlyn or you might find yourself missing some messages, which could be disastrous for your career. She had that kind of power.

Arlyn also had one of the most sexy telephone voices anybody had ever heard. I'm sure that she worked on it quite a lot to get just the right inflection. All the musicians agreed that if she looked as good as she sounded, then Arlyn would be a great date. But that was just it; no one had ever seen her.

However, unlike some of my fellow studio players, I was not so eager to date someone whom I had never met. I knew that voices could be deceiving. Not to mention that getting romantically involved with someone upon whom you depend for jobs is a recipe for disaster.

Nevertheless, Arlyn did take a liking to me when I first joined. She had heard good reports about my playing from some of the other musicians and contractors, so when anyone asked Arlyn for a recommendation, she felt confident in suggesting me. Consequently, over time, she and I became quite *phone friendly*. I always made time to chat with her and found her to be smart with a great sense of humor. Of course, she would occasionally hint at getting together on a more personal level, but I always avoided that by turning it into a joke. Keeping things professional was of the utmost importance to me.

One time, however, Arlyn invited me to join her and some of the other girls from her service at Donte's Jazz Club on Lankershim Boulevard in North Hollywood. I accepted the invitation because I couldn't think of any polite way to get out of it. Since it wasn't a date, but rather a gathering of many, I felt it would be safe. Arlyn told me that she and her friends would all be sitting at one of the front booths and that I'd spot them right away when I walked in. No truer words have ever been spoken. All I can say is that I couldn't have missed them even if I had been legally blind.

Arlyn, tipping the scales at what looked to be more than three hundred pounds, easily took up half the booth all by herself and the others weren't much smaller. I walked over and said, "Arlyn?" not knowing which one she was. She answered and I immediately recognized her voice, but you could have knocked me over with a feather. In my mind, I never could have put that face and body together with the voice I knew so well from the phone. I was flabbergasted. If I had ever consented to go on a date with her, it would have been the end of me, for sure.

But I quickly pulled myself together and acted the gentleman that I am and introduced myself to the *girls*. One of them then got up and Arlyn invited me to sit down next to her, which I did. I'm sure Arlyn prearranged this little seating switch. I was squeezed in next to her and she was totally delighted that I had shown up. So I bought a round of drinks for the table and we all chatted and had a grand old time. But I did excuse myself early because I really did not want to wind up alone at the table with Arlyn, which is what I think her next move was going to be. That was a really close call.

However, not everyone was as lucky as I had been. A violinist friend of mine told me that there was one new violin player in town that had just gotten on the service and he had not been so fortunate. Evidently, the new guy was single, alone, and had not heard about Arlyn's considerably generous girth and wily ways. Taken in by her sultry telephone voice, he fell for her hook, line, and sinker. Slight of stature—one might even say skinny—he thought he was going to be meeting a Mary Tyler Moore lookalike. But what a surprise he got.

Arriving at her house at the appointed hour, the scrawny violinist heard a voice from inside say, "Come on in." So he entered Arlyn's living room. The lights were very dim. He didn't see her anywhere and so he called to her "Where are you?" to which she replied, "Here, in the bedroom, come on in." Now if this sounds eerily like my first encounter with Joanna Moore at her house, you're right—except far more comical.

Thinking he had struck gold, the little violinist found the bedroom door and eagerly opened it. With the lights off, all he heard was Arlyn somewhere in the darkness with her velvety voice saying, "Come and get into bed with me." Now really excited, he quickly removed everything and slid under the covers. Reaching over to take her in his arms, it was only then that he realized he was in bed with a beached whale and not a pin-up girl. But by then it was too late. He couldn't back out. If he did, he would never get another studio call for the rest of his life.

So the pint-sized fiddle player dutifully climbed on top of undoubtedly the fattest telephone operator in the history of the planet, took a big breath, and dived in for the duration. I'm sure he was just a little snack for the ravenous Arlyn. But you know, everybody deserves love wherever they can get it. And if she found a little romance there in the darkness, then I think that's just swell. Who knows, maybe the violinist hit a really high note that night.

I stayed on with Arlyn's Answering Service all through the '60s and into the '70s. It was a very sad parting of the ways the day I finally called Arlyn and told her that I would no longer need her extraordinary service any longer. It was a new era.

THIRTEEN

Sonny, Cher, and Jackie O

Long before she became famous, Cher and I first met around 1960 at my old girlfriend's house in Toluca Lake, a wealthy neighborhood immediately adjacent to Burbank. She and Cher were teenage schoolmates at a private high school in the Valley and Cher happened to be at her place one afternoon when I stopped by. Ironically, the as-yet non-musical Cher was just Cher La Pierre to us, a chum hanging out at my girlfriend's house, and none of us ever had the thought that Cher would wind up being a world-famous singer and entertainer.

As the years passed, I subsequently became one of the busiest pianists in town. And as fate would have it, one day I was called to Gold Star Recording Studios to play on a session and there, of all people, was Cher, standing with some of the other background singers waiting to start the rehearsal of the tune. We both spotted each other across the room at about the same moment, and I blurted out, "Cher?" and she said, "Mike?"

Neither of us could believe that we were looking at each other in the same room. I didn't know how Cher got there, and she didn't have any idea about what I was doing there, either. It was quite a surprise for both of us as we had never been in each other's company as adults before. We only met each other as teenagers.

Cher and I gossiped for a little bit, but the session was getting started, so we each took our respective places and went to work. Seeing Cher there doing backing vocals on a Phil Spector date made me flash back to the odd circumstance of our first meeting so many years before. But there existed little time for any of those thoughts because, once again, the chord sheet was there on the piano in front of me and I needed to immediately figure out what I was going to play. Cher and I did talk a little again during the break, but at the end of the session, she left rather quickly and I had to move on to my next studio job, anyway, whatever and wherever it might have been.

When I later met Sonny Bono, Cher's much-older boyfriend, mentor, Svengali, and eventual husband, it was a bit difficult for me to figure out exactly what his job description was. I had seen him around Gold Star where he seemed to be Spector's personal gofer. Sometimes Sonny would play the tambourine or other simple percussion instrument on recordings, while other times he ran errands for Phil; it was all sort of a blur. Mostly he just seemed like a flunky.

But I soon discovered that Sonny was a lot more talented and driven than my first impression led me to believe. I had been called by Arlyn's Answering Service to play on a session, but other than the date and time, they didn't have any particular info for me. I, of course, accepted it; Gold Star was my home away from home in those days and I loved going there. I thought the call was probably for just another Spector date. But when I got there, I was surprised yet again. It wasn't a Phil session, but a Sonny and Cher session.

Yes, Sonny Bono, the guy who played the world's worst tambourine and ran out to get hamburgers for Spector in the middle of the night was now producing a session all his own, this time with Cher and him on co-lead vocals. Sonny employed most of the same musicians that Phil used, too (i.e. the Wrecking Crew), and the studio was also set up about the same way, the only real difference being that Sonny used a different engineer. Instead of Larry Levine, who was Phil's regular engineer, Sonny hired Stan Ross, one of the two co-owners of the studio. The ever-affable Ross knew everything there was to know about the place; he and Dave Gold, his partner, had built it themselves.

Watching Sonny through the glass, it quickly became evident to me that though he was trying to copy Spector's production style, he also had his own thoughts about what the song should sound like. Of course, just like Phil, Sonny liked to yell out instructions on the fly to the musicians over the talkback microphone as we faithfully repeated sections of the music over and over. I can't remember the exact tune we worked on that day, but the session went on for hours. Sonny was going through the roof with excitement, too; he especially loved the sound of my electric harpsichord. I felt like we were all onto something new, something big. And I was right. Sonny and Cher soon had hit record after hit record, such as "I Got You Babe," "The Beat Goes On," and "All I Ever Need Is You"—with me playing the keyboards on every one of them.

Sonny and Cher were also playing a lot of shows in and out of Los Angeles and they asked me to go on the road with them, as well. But during those first several years, from about 1965 through maybe 1969, Sonny couldn't pay me (or wouldn't pay me) enough to make me take a break from my studio work to travel out of town. So he found some young players that needed the job and that worked for him for the first part of his and Cher's career together. However, having told Sonny that I would be happy to play live with him as long as the jobs were around the L.A. area, I agreed to perform with Cher and him at the Hollywood Bowl in 1966, their biggest gig yet. Sponsored by the local AM radio powerhouse 93-KHJ as the "Sonny & Cher Appreciation Concert," the bill also featured major acts such as Donovan, the Mamas and the Papas, Otis Redding, and the Turtles. The Hollywood Bowl job was also unique for me in another way. By that time, I had been hired by producer Jimmy Bowen as basically his assistant producer over at Reprise (the Frank Sinatra-owned record label) where Bowen had given me the assignment of producing a couple of songs for a new three-chord, teenybopper band named Dino, Desi & Billy. Dino was the son of Dean Martin, Desi was the son of Desi Arnaz and Lucille

Ball, and Billy was a friend of theirs from school. They had recently signed a recording contract at Reprise (no surprise there—Dean Martin was also on the label), so it was impossible for Jimmy Bowen to turn Dean down when he asked Jimmy to give his kid a shot.

Though Jimmy Bowen showed enormous talent production-wise, perhaps more important, he was also a master politician who knew just how to juggle the fragile egos and overblown demands of Hollywood's musical hierarchy. So in an effort to placate Dean Martin, one of the biggest stars in the world and Frank Sinatra's best friend, Dino, Desi & Billy suddenly became the opening act for Sonny and Cher's big show at the Hollywood Bowl.

Now needing to do double duty (I played the keyboards for Dino, Desi & Billy, too), I arrived early and performed first with them and then, when they left the stage, rushed back into the dressing room, threw on my Sonny and Cher costume and went back out. By having two sets of clothes and then changing them for each act, the audience never realized I was the same guy playing with both groups, something that amuses me to this day.

During this time, in the fall of 1965, a couple of small-time go-getters named Charlie Greene and Brian Stone were managing Sonny and Cher (the ever-ambitious Greene and Stone would go on to manage Buffalo Springfield, Iron Butterfly, and the Troggs, as well). The pair had an office on Sunset Boulevard, and I went over there from time to time to discuss business with them. I happened to be there one afternoon when a phone call came in from New York; apparently, somebody wanted to hire Sonny and Cher to fly to the Big Apple and play at a dinner party being given for Jackie Kennedy, with money being no object.

When Greene got off the phone, he had the most incredulous look on his face. He then proceeded to tell those of us who happened to be there with him what had just gone down. Jacqueline Kennedy, who had been in mourning ever since President Kennedy was assassinated well over a year before, had made it clear that she had no interest in going out in public.

This naturally left her friends quite concerned about her. A good friend of Mrs. Kennedy's somehow eventually talked her into attending a small dinner party with the proviso that Jackie would only come if her friend could get Sonny and Cher to sing at the gathering.

When Sonny heard about the proposed Kennedy gig, he enthusiastically agreed to do it. He then asked me and four other musicians who played on Sonny and Cher's records to go along. Sonny made clear that we wouldn't get paid anything because he and Cher had agreed to do it for free. But all expenses would be covered, so at least it wouldn't cost us anything.

For my part, I was thrilled. It would be an opportunity to actually meet Jacqueline Bouvier Kennedy and maybe in some small way show her how much I admired her husband and how truly stricken I was when he died. If I could do something, anything, to help her or make her life better, then I was ready to go.

We flew first class to New York City, checked in to a wonderful hotel, and the next thing I knew, I was riding up the elevator inside the Waldorf Astoria Hotel to the very top floors. I had heard of the Waldorf, of course, and was equally aware of its reputation as one of the most expensive and exclusive hostelries in the world. But what I didn't know was that there existed yet another section of exclusive apartments built on top of the hotel where the *really* rich and famous people lived, called the Waldorf Towers.

Getting off the elevator, we walked down a hallway past highly polished dark oak doors through which some of the most famous people in the world had passed. There were brass plaques screwed into some of them with inscriptions that read something similar to "Franklin Roosevelt stayed here June 3rd, 1944."

As we walked up to the designated unit, a butler immediately greeted us. As we entered through the foyer and passed a doorway, I saw a small group of guests sitting at an ornately decorated dining table, including Jacqueline Kennedy. We were then shown into a bedroom where we removed our jackets and gloves etc. From there, we proceeded to the living room where we set up our instruments and waited, with the organizer having rented a small harpsichord for me to play.

After a while, the guests filtered into the very small living room. I remember that I was amazed at how small the apartment was compared to our homes in LA. I knew this was the crème de la crème, but really, it felt like the whole apartment was maybe about 500 square feet.

Jackie's escort for the evening was a quiet, elderly gentleman. When everybody sat down, there was only one chair left for the both of them, and Jackie, being the tremendously elegant and generous lady that she was, graciously insisted that man with her take the chair. She then quite contentedly seated herself on the carpet in front of his chair. So there she was, one of the most beautiful and celebrated women of the century, dressed in a pink, full-length silk evening gown sitting on the floor and still looking fabulous. No wonder she entranced everybody; Mrs. Kennedy was the essence of class.

We then played our set with Sonny and Cher singing "I Got You Babe" and their other hits. After about forty minutes, we finished the little show. And though there was polite applause from everybody after each song, with the exception of Jackie, who was clearly enthralled by Sonny and Cher, I am not sure just how much the guests really enjoyed our performance. They all seemed a bit stiff. Nor did I get the feeling that they really approved of rock and roll in general, let alone Sonny's wild furs and Cher's long hair and tight fitting hip-hugger pants.

However, Jackie was obviously thrilled by the performance, and when it concluded, she came over and walked down the line we made standing side by side, where she shook our hands and said what a pleasure it was to meet us. I could hardly contain myself as I took her hand in mine and introduced myself. Her eyes were bright and she looked straight into mine as we talked. For those few fleeting seconds, I felt like I was the only person in the room, maybe the world. That's the kind of charm and charisma she had. She made it a magical moment, one that I will never forget.

Thank you so very much, Mrs. Kennedy.

FOURTEEN

Joining Groups

Though during my session days in the mid-'60s I played in support of every conceivable style of popular music artist—from the likes of Sonny and Cher to Frank Sinatra to Tina Turner—I also occasionally found myself hired to become a *secret* member of a fake rock-and-roll group, too.

Concocted by Hollywood-based producers such as Joe Saraceno, Kim Fowley, H.B. Barnum, and Bob Keane, among others, these kinds of bands were given goofy, made-up names like the Darts, B. Bumble and the Stingers, and the Marketts. The goal was to have my fellow studio musicians and me (now known as the famed "Wrecking Crew") play in various combinations on a whole slew of simple, quickly-produced songs that the record labels would then release as 45s under phantom band names, always on the cheap and with an eye toward hopefully getting lucky by scoring a hit single out of the deal.

Probably the best-known fake group I was in was the Monkees. That group was the total fabrication of two wannabe producers, Bob Rafelson and Bert Schneider. Their idea was to create a little four-piece rock-and-roll band and a corresponding TV series that would hopefully cash in on the teen craze known as the Beatles that gripped the record industry at that time. They hired young actors to play musicians, but who weren't really musicians themselves; they just had to look the part. The head of music at Screen Gems (the company producing the series), Don Kirshner, assigned the songwriting team of Tommy Boyce and Bobby Hart to produce many of the Monkees' early singles and albums, along with the music for the series itself. Boyce and Hart, in turn, hired studio musicians to actually record the songs, me being one of them. I never kept track of how many Monkees records I played on, but it was a bunch. We rarely saw the actual Monkees, either. The four of them were busy filming while we were recording their songs.

As you may have learned by reading the recent bestselling book, *The Wrecking Crew*, or by watching the documentary of the same name, many of the well-known bands in Los Angeles during the '60s couldn't really play well enough to actually make their own records. Lots of them were world-famous, too: the Byrds, the Turtles, the Ventures, Chad and Jeremy, the 5th Dimension, the Osmonds, and countless more. So the producers often hired studio musicians such as myself to cut the tunes instead. The vocalists would then overdub their voices after the fact on top of our pre-recorded instrumental tracks. When these bands later performed on popular TV shows such as *Shindig* or *American Bandstand*, they usually merely lip-synced (i.e. mouthed) the words and pantomimed their way through "playing" the instruments as best they could. It was all done Milli-Vanilli-style, long before anyone ever heard of that much-maligned pair of '80s fakers.

Of course, the record-buying public had no idea that many of the bands they were so in love with couldn't even play their own music. Though I had my own opinions about this farce—and none very good—I learned to just keep my mouth shut. Yes, it secretly frustrated the hell out of me to see other much-less-talented musicians getting all the fame and glory while I played in the background, hoping to be discovered as a solo artist. But, in the meantime, they paid me well. And though I never became a breakout pianist/singer on my own, my long and winding career in music took me in some amazing, highly successful (and sometimes mind-blowing) directions nonetheless.

But let me be clear: being a studio musician entailed much more than simply playing on other groups' records, whether they were fake like the Monkees or real, such as with Loggins and Messina or Seals and Crofts (both of whom I joined in the '70s). I played piano, organ, and harpsichord on many wonderful recordings for plenty of famous singers, Barbra Streisand, Jose Feliciano, and Nancy Wilson, among them. I also played on countless movie soundtracks and commercials. I worked, too, for some of the most talented arrangers and producers in the world. Everyday in the studio was an adventure for me. I never knew what I was going to have to do or even if I would be *able* to do it. So I always felt a little nervous, stayed on my toes, and made it a practice to listen intently to every word that anybody said to me, knowing that if I screwed up—if I made just one mistake or couldn't cut it—my career could be over as a studio player in the blink of an eye. There was no room for errors. Yet, I also had the time of my life.

FIFTEEN

Frank Sinatra

Everybody wants to know about the song "Strangers in the Night."
I get asked all the time about how I got the chance to play on it, what Frank Sinatra was like, how I felt, etc. Between Sinatra, Sonny and Cher, and Phil Spector, one might think that nobody else in the world ever made a record, at least that I played on. And people ask me about Sinatra far more than the other two.

For me, it was a sort of pivot point, career-wise. It was the moment when people really started taking me seriously as a first-call studio musi-cian, the guy producers suddenly had to have. "Strangers in the Night" came out in April of 1966, and soon after, I was asked to be Johnny Mathis's musical director. By 1969, I was Nancy Wilson's musical director. Two years more and I became Sonny and Cher's musical director. All were exception-ally well-paid, esteemed positions that a few years before I could have only dreamed of obtaining.

Was it all a natural arc, a path that I was already traveling? Or did the fact that I happened to play on two of Mr. Sinatra's biggest hits of all time ("Strangers in the Night" and "That's Life") have something to do with my fast-rising career trajectory? I have no idea. But I did know one thing: before I got the call to play on my first Sinatra recording date, I didn't believe that I had arrived.

Please let me explain. No matter whom I played for, and there were many famous people, I always felt insecure, never feeling like I had really *made* it. It was perhaps because of my father's fall from fame in the '50s, right about the time I began to understand what was really going on in my family. When I was a little boy, everything seemed bright and rosy. My mom always took great care of us, and we lived in beautiful homes in both Malibu and Beverly Hills.

But then when I was about twelve, my parents split up and my brother, mother, grandmother, and I all moved to Palm Springs. We started living in our little twenty-foot house trailer that had previously only been used for a couple of short vacations and road trips to places like Pismo Beach. All by herself, mom hitched it up to her car and drove it the hundred-and-fifty-odd miles from our house in Malibu to Palm Springs and rented a space in the local trailer park at the east end of town. It was then that the rude facts of life started to open my eyes to the reality of what was happening: that my father was no longer the big star, money was really limited, and my mom had to go to work for the first time since I was born. It left me feeling anxious ever after, as though the ice could break at any moment under my feet.

Consequently, as I started to get busy as a studio musician during the mid-'60s, I never felt secure, no matter whom I played for nor how much money I earned. I kept remembering what happened to my dad and our family. I saw that I was getting to be popular, but there were still other pianists out there who I thought were more in-demand than I, such as the early Wrecking Crewers Don Randi and Leon Russell. For every session I played on, they played on two.

Now, Don Randi was a great friend to me, and he helped me get established in the first place by giving me his Sunday night jazz gig at Sherry's on the Strip. So I have no complaints. He was wonderful to me. He also recommended me to producers and arrangers all over town whenever he was over-booked. In effect, I became his main substitute and he was always delighted when he got a good report back on me. He went out of his way to encourage me whenever we crossed paths at United or Western and would tell me, "Hey, Rubini, so-and-so told me they really liked the way you played on that date I gave you. That's good because I know I can always count on you when I'm in a jam."

Of course, Randi didn't want me to take *all* of his work from him, particularly the high-profile dates, which I would never have been called for anyway. I finally got to a place in my mind where I felt that I was doing pretty well for myself and that my future was pretty much secure, but then one day Don burst my bubble by walking up to me with that big toothy smile of his and said, "Guess what? I just got called for my first Spector session." And I knew then and there that I still had not arrived. Phil Spector was the rock-and-roll gold standard. He was the hottest, most successful producer in the music business during the early-to-mid-'60s. If you played for him, then everybody in town would want your services.

So I remained on the B-list. Worse yet, Spector commonly used three or four piano players on each of his recording sessions, and I wasn't even on the list at all. I was crushed. For the next several weeks, I moped around feeling really depressed and sorry for myself. Every musician in town wanted to play on those dates. That was the real "in" crowd.

And then it happened.

Out of the blue, I received a message one day from Arlyn's Answering Service to play for Phil Spector on such-and-such date. I think that Don Randi may have told Spector's contractor my name and so they called me. Hallelujah, I had arrived! I was dancing on clouds for the rest of the week.

Finally, the big day arrived. I walked into Gold Star and, sure enough, there were Don and the Wrecking Crew guys (and one gal, as in Carol Kaye), plus the legendary Phil Spector himself, who was nothing but friendly to me, by the way. I said my hellos to those I knew, laughed at a few musician jokes, and then we all settled down to business. Though I can't remember what song we recorded that fateful day—almost certainly nothing that became a hit—I nevertheless went home that night so excited that I never did fall asleep.

As time went by, Don Randi and I would pass each other in the hallways of various recording studios around town and usually stop and chat for a moment. One day, Randi pulled me aside and said, "Hey Rubini—guess what? I just got my first Sinatra session!" I looked at Don and thought I was going to have a heart attack. It all came crashing over me like a tidal wave. I realized in that moment that *I* hadn't arrived; *Don* had arrived! Playing for Spector was great, the top of the rock-and-roll heap, for sure. But there was only one Sinatra.

Once again, I was devastated. How could Don Randi be so lucky? Of course, he was a great pianist and had been around much longer than I, so I couldn't begrudge him his good fortune. But I was young and hungry and wanted to be on the A-list too. Call it jealousy or insecurity or whatever you want, but I hated the way it made me feel. Hollywood, whether in the form of film or music, is an intensely competitive place and his Sinatra news made me once again feel like I was on the outside looking in. I had totally forgotten how I thought I had arrived when I got my first Spector session. In my own obsessed way, I knew that I had to play for Sinatra or I would never consider myself a success.

Then, one day, many months later, the miracle of all miracles happened—I got the Sinatra call that up to then had only been a dream. It came from Jimmy Bowen, a hot young producer for whom I had been working. Bowen was going to cut a song called "Strangers in the Night" with Frank and wanted me to play the piano on it. Sinatra desperately wanted back on the Top 40 charts, to be contemporary and relevant again. "Strangers..." was carefully chosen by Bowen to hopefully do exactly that. And when Frank Sinatra hired you for a project, you were expected to come through. So the pressure was on for Bowen.

In keeping with the importance of the recording session, Bowen hired the great Ernie Freeman to do the arrangement and also blew out all the stops budget-wise. No expense was spared. The night I walked into the studio at United Recorders, I was greeted by no less than about sixty guys in the orchestra. It was a huge date by anyone's standards, let alone Jimmy Bowen's; usually he had about seven or eight musicians on hand. But this time around, practically every string and horn guy in town was there.

As I walked up to the Steinway concert grand piano, however, I noticed a man already sitting there looking at some sheet music. Pleasantly introducing himself as "Bill Miller," he went on to say that he was Mr. Sinatra's pianist and would be playing the session, which left me flabbergasted. Here was my big chance to play with the Chairman of the Board himself and someone was taking my place. I didn't know what to do; I certainly couldn't argue with Bill about who was supposed to be sitting on the piano bench.

So I walked back to the control room and quietly stood behind Bowen, who was busily talking with Eddie Brackett, his regular engineer. They were discussing some recording problem together and I just stood and watched them, not wanting to interrupt. After about a minute, Bowen became aware of me standing behind him. He turned around and said in a voice that clearly indicated he was pressed for time, "Rubini, what the hell are you doing in here? You should be out there at that piano."

As politely as I could, I told the Texas-born Bowen that I *had* already been out there, but that Bill Miller announced to me that he was going to be playing the session and that I should just go sit somewhere else. Bowen, the ultimate diplomat and always ready for any dilemma, thought about this for around three seconds and then said, "Come on, follow me."

Bowen zipped out of the control room and back into the studio, with me following along about six feet behind him like a lap dog. He walked right up to the piano and, I swear, proceeded to hand out the biggest line of bullshit I have ever heard in my life. With a perfectly straight face, he ever so pleasantly told Bill Miller—Frank Sinatra's personal pianist, mind you—that he knew that Bill was the greatest piano player ever, but that he (Bowen) had already hired me to play on a special part for the record that wasn't written on the sheet music. Because of that, there wouldn't be enough time to show anyone else how to do it. Therefore, would he (Bill) mind too terribly much if I (Michel) just played on this one song?

Bill Miller thought about this for a couple of seconds and decided that he didn't want to argue with Bowen. After all, Bowen was the producer and it was his date. You don't argue with the general when you are only a private. So the ever-gracious Miller got up from the piano, and I sat down. Bowen and Miller then walked back to the control room together. What a politician Bowen was. He could talk the shine off a new pair of shoes.

With that little disruption out of the way, I sat down and looked at the music for the first time. I had never rehearsed a special part with Jimmy in the office. That was all baloney. Bowen just wanted me to do my usual thing. He knew I'd play exactly what he needed for the record.

We rehearsed the song for about an hour until everybody had played the arrangement about a dozen times. At this point, we all knew what we were going to do by heart. We could have played it in our sleep. After a ten-minute break, we all came back and waited.

A few minutes later, Frank Sinatra showed up with his entourage. He entered the studio followed by a bunch of people, mostly couples, who were in evening dress. They all looked like they had stepped off the pages of GQ magazine or had maybe just left the casino. The men wore dark silk suits and ties and the women had on cocktail dresses and/or evening gowns with furs to match. Diamonds, too, sparkled from every lady's ear and neck.

Marching in behind Sinatra, they were directed to about thirty nearby metal folding chairs, where they all sat down and quietly watched us. It was quite surreal; I had never before played a session where the artist brought his own audience. Of course, this *was* Frank Sinatra.

With the vocal booth placed right next to the piano near the back wall of the studio, Sinatra walked up to me, stuck out his hand, and introduced himself (as if he needed to do such a thing). Naturally, I stood and shook his hand in return, told him my name, and said that it was a pleasure and privilege to be playing for him. Though he looked at me somewhat quizzically while probably wondering where Bill Miller was, much to my relief, Sinatra didn't have me thrown out. He actually couldn't have been more cordial.

Standing in front of his microphone, Sinatra then chatted a bit with Bowen and Ernie Freeman. After some sound adjustments, we finally started the song. Frank came in on cue and we did a take, but at the end, he got a little confused. On the records of the '40s and '50s, the arrangers always wrote real "cold" endings to the songs, they didn't just fade out. Sinatra thought "Strangers..." was going to end like that. Nobody had told him it was going to gradually fade. This was the rockin' '60s, after all, and almost all the pop/rock records faded out.

Normally, as a song fades, the singer will repeat the tag line or chorus over and over as the engineer slowly lowers the recording volume. Which is what was supposed to happen on "Strangers in the Night." But either Sinatra just didn't know he was expected to do that or else he had failed to prepare a proper ending to match the fadeout.

After Sinatra stopped singing, he and Bowen then had a hushed discussion near me about what was happening. I could see that Sinatra was not happy. Bowen finally asked Frank to just vamp (i.e. make up) something at the end to sing over the top of the music. I think Bowen was secretly praying at that moment that God would deliver him from Sinatra's impending wrath, which could be withering, if not career-ending, when he was displeased about something.

We cut it again and Frank scatted something at the end that was not great, to say the least. Bowen and Sinatra talked once more, this time through their headphones, and an increasingly impatient (and likely embarrassed) Sinatra said he would do one last take, but that was it. Take it or leave it. He had a plane to catch. So Ernie counted it down and we recorded a third and final pass at the tune. This time, however, when we got to the end, Sinatra, the old pro that he was, cut loose with the now famous, "Doo-be-doo-be-doo" scat line. We played the music around for about thirty seconds with him singing over the top of us and then Ernie stopped the band just as the engineer faded the volume down to zero. And that was it.

Sinatra asked Bowen if he had what he needed, said goodnight to me, and then walked over to his guests. Just before departing, Sinatra turned to all the musicians and said, "Thanks, boys—great job." His entourage then rose as one, just like the good little soldiers they were, and followed him right out the door of the recording studio and into the night.

As the orchestra took a break, Bowen walked out into the studio. He and I stood together in front of the big Altec playback monitors (speakers) as Eddie Brackett rewound the tape and then replayed the whole song for us. When it got to the fadeout, just as Frank began singing the "Doo-be-doo-be-doo" part, Bowen turned to me and asked, "So, Rubini, what do you think?"

After a moment of reflection, I replied, "You know, Jimmy, this is either the worst fade ever recorded and it's going to be a total bomb, or people are going to pick up on it and think it's really cool and it'll sell a million copies. One or the other."

Well, we all know what happened from there. "Strangers in the Night" became a giant success, going all the way to number one on the Billboard Hot 100 singles chart in 1966, in the process knocking the Beatles' "Paperback Writer" right out of the top spot and also winning a Grammy for Song of the Year. You can't get any more contemporary than that. I guess Frank and Jimmy knew what they were doing. And I'm fortunate to say that I was there when it happened. That's when I knew I had finally arrived.

SIXTEEN

Psychedelic Harpsichord

A s I became busy doing recording sessions during the '60s, producers and arrangers frequently started asking me to play keyboards other than just the piano. Which I was happy to do, of course, because whenever I played a second instrument on the same session, I got paid about fifty percent above the regular union scale. So I could often be found offering up my skills around town on the Hammond B3 organ, various electric pianos, and also on a vintage Chamberlin that I owned, which was an electronic tape-playing keyboard that had pre-recorded sounds triggered by pressing a key.

But it didn't stop there. To earn additional income, I also owned a full-size grand Sabathil acoustic harpsichord, an electric harpsichord, and two electric pianos that I rented out for sessions. It was a side business that just sort of developed. The demand for those sounds in the L.A. studios started with the flower power movement up north in San Francisco where harpsichords were commonly being played in unison with twelve-string acoustic guitars on various hit records. It all sounded very flowery and delicate, like the embroidered blouses the girls wore at that time. Mozart would have loved it.

There was a company in Los Angeles, Modern Music, that rented out harpsichords for recording sessions. When I initially inquired about how much the record companies were paying for these rentals, I found out it was as much as a hundred and fifty dollars per session, plus the cartage fee to deliver them to and from wherever. Since I was playing these very instruments several times a week, I quickly did the math and figured out I could buy a harpsichord of my own and pay for it in about twenty sessions. That was about six or seven weeks by my estimation. After that it would be all profit.

Feeling the entrepreneurial spirit, I had asked a few of my producer and arranger friends if they would rent my harpsichord instead of Modern's and they all said yes. So I drove on down to Finnegan's Pianos on La Cienega Boulevard and bought a Sabathil, one of the best in the world. It cost me about two thousand dollars, too, more than a lot of new cars went for at the time. But, just as I figured, I had it all paid for within three months.

From that point on, I made as much as a thousand dollars a week just renting the harpsichord to studios. Can you believe it? And that was in 1960s' dollars. I even had my own personal tuner. That harpsichord became the most-listened-to harpsichord on the radio during the latter half of the decade. And I played it myself on many Monkees sessions, Chad and Jeremy sessions, Phil Spector sessions, and most distinctly, on Sonny and Cher sessions.

Ever the tinkerer, at one point I came up with the novel idea to electrify my harpsichord by placing several contact microphones inside and running them through a preamp that then plugged into a big Fender Super Reverb guitar amplifier. After adding a few cool effects like a fuzz tone pedal and a chorus box, I had the first electric/psychedelic harpsichord in the history of recorded music. One day I brought this customized unit to one of Sonny and Cher's sessions, and when Sonny heard it, he went nuts. He thought it was the greatest sound ever. We then worked out a way of having me play rolling chords on it that were blended with one or two twelve-string guitars being strummed or picked in the same rhythm pattern. Sonny added a ton of echo to the final product and that became the centerpiece of Sonny & Cher's unique rhythm sound.

As the '60s came to an end, the delicate plucking sound of the harpsichord finally went out of style, being replaced by heavy-metal power-chord rock and roll. With little demand for it anymore, I took the goliath piece of gear back to Finnegan's where Bill Finnegan told me he couldn't buy it for cash, but would gladly put it up for sale on a consignment basis. That sounded fine to me, so I left it there in his store.

After having checked in with Bill a couple of times over several weeks only to find that my big, beautiful electric harpsichord still had not been sold, I subsequently forgot all about the thing for at least another six months. One day, though, it popped into my head, so I gave Bill a call to see what was up. Only no one answered. After a few more days of receiving no response, I finally drove down to the store to see him personally.

Much to my surprise, when I arrived there was a big sign in the window that said, "Out of Business" and "Building for Lease." I dashed to a payphone and dialed the number listed. The man who answered at the leasing company informed me that Finnegan's had gone bankrupt a couple of months before and had moved everything out. I then asked as to the whereabouts of all the pianos, organs, and especially my one-of-a-kind Sabathil and Son grand harpsichord. "I have no idea," came the reply. And that was that. Bill Finnegan took my expensive harpsichord and just disappeared with it into thin air, gone forever. I never did find out what happened to it, either, but I've always been grateful that it served me so well.

SEVENTEEN

Ginger Baker

Her name was Mrs. Baker. At least that's what she said when she introduced herself to me. Although "Rainbow" (not her real name) wasn't actually married to Ginger Baker—the famous rock drummer from the band Cream with whom she was cohabitating—she was definitely his live-in dope dealer.

Rainbow, a real groupie type, hit on me at a Cream concert I attended in 1967 in Los Angeles, probably because I had just finished my own performance next door at the Shrine Auditorium and was still dressed in my tux. Everyone else in attendance to watch the superstar band (whose members also included Jack Bruce on bass and Eric Clapton on guitar) wore grubby jeans, old tie-dyed t-shirts, and were generally stoned out of their minds while listening to Ginger pound his drums during one of the longest and most bombastic solos I had ever heard.

Beautiful, exotic, and clearly bored with everything going on, Rainbow asked me to take her back to her hotel before the show even ended. Never one to turn down a pretty face, I said okay, and we hopped in my Ferrari and zoomed off.

After the two of us arrived inside the swanky suite she shared with Ginger at the Chateau Marmont, one of L.A's trendiest hotels (and the notorious location of the comedian John Belushi's tragic drug overdose death many years later), Rainbow then phoned her personal masseur to come up and give me a massage.

When he arrived, I excused myself momentarily and went into the bathroom. I noticed that the medicine cabinet was a bit ajar and out of curiosity opened it to see what was there. The thing that caught my eye immediately was a kitchen spoon with what appeared to be a pile of powdered toothpaste in it. I mean, what else could it be? Because if it was something else, then I had to ask myself a serious question, like what was I going to do next?

Since I couldn't stay in the bathroom all night long pondering this question, I just assumed it must be powdered toothpaste, which then allowed me to go back out to the living room, get undressed, and lie down on the table. The masseur then went to work on me.

While I lay prone on the table wondering what was going to happen next, Ginger himself came bursting through the door into the living room with his trademark red hair exploding out of his scalp and with a crazed look in his eyes. Heading right toward me, Rainbow intercepted him just before he could ask who I was (or worse) and steered him into the bathroom instead, where after a moment or two of frenzied conversation she produced a syringe and deftly drove it into his arm, presumably filling his veins with a dose of heroin. As I lay there taking in this bizarre scene, the masseur never looked up or lost a beat. He had obviously seen it all before.

With her arm around his waist, Rainbow then guided an incoherent Ginger into the master bedroom where he collapsed onto the bed with a groan of opiate-induced pleasure. Waiting until he began snoring his way into a drug-hazed coma, she then came out, bade the masseur goodbye, and led me into the other bedroom.

Now I knew what picture she was drawing in her mind, but for me, it wasn't so easy to pick up the brush and stroke away with her on the same canvas. Ginger Baker was right there in the next bedroom sawing the thickest logs in the forest, and frankly, it was distracting. And what if he woke up?

No, this wasn't going to be a great impressionistic sexual masterpiece we were about to paint. I was way too nervous, and then she got weird, as if this whole thing wasn't already weird enough. She started haranguing me and then went into the bathroom with the door open and started brushing her hair while still yelling at me, but not looking at me either.

Rainbow was staring into the mirror and her voice just kept going up and up. Finally, she was becoming hysterical and I got scared. What if security showed up and there I was with Ginger Baker in bed and heroin all over the place?

Oh yes, I forgot to mention that Rainbow also told me that she was not a heroin user; she was a morphine addict. An *addict*? I had to make a decision fast.

Luckily, she didn't seem to know if I was there anymore, anyway, although she was still screaming at me. So, I said rather softly to her, "Rainbow, I'm going now, see you later." And with that, I started crab-walking my way sideways toward the front door.

I fully expected her to turn around any second to see that I was no longer standing there and then rush out into the living room and scream at me even worse. But God and country were on my side; she remained transfixed by the mirror.

Opening the front door, I let myself out into the hallway while she bellowed incoherently. Even once it was closed, I could still hear her.

Now, the Chateau Marmont was and is an old hotel, the walls are thin, and sound travels through them like a wind walker. I pressed the elevator button and waited. She was still screaming. The elevator arrived, I got in and down I went to the garage. The elevator shaft was like an echo chamber, with Rainbow's voice reverberating off the walls, but became softer with each descending floor.

Mercifully reaching the bottom, I then stepped out into the dimly lit garage and paused to listen. Sure enough, I could still hear her up there in the room screaming at me or the mirror or perhaps some unimaginable terror.

When I got into my car, the sound of Rainbow's voice finally grew silent, and I drove home in grateful solitude and more than a little shaken. Spending some quality time with the Baker "family" had turned into one of the strangest evenings of my life.

1.   Handsome and debonair, this is a publicity headshot of my father, Jan Rubini,
      taken during the 1930s. A world-famous violinist, he very much wanted me to
      follow in his footsteps and build a career in classical music. Though I was a clas-
      sically-trained pianist, I ultimately decided to go the rock and roll route instead,
      much to his chagrin.

2. Though Terry Walker was this beautiful actress's stage name (and, for a little while, "Alice Dahl"), she actually began life in Alaska as the solidly Norwegian Alice Norberg. Of course, I simply knew her as mom. After appearing in lots of movies during the '30s and '40s with stars such as Bela Lugosi, Buddy Rogers, and Milburn Stone, she eventually married my dad, stopped acting, and settled into a life of domesticity in Malibu.

3.   The original family band, right? Wrong. This is my mom, dad, brother David, and
      me (at the piano) all pretending to play as a unit for the camera in our yard
      in Malibu. In some ways, I think my father always wanted the four of us to be
      a close-knit "Father Knows Best" kind of household, except we were anything
      but. With his serial philandering and long absences on tour, my mother's heavy
      drinking, and my notable independent streak, we were in actuality all headed in
      very different directions.

4.   "Look, look into my eyes," my father seems to be telepathically commanding me in a late 1950s publicity photo of the two of us. By the age of fifteen I had become his regular piano-playing accompanist on concert dates all over the country, causing me to graduate a year late from high school.

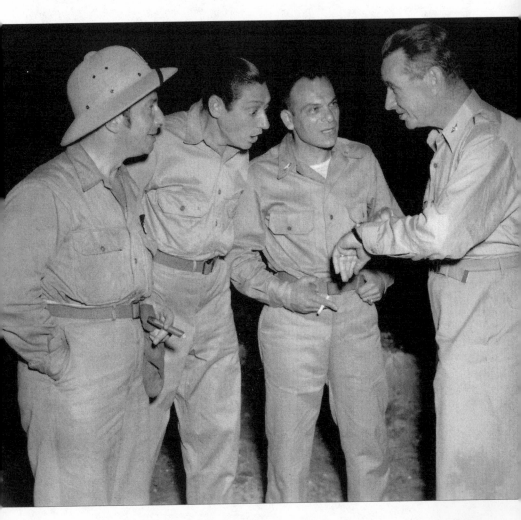

5. Two paisanos walk into a war: my dad (far left) and a young Frank Sinatra (second from right) chew the fat while touring to entertain the troops during World War II. Twenty years later, I would have my own memorable encounter with the Chairman of the Board on "Strangers in the Night."

6. Quite a pair, aren't they? My father and the native South African girl, I mean. The look on his face is priceless, too. Dad's insatiable interest in the female form was no secret. And, for better or worse, I have inherited his "appreciation."

Wednesday, Nov. 20, 1957 ★ **Los Angeles Herald & Express A-3**

Hollywood High and Griffith Park

Snake Swaps Told In Zoo Keeper Case

The fine art of snake-swapping as practiced by the students of Hollywood High School and the Griffith Park Zoo was outlined for the Civil Service Commission as it probed the firing of senior animal keeper Aaron Krieger.

Giving the reptile report was Michel Rubini, 14, who told of a series of snake trades with Krieger and Chief Animal Keeper Loren Mike Wendt.

Testifying as the assistant city attorneys Walter W. Carrington and Weldon Weber sought to show Krieger made reptile deals without authorization, Rubini recalled how he had swapped a rainbow boa for a South American boa.

BEST OF BARGAIN

"They got the best of the bargain," he said, "The snake I gave them sells for $25 and the one they gave me is worth only about $10."

Snakes, which he called "the most misunderstood creatures in the world," were swapped regularly between the zoo and the high school youths to keep the zoo's snake pits filled, Rubini said.

Also testifying was Miss Catherine Van Ingen, former zoo office clerk, who disclosed arguments between Krieger and Wendt over the running of the zoo and Krieger's opinion of Wendt's ability.

Richard E. Bullard, city superintendent of horticulture, testified for 2½ hours, reading reports of Krieger's work in which Krieger had commented on friction between himself and Wendt.

The hearing, which resumed today, deals with Park Department charges of insubordination, use of abusive language, failure to improve his work and reptile trades with private parties by Kreiger.

7. Maybe it was my feeling of being an outsider among my own peers. Or perhaps I just identified with critters that were wild and free. At any rate, I became obsessed during my adolescence with all things slimy, slithery, and often dangerous. In this capacity, I amassed quite a collection of exotic reptiles, even trading them with an animal-keeper friend up at the Los Angeles Zoo who they eventually (and unfairly) tried to fire. As this old newspaper clip details, I did my best to defend him.

The Desert Sun—2ª

PALM SPRINGS, CALIFORNIA

Thursday, May 19, 1955

Throng Thrilled by Young Pianist

Members of the local press and radio who gathered at the Biltmore hotel Monday evening at a cocktail party hosted by Sam Levin were treated to a rare musical treat.

During the cocktail hour which commemorated the third Summer season's continuation of operation saw Michel Rubini, 12 year old son of Jan Rubini, famed violinist, sit down at the grand piano to perform in such a manner as to hush the crowded room.

The youngster showed a finely developed sense of music appreciation and this was indicated in his renditions of Toccata by Katchaturian and Rachmannanoff Prelude in C minor. The 12-year old imparted his evident love of music in his playing of the two intricate pieces of music to a degree that if one did not know a 12 year old boy was playing, it would have been presumed that a famed pianist was at the keys.

And by the way, the Summer kick-off of the Biltmore's summer operation was a huge success.

8.   This article really should have been titled, "Man Who Pulled Out Schlong Thrilled by Young Penis." Though I was happy at the tender age of twelve to get the gig, the pervert who recorded my performance that day to later play on the radio had also exposed himself to me beforehand and wanted me to do the same in return. I refused.

9.   Ever heard of Fats Domino? Well, ladies and gentlemen, here is "Slim" Rubini, all sixteen years of him, in New Orleans in 1959. After a bit of chatting, the drummer had asked me to come up onstage and play something, probably because he wanted to have a little fun at my expense. Though I was nervous, and definitely didn't look the part given my formal attire, I'm sure I surprised him (and everyone else) by holding my own.

10. Though the college no longer exists (it was located somewhere out in Rancho Cucamonga), this marquee lists an upcoming appearance by my father and me during our violin-and-piano concert tour in 1959. While playing gigs all across the country had its moments of fun and was a prestigious thing to do, what I really wanted was to get back home to my girlfriend in Los Angeles. Hey, I was a teenager!

11.   Yes, that is indeed my pet coyote pup. Oh, you're still looking at the charming young lady? Well, she was a "friend" of mine in the early '60s at the Hollywood Modeling Studio, where let's just say that posing for photos was the least of what went on around there.

12. "Imagine me and you...so happy together!" While I did play piano on a song or two for the Turtles during the '60s, I actually spent more time with the real-life sea-dwelling kind. These are a couple of my little buddies from my personal reptile collection back then.

13. This is a late '60s shot of me sitting with the legendary jazz singer, Nancy Wilson, as we took a ferry ride together from Kowloon on the Hong Kong Peninsula to the Central District of Hong Kong where our hotel was located. The world-famous Ms. Wilson had hired me as her musical director for a big tour of Asia, which proved to be unforgettable—as were her vocal performances every night. To me, Nancy, Ella, and Lady Day were/are the three greatest of all time.

14. When I first saw this marquee on the Vegas Strip in the early '70s with my name on it I felt like Jimmy Cagney in that classic scene at the end of White Heat where he shouts out, "Made it, ma, top of the world!" Except, of course, I didn't burn to death.

15. Here I am in action inside Houston's Astrodome as Sonny and Cher's musical director somewhere around 1974. I took great pride in my hip stage appearance back then. Can you dig my trendy denim tux, plus Afro and beard?

16.   "Easy there big fella, we'll play "I Got You Babe" — don't worry!" This is a shot of Sonny, Cher, and me with a baby gorilla before one of our shows in the early '70s. True to our personalities, Cher was cautious, Sonny was amused, and I immediately began whispering sweet nothings in its ear. After a few moments, we became inseparable friends.

17.   "All I Ever Need is You"— this is a shot I took around 1972 of Cher with her
      then-daughter Chastity. Chaz, as he is now known, famously transitioned to
      being a male some years ago. But what a cute little girl she was back in the day.
      Cher's blue contact lenses are also quite striking.

18. Okay, one last Sonny and Cher photo—I swear. This is the three of us floating off the beach at Waikiki with Diamond Head in the background in the early '70s. By this time, with their TV series, The Sonny & Cher Comedy Hour, receiving huge ratings, they were flat-out superstars.

19. Back in the '70s, millions of red-blooded American males went crazy over Farrah Fawcett ("Charlie's Angels") and/or Suzanne Somers ("Three's Company"). Me? As sexy TV stars went, I much preferred the gorgeous Lynda Carter ("Wonder Woman"), shown here in a photo I snapped. And I didn't have to watch her series to see her, either. She and I were "friends with benefits" on and off for several years.

20. Ready, set—jump! Lynda Carter always did know how to reach high to achieve her dreams. Before she landed the plum title role on "Wonder Woman" Lynda was also Miss World USA. This is an impromptu moment where I asked a bunch of children to leap in unison with her at a personal appearance during her reign.

21.   Here I am with my friend, the brilliant singer/songwriter Harry Nilsson in Hawaii
      in 1970. While there, he asked me to drop some acid with him and then pro-
      ceeded to tell me about this odd idea he was concocting about a make-believe
      land where everyone had pointed heads. Though I chalked it up to the LSD he
      and I had taken, Harry, as usual, ended up making something spectacular out
      of his brainstorm: "The Point," an animated TV movie featuring the Top Forty hit
      song, "Me and My Arrow," which I also played piano on.

22. This is another shot of Harry Nilsson and me from the early '70s, this time standing in North Hollywood in front of our favorite coffee shop, a unique diner that
had been constructed inside of an old railcar.

23. Nope, this is not a Monkees session. Though I did play on many songs for that
band during the '60s, this is a photo of me on my almost three-month-long journey throughout South America in the mid-'70s where once again I just couldn't
resist playing with another furry young fellow.

24. "Okay, boys, let's take it from the top!" I know it looks like I'm conducting an iguana vocal session of some kind, but I'm actually feeding them in the wild on the Galápagos Islands.

25. What can I say? I was in lust, maybe even love, with the young, innocent Maria
     from the moment I laid eyes on her in a hotel restaurant in Rio de Janeiro. Our
     time together may have been brief, but it was intense and I have never forgotten
     her.

26. What? You've never had a scrub-job at the hands of a native Ecuadorian woman in the middle of an Amazon tributary before? Well, take it from me, it's sheer bliss. This was but one of the many "firsts" I experienced on my mid-'70s solo sojourn throughout South America.

27. Holy glam rock, is that Ziggy Stardust? Or maybe Mott the Hoople? No, it was actually me in the mid-'70s when I starred in my own self-produced full-length concert film that ended up helping me score a big record deal with Motown as a solo artist.

28. Like a priceless Gauguin painting come to life, this is the forever captivating Suzanne de Passe during our Hawaiian vacation together in the mid-'70s. Aside from stealing my heart, as the brilliant president of Motown Productions, Suzanne also played a major role in helping my solo career finally get off the ground. She remains a powerful presence in Hollywood to this day.

29. John and Yoko eat your hearts out! This is the gifted dancer, choreographer, actress, and businesswoman Adele Yoshioka and me posing au naturel while we were a couple in the early '70s. If she looks familiar it's probably from her role as Clint Eastwood's girlfriend, Sunny, in my favorite Dirty Harry movie, Magnum Force.

Barney Kessel
Larry Knechtel
Lincoln Mayorga
Lew McCreary
Mike Melvoin
Jay Migliori
Ollie Mitchell
Lou Morell
Joe Osborn
Earl Palmer
Don Peake
Bill Peterson
Bill Pitman
Ray Pohlman

Emil Richards
Lyle Ritz
Howard Roberts
Mike Rubini
Leon Russell
Jessie Sailes
Louie Shelton
Billy Strange
Tommy Tedesco
Nino Tempo
Tony Terran
Julius Wechter
Bob West
Arthur Wright

30. Known as "Mike" Rubini, in my early twenties I became a mainstay within the Wrecking Crew, a supremely skilled group of studio musicians that played all the instruments on seemingly every other hit record that came out of Los Angeles during the '60s. It was a time, place, and circumstance that I'm immensely proud and grateful to have been a part of. This plaque, commemorating our work, is from Guitar Center's famed Rock Walk in front of their flagship store in Hollywood on Sunset Boulevard.

EIGHTEEN
Johnny Mathis

Because of all my classical training and my early fascination with R&B and jazz, by the time I turned twenty-one I felt more than prepared for whatever musical challenges or opportunities might come my way. Of course, my true readiness might have been debatable, but nothing in my personality would have stopped me from saying yes to anything that sounded like a new experience. I never had any formal training as a conductor, though I had been watching my father do it from the time I was a baby. I had also seen many wonderful conductors leading symphony orchestras around the world. Not to mention that as a session musician I watched arrangers conduct bands practically everyday. For me, it was a natural thing. I had absorbed years of free lessons. So when internationally acclaimed pop singer Johnny Mathis ("Chances Are," "It's Not for Me to Say," and "The Twelfth of Never") asked me to sign on as his musical director in 1968, I didn't hesitate.

Having played for a couple of years on Mathis's recordings, I had in fact only met him once socially, back when I was about eighteen. He lived on the same street as Milton Golden, my father's lawyer, who was one of the more notable characters in Hollywood during the '50s. In 1962, Milton wrote a much-talked-about, thinly veiled novel titled *The Hollywood Lawyer* detailing the sexploits and sordid secret lives of many of the movie stars of the day (my father being one of the case histories in it). Only the names were changed to protect the not-so-innocent.

One day while my dad and I were visiting Milton at his lush home overlooking the Sunset Strip, he told us that Johnny Mathis was his neighbor and suggested that I walk over to Johnny's house and introduce myself, with the thought being, I guess, that Johnny might offer me a musical job or something. Knowing no fear at that time, I did what I was told and walked up to Johnny's front door and knocked. After a moment, Johnny himself answered. That's when I realized that I was staring into the face of a superstar, and I started to stutter.

With me managing to barely blurt out that I knew Milton Golden, much to my surprise, Johnny's face suddenly lit up and he invited me in. I walked into an opulent home that had a swimming pool just inside the front door right where I thought the living room would have been. We walked around the pool and he led me to his living room where we started chatting. Though I was definitely nervous, he was easy going and seemed interested in having someone new to talk with. After a nice visit, I said my farewell and we left it on a very pleasant note, with him saying to come back anytime and that maybe we would meet again sometime in the future.

After my first introduction to Johnny Mathis, I actually returned once more a month or so later while my dad was visiting yet again with Milton, and this time there was a rather noisy party going on at Johnny's place. I knocked on his door, he greeted me warmly, and, much to my shock, I saw nothing but men behind him. Johnny ushered me into the kitchen where he offered me a drink and afterward we went into the living room. He sat in his favorite chair and looked over the scene as though he was king of the hill. We chatted for a while and then he invited me to see the rest of his home. As we walked into his master bedroom, I saw two guys on the bed making out, but I wasn't supposed to have seen that.

Quickly, Johnny took me back to the living room where we sat down again, and after a few minutes, I saw the two guys run out of the bedroom buck naked, both with their members at full salute waving happily in front of them. They jumped into the swimming pool with a big splash, giggling and laughing all the while. Johnny also saw it and apologized for the behavior of "some of his guests." I tried to act nonchalant and brush it off like it was no big deal. But, in fact, it was a big deal; it creeped me out so much that shortly thereafter I made my apologies and left his house, never to return.

Several years later, when I saw Johnny on the first recording session I played for him, he looked at me and immediately remembered who I was. He came over and greeted me with a big smile and asked what I was doing there. I think he was a little surprised, but he welcomed me to the band nonetheless and then moved on to say hello to some of the other musicians. After that, based on my playing, I was called repeatedly to play for Mathis and came to know him fairly well on a professional basis.

In 1968, Johnny's manager at the time, Ray Haughn, asked me to stay after a session to talk. He wanted to know if I would be interested in becoming Mathis's musical director and conductor. Stunned but delighted, I accepted on the spot. It turned out that the current musical director was retiring and they needed to replace him quickly because Johnny had a European tour coming up in the fall. Soon after, I met with Ray up in Johnny's office and I inked a very generous deal. Ray then set up a meeting for me with Johnny's previous musical director to go over all of Johnny's arrangements. By the time we finished, I knew Johnny's show like the back of my hand.

Johnny, Ray, Johnny's houseboy (whose name escapes me), and I boarded a plane that October and flew to Munich, Germany. We checked into a lovely hotel there and got situated. But then Johnny's schedule called for exactly one radio interview and no live performances in Munich for about a week, so I was at loose ends because they told me that I wouldn't actually be working until we got to London at the end of the tour.

Since I was under contract as a recording artist with Liberty Records, before leaving the United States I told the execs at Liberty that I was flying to Europe with Mathis and gave them my itinerary. They then called ahead to their sister company in Munich and told them I was coming. They surprised me by treating me like I was a huge star, even though I had only released one, non-charting record so far during my fledgling solo career. Nevertheless, the record label rolled out the red carpet. They sent a car for me, and after a wonderful lunch, they took me back to the office and introduced me around to all the staff.

From there, it was off to a championship hockey game where we all got drunk on Schnapps, something I had never tasted before. Though having heard the word used occasionally in a Humphrey Bogart movie like *Casablanca*, I had never tried the stuff. The record label folks passed around bottles of this flavored liqueur and drank it like water. It really surprised me how much these buttoned-down, conservative German executives changed from the day into the night.

Fueled, no doubt, by my level of Schnapps intake, I developed an instant mutual infatuation with a gorgeous blond secretary who had come to the game with us. In the heat of the moment, I thought I wanted to marry her, even though she spoke no English and I spoke no German. She was that stunning; our language barrier meant nothing to me. But the label heads quickly put a damper on our budding romance, politely telling me the following day that, in essence, the young woman was far too innocent for my roguish ways. Apparently, she was just a young single mother with a little child and was very sweet and impressionable. Everybody in the office looked out for her and they could see that she saw me as a huge American recording star. Looking back, they were probably right in protecting her. It would have likely ended poorly, being just a one-night stand or something. But I sure was crazy about her.

Our group left Munich a couple of days later and flew on to Hamburg. In Hamburg, Johnny met with the head of his label and also with Bert Kaempfert, a famous composer and recording artist, to talk about the possibility of recording some of Bert's songs together in the future. We all went to the recording studio where Bert was cutting his new album. From the moment I was introduced to him, we got on famously. We were both the same type of people. Being musicians of the same ilk, we chatted about producing records, the differences between the American and German studios and recording techniques, etc. Though I didn't mean to take center stage, Bert seemed more interested in talking with me than with Johnny, at least at that moment. Unbeknownst to me, this aggravated both Johnny and Ray. Luckily, Bert finally turned his attention to Johnny and they had a lovely conversation about getting together down the line to record some songs. All around, it turned out to be a great day.

It would also prove to be my last as the musical director for Johnny Mathis.

Early the next afternoon, I was summoned to Johnny's hotel room for a business meeting. I dutifully went up to Johnny's suite at the appointed time and knocked on the door. After Ray answered and let me in, I immediately noticed that Johnny and his houseboy were joking around together and something didn't seem right. Johnny said something about his houseboy's balls and then grabbed them like he was juggling. Johnny then looked at me oddly. Johnny, Ray, and the houseboy then burst out laughing as I stood there in the foyer, clearly not getting the joke. I believed it to be an invitation to a four-man orgy or something like that, which I wanted no part of. I basically froze, not knowing what to do. This was my employer, after all. Mumbling something about coming back later when they wanted to discuss business, I awkwardly backed my way out, shutting the door behind me.

Shaken by what I had seen, I returned to my room in order to sort things out. Feeling trapped, I quickly took the elevator downstairs and left the hotel. I didn't know where I was going or what to do, but I needed time to think. I walked the streets for better than an hour, stopping at a teashop at one point to order a cup. As it began to get dark, I reluctantly headed back to the hotel, still not knowing how to handle what had happened. Johnny and his two assistants had drawn a line in the sand that I could not cross. Nor did I know what to do or say the next time we saw each other. The whole thing was a big mess.

With a heavy heart, the answer to my dilemma came sooner than I expected. Upon entering my hotel room, I immediately saw an envelope lying on the floor just inside the door. Picking it up, I tore it open to read that I was now being fired for not showing up to rehearsals, which was a ridiculous statement. There had never *been* any scheduled rehearsals. Johnny had no performances planned until we got to England, which wasn't for two more weeks. The envelope also contained a first-class plane ticket back to the United States.

Shock would be an understatement. And the more I thought about it, the angrier I got, too. What had they been thinking? That they were going to fly me all the way to Europe just to seduce me in some hotel in Hamburg? Did Mathis and his minions really think that I was that stupid, easy, or corruptible?

Soon, my furiousness gave way to calm, however. I realized that this was a changeable ticket, meaning I could actually fly anywhere I wanted. With more than two weeks before I had any commitments back home, I decided to cash in the ticket and take a two-week European vacation for myself, which is exactly what I did.

First visiting the J. C. Neupert harpsichord factory and museum in Bamberg, I bought one of their flagship models and shipped it back home. The next day I took the train from Bamberg to Hamburg and got on a plane to Rome where I met up with an old friend. Bamberg to Hamburg, hmm . . . sort of sounds like a Broadway musical dance number, doesn't it: Bamberg to Hamburg, Hamberg to Bamburg.

My week in London goes down in history as one of the best of my life. To begin with, I threw my back out the day I arrived and felt so uncomfortable that I slept on the floor of my room. At some point in the early morning, a young housekeeper opened the door to my room because she thought it was vacant. She saw a body lying on the floor and thought it was a dead man. She gasped and ran from the room, but not before I caught a glimpse of her. She didn't look like any housekeeper I had ever seen. This girl was beautiful.

Calling down to housekeeping, I asked them to send her back up to my room. She arrived about five minutes later, and I apologized for frightening her, explaining about my back and why I was on the floor when she came in. We had a good laugh, and she told me a little about herself. She was twenty-two, a beautiful brunette from Spain, who was working at the hotel to help pay her tuition at school there in London. I, of course, asked her out. Initially, she refused because of the hotel's strict rules against fraternizing with the guests, but I convinced her to meet me outside the hotel, and off we went to have our share of romantic fun.

While strolling down the street the next day in the heart of the swinging Piccadilly Circus area of London, who in the world should I bump into but Perry "Bunny" Botkin, a wonderful arranger/producer I worked for a lot in Los Angeles. I asked what he was doing there and he told me he was arranging a series of recording sessions for Time/Life's well-known series of music collections. Bunny invited me to go with him to the Playboy Club for a press party that was being thrown for the strange-looking (and singing) performer, Tiny Tim, who was performing at Royal Albert Hall. One of the Beatles, I believe George Harrison, had also loaned Bunny his Austin Princess limo for his use while in London. Bunny, in turn, made that luxury ride available to me, so I subsequently scooted around town in a Beatle's limo. It was a real kick.

Bunny and I went to the Playboy Club that night and sat in a booth with one of the Beatle's publicity men. After some getting-to-know-one-another conversation, the publicity guy offered us a chunk of his hash. Hash was all the rage in London at that time, mainly because it was being produced in the Middle East and was more readily available than marijuana. Paranoid guy that I was, I politely turned him down. But he lit up right there at the table and started to puff away. Marianne Faithful—Mick

Jagger's gorgeous girlfriend at the time and the singer of the hit single "As Tears Go By"—turned out to be sitting in the booth next to us. When she smelled the hash, she leaned over and asked for a hit, to which she was immediately accommodated. It was a jolly good time for all.

Toward the end of the party, the publicity guy asked if we wanted to join him at George Harrison's house to continue the party and smoke even more hash, but I once again turned him down. Being cautious by nature, I just didn't want to have any trouble, legal or otherwise, while visiting merry old England.

However, the next night was the cherry on the cake. There were two concerts happening and I had to make up my mind which one to attend. The first was none other than Johnny Mathis's show that I had originally been hired to conduct. The other was Tiny Tim's. I had to think long and hard about this, because the temptation to attend Mathis's concert, sit in the front row, and wave at him was almost irresistible. Imagine the look on his face had he walked out on stage and seen me sitting there after firing me and telling me to go directly back to the United States. It would have been priceless.

But I thought better of stalking Johnny Mathis at his own show because I didn't want to appear petty. Besides, I had already worked on Tiny Tim's albums back in the States. And Bunny Botkin had given me his tickets because he was going to be elsewhere. So I had prime seats, George Harrison's limo, and the hot housekeeping girl on my arm—what could be better?

We arrived at Royal Albert Hall, which I had always wanted to see, and I was just shocked at how the rowdy teenagers had taken over the grand old palace, showing it no respect. They were smoking, yelling, tossing balloons in the air; it was appalling.

In any case, the show started, and there was of course the obligatory opening act. It was some guy I had never heard of, somebody named Joe Cocker. He came out and did his set, and all I could think of was how the band was good, but this guy looked like he had some kind of palsy. He also sounded like he had blown out his vocal cords years before.

However, Cocker was nothing if not entertaining, and when he started singing the last song of his set, I had to listen. The audience had by then calmed down and Cocker launched in to a cover of the Beatles tune, "With a Little Help from My Friends." When I heard that, I said to myself: now, that's a hit. Not yet released in the United States (but already out in Europe), sure enough I was right. When I got home, the radio stations in Los Angeles were just beginning to play it, and "With a Little Help from My Friends" soon indeed became a career-making smash for Mr. Joe Cocker.

After Joe's set, there was an intermission and then Tiny Tim's set began. The lights went down and a big cloud of smoke emanated from the stage. The music started and the lights came up and whom did I see standing on the stage conducting the band but Richard Perry! Back in L.A. I worked with Richard all the time, but he was not a conductor; he was a well-known rock-and-roll producer. Yet there he was, all decked out in an all-white silk tuxedo, complete with tails, and waving an ivory baton. I couldn't believe it. I knew Richard had a large ego, but this was unbelievable. What's more, it was like Old Home Week. I was running into everyone.

After the band's overture died down, Tiny Tim came walking out onstage in his cute little outfit with his black, stringy hair and ukulele. Other than being overshadowed by Richard Perry in all his white-on-white glory, Tiny was very charming and sang his little falsetto heart out.

With one day left in London, I decided to go shopping and wound up in a wonderful men's haberdashery close to Piccadilly Circus. I wanted to buy a great Scottish wool sports jacket and a topcoat for those few, chilly winter days in Southern California. After I made my selections, I went to pay and the gentleman asked for my name to put on the receipt. When I told him it was Michel Rubini, he paused from his writing and looked up at me. "Are you by any chance related to the great violinist, Jan Rubini?" I replied that, yes, Jan was my father. With that, the gentleman behind the counter looked as though he had seen a ghost. Finally recovering, he then announced that he was my first cousin and that my father was his uncle. He was the son of one of my father's sisters. I was dumbstruck. Here I had traveled halfway around the world, been fired by Johnny Mathis, planned an impromptu trip through Germany, Italy, and England, and wound up in one out of a hundred men's stores in London, only to end up paying my very own cousin for the clothes I wanted to buy. It's really a small world sometimes. My cousin invited me to have dinner with his family and him the next night, an offer that I readily accepted.

He picked me up at the hotel the next day and we headed out to his home where I was greeted by about fifteen of my relatives that I didn't know from Adam. They were all thrilled to meet me and asked me a hundred questions about my father and his life in the United States. They hadn't seen him since they were kids. It was all very pleasant, and we had a good time. After dinner, my cousin put me in the car and took me to the airport, and I continued on my journey.

Finally arriving back in Los Angeles over a week later after a circuitous route by air to Gibraltar and then by ship to New York, I managed to put the distasteful experience with Johnny Mathis and Ray Haughn behind me. Though only after some nasty legal stuff with the Musicians Union, whose board supported me one hundred percent in my claim to be paid in full based on the contract I had signed with Mathis.

A couple of years went by, with me working steadily for all sorts of musical luminaries in the studios. Then, one day in 1970, out of nowhere I got a call to play once again for none other than Johnny Mathis. Never one to turn down a paying job and curious as heck, I sat there at the piano in the studio wondering what was going to happen when Johnny saw me. Would he throw me out? Was he looking to make amends? The question was answered when, as per his custom, Johnny came out of the control booth before the session to say hello to all the musicians. He didn't see me right away, but as he walked up to the piano, he spotted me and a big smile came across his face. He said, "Hi Michel, great to see you!"

I responded in like fashion and then Johnny walked on to finish his rounds. That was it. No yelling, no apologies, no nothing. It was like we were simply old friends.

We got down to business and recorded Johnny's songs, the session finished up on a good note, and I drove home, a bit mystified. I thought about it for some time after, wondering if Mathis was the best actor in show business or whether he had a terrible memory and had blocked out the whole incident in Germany. Or perhaps there was another option. Since Johnny seemed so genuinely pleased to see me, it made me wonder if he even knew what had transpired. After all, I never had an argument or disagreeable word with Johnny himself. It made me think that perhaps Ray Haughn, his manager, had written the note that I found under my door and then lied to Johnny about what had happened, maybe saying that I had gotten sick and couldn't continue the tour. That would have let Johnny off without feeling insulted or rejected by me, solving the problem for everybody.

Good old Ray, he did what great managers do; they protect their clients. And I really have to thank Johnny for paying for the best European vacation I would ever have.

NINETEEN
Nancy Wilson

About a year after my musical director position ended so abruptly with Johnny Mathis in Germany, I was asked once again to perform the same role, but this time for arguably the world's greatest jazz singer at the time, Nancy Wilson. Having played on her records for a few years during the late '60s, the beautiful Ms. Wilson apparently had kept her eye on me, but much to my disappointment, only in a musical sense. With deep, rich, café au lait skin that looked like satin, a figure any woman would kill for, and a sophistication and grace that appealed to my every sense, Nancy was simply stunning. She knew her music inside and out, too, which only made me respect her that much more. The idea of traveling around the globe with Nancy Wilson certainly sounded like a great adventure and opportunity to me, so off we went.

Nancy had a wonderful road manager, Sparky Tavares, who latched onto me like a grandson and made me feel like I really belonged to the family. He took care of Nancy like the queen that she was, and the very first job that we did together was a one-month tour of Asia, starting in Japan and finally ending in Hong Kong, with stops in the Philippines and Singapore. Nancy had also hired a drummer and bassist, so our little traveling band was comprised of Nancy, Sparky, and we three musicians.

Upon landing in Tokyo, we were greeted by the tour promoter, a most wonderful and interesting man by the name of Tats Nagashima. Tats was the most famous promoter in the Far East, and he certainly knew how to take care of his artists. During our visit, he booked us to play at several major nightclubs, ending with a concert inside a large auditorium to a standing-room-only audience. These venues were more or less Japanese copies of famous nightclubs in New York and borrowed their American names, too. So we played at familiar-sounding places such as the Stork Club and the Copacabana, which were all first class.

On our second night in Tokyo, Tats invited Nancy, Sparky, and myself to a very special restaurant to experience the legendary (and authentic) Kobe beef that I had only read about in novels. This delicacy could usually only be found in Japan back in the day. The restaurant had just two tables and two chefs, too; in other words, one for each. That night we were the only patrons, and what an experience it was as we feasted on the world's most expensive and delicious beef, along with a variety of other Japanese culinary delights.

We stayed at the Tokyo Hilton and the service there was impeccable. I saw that they offered massages, so I called down to the spa and asked to book a session. With so much of my life spent hunching over a piano keyboard, a good massage often made my back feel a lot better. My masseuse's name was Keiko, and though she spoke a little English, she was too shy to really say much of anything. I did find out later that she had gone to university, studied for four years to get her license, and was totally dedicated to her profession. The session itself was unlike any massage I had ever had.

First, I went into a little changing room and removed my clothes, then I was given a large towel to wrap around myself. Following that, Keiko asked me to step into a shower stall where she turned on the water and asked me to wash myself. I must say that I was a little disappointed because I had fantasized about a soapy scrub-down from head to toe by her, but it was not to be. This was a completely legitimate operation inside the Tokyo Hilton Hotel, which meant no *funny stuff* was allowed. I found out later that *they* were secretly watching all the time, so Keiko's reticence made total sense.

After I finished my shower, Keiko led me to a table where she proceeded to give me the best deep tissue massage I had ever received.

However, nothing inappropriate took place. It was simply just a talented masseuse applying her skills. In fact, the experience was so transformative that I made another appointment with her for the next day.

During my next appointment, I asked Keiko to attend one of our performances with me, but she declined, saying that it was impossible because she was forbidden to fraternize with hotel guests. Feeling that she was somehow interested in me, I booked yet another massage. On this occasion, the third time was definitely the charm. Keiko clearly felt more comfortable and even found the courage at one point to ask me in a very soft voice if she could feel my beard. A strange request to be sure, but I guess she had never met a man with a curly beard before and just wanted to feel what it was like. Of course, I let her feel away all she wanted. So while I lay there naked and prone on the massage table, she, very gingerly, ran her fingers through my beard and started pulling on my whiskers a little. It was actually very funny. Given our growing fondness for one another, I asked her again to please go out with me. This time she consented.

We made an arrangement to meet outside the hotel late that night and she took me walking with her. Neither of us said much, but it didn't matter; we were getting along just fine with the little bit of English she did speak. We walked up a steep hill, at the top of which a temple had been built. Like something out of a movie, we then stood together under an archway at the entrance with only the lights of Tokyo far below illuminating our bodies. I just couldn't let the romance of this magical moment slip away, so I kissed her. From there, I advanced a little further, and Keiko didn't stop me, either. There we were, alone in the dark, making out like two teenagers in heat with the stone statues of the Buddhist gods powerlessly glaring out at us from inside their temple. Needless to say, this was a unique experience and one that I thought could never be topped.

Oh, how wrong I was.

Keiko and I met again the next afternoon, and this time she took me by taxi to an area called the Shinjuku District, a place teeming with dozens of bustling restaurants and nightclubs. After stepping out of the car, we began walking. Figuring that she was taking me on some kind of sightseeing trip, I just followed along. Keiko finally pointed to a door with a Japanese sign on it and indicated that we should go inside.

Entering what looked to be an upscale boutique hotel of some sort, Keiko told me to pay the lady sitting behind the front desk. Doing what I was told, I pulled out a wad of yen and Keiko took several bills and handed them over. I still had no idea what we were doing, but Keiko obviously did and that was good enough for me. The lady then took us down a hallway to a room that she opened with her key. She did not give me the key, however, which I thought seemed strange.

Keiko led me into the room and the door closed behind us. The room was decorated totally in traditional Japanese style except for a small glass display case in which resided various *objets d'amour* (sex toys). In the middle of the room sat a low wooden table and my date told me to take off my shoes and sit on the floor next to it. I did as I was told, and she then proceeded to perform a complete Japanese tea ceremony for me. I was utterly speechless. I had gone on a date, expecting to probably go to a restaurant and have dinner and then maybe visit a nightclub. Instead, here I was in a Japanese "love hotel"—a place that rented its rooms by the hour—being served Japanese tea by a beautiful, delicate masseuse from the Tokyo Hilton Hotel who barely spoke a word of English.

Let me be clear, though: Keiko was in no way a prostitute or sex worker of any type. She never asked for money or tips or presents. She was doing this for her own personal reasons. Naturally curious, I asked her about the items in the display case, and she indicated that she did not want to discuss that. I took her lead and kept my mouth shut; I didn't want to do or say anything that might jeopardize the moment. After we finished sipping the tea, Keiko asked me to get up and follow her. We went through a partition and there in front of me was a Japanese rice bed with a strange looking wooden box that had a slot in it where you could drop in coins. I thought maybe it was like an old-fashioned Vegas slot machine or jukebox, but Japanese style. To our left was a dimly lit, romantically appointed bathroom. It was also the first I had ever seen where the tiles began on the floor and continued all the way up to the ceiling. The shower had no curtain, and there was a drain in the middle of the floor. One could take a shower and splash water everywhere and it would all wash right down the drain—pure genius.

Then there was the tub, just like in the Geisha movies I had seen—almost square, made out of some type of dark metal, about three feet wide, four feet long, and about two-and-a-half feet deep. It was just big enough for one person if you pulled your knees up toward your chest. There were terrycloth bathrobes hanging on the walls, too, along with toothbrushes and toothpaste, combs, and brushes—just about everything a person could want grooming-wise.

Keiko started filling the tub with hot, steamy water. She then stepped up to me and slowly began undoing my shirt, button by button. Then came the pants along with everything else, until I was standing there completely nude, which left me stunned. Was this the same girl who had refused a date with me at the Hilton only two days prior? Clearly there was a lot about Keiko and the Japanese culture that I didn't know anything about, but I was certainly getting a crash course now.

Asking me to get into the tub, which I did as fast as I could, Keiko then stood in front of me and slowly undressed herself, folding each item of clothing carefully and putting it on a shelf. Once completely nude, she leaned over the tub and with a large bar of soap proceeded to wash me. I was in the tub, and she was outside of it. This was part of the Japanese ritual; the woman always washes the man.

After I had been scrubbed and scoured to her satisfaction, Keiko politely asked if she could enter the tub with me. I didn't know exactly where she would fit, but I welcomed her nonetheless and she carefully climbed in until our bodies were submerged and our legs became intertwined in some geometrically impossible position.

It was heaven on earth being wrapped in her arms in that tiny tub. But then, after toweling off our bodies, came the next step. Keiko led me back out to the bed, which was only about five inches thick and right on the floor. I had never been on a Japanese mattress, but I was getting a welcome education. As we lay upon the bed, I again spotted that strange box with the coin drop. It had some Japanese words on the front. But of course, I couldn't read it, so I asked Keiko what it said. With a pained look, she immediately replied, "Very bad, very bad."

As she tried to pull my attention away from it, it just made me more curious. What would happen if I *did* put coins in it?

I asked her for a better explanation but she sort of furrowed her brow and again said, "No, no—very bad, very bad!"

So now my curiosity was definitely piqued. That is probably my most marked trait, aside from my love for music and beautiful women. I am insatiably curious by nature.

Against Keiko's protestations, I retrieved a coin from my pants pocket and dropped it into the slot. Much to my surprise, a Japanese instrumental recording of Johnny Mandel's award-winning song "The Shadow of Your Smile" started to play. It was tinny-sounding, with a lot of what I would call cheap reverb, but it was definitely Johnny's song. I didn't see what Keiko was so upset about; the hotel just wanted to provide a little music to help set the mood. But as I looked at Keiko, she had her hands over her ears and was shaking her head "no, no, no." I didn't get it. What was wrong with "The Shadow of Your Smile"?

But then something changed; the music dipped in volume and a little female Japanese voice started to speak. Very soft and refined, it sounded like a little girl. Of course, I couldn't understand what she was saying, but it was sort of like she was speaking to a friend, a man-type friend. At first she was speaking rather softly, but then she said something that evidently she thought was funny, sort of giggling like a young girl. Then, as if an invisible man replied, she responded with something throatier and then made a sound like "ooh," as though he may have shown her something special that really impressed her.

As this went on, the woman's voice on the recording became more breathy and higher pitched. After a few quick inhales, she muttered a few more words and then the "ooh" came again. She was definitely picking up the pace, too. Meanwhile, in the background, the beautiful melody of "The Shadow of Your Smile" continued to play. Soon the woman's voice became even more high-pitched and the words came ever faster, complete with panting and little moans. Whoever this person was, she was clearly enjoying herself. I looked at Keiko again to ask for a translation, but she just covered her ears while cutely rocking back and forth in the nude on the futon next to me.

In any case, the voice finally reached a climactic pitch, with the woman letting out a long, deep moan of intense pleasure. As the sound of her voice faded slowly into oblivion, Johnny's last phrase of "Shadow..." rose in volume, then slowly retarded to an end with the violins playing the last few notes of his famous melody. Following that, the coin quite unceremoniously dropped with a loud *thunk* into the tin moneybox and the machine turned off.

Looking at Keiko, I could see that she was mortally embarrassed. Of course, she knew full well what the girl had been saying. But, to me, the funniest part about this whole episode was that I didn't understand a word of it and Keiko had been acting as though I did.

Now, though, I had a predicament. I had done something clearly not on her schedule of activities for the night, and I feared that I might have permanently broken the mood. Remember, I still hoped to be soon making passionate love to this lovely young Japanese woman. But, fortunately for me, Keiko didn't need too much in the way of persuading. Just a few good-natured pleas of forgiveness on my part, along with an affectionate hug, and we were quickly back on track toward enjoying a fabulously sensual night together that I will never forget.

A few years later, after moving back to Malibu, I actually ran into Johnny Mandel one day and decided to tell him the story. I asked Johnny if he had ever received any royalties for jukebox plays in Japan. He said he didn't think so and asked me why. By the time I finished telling him my "Keiko and the porn jukebox" tale and how the last five notes of his song played just after the mysterious female had her orgasm—with the coin then dropping into the moneybox—Johnny simply roared with laughter.

But that was hardly all the drama that came my way on the big Asian excursion.

Sometime prior to our trip, Nancy Wilson, the star of the show and my boss, had become involved in a romantic relationship with the actor Robert Hooks. Evidently, Mr. Hooks liked to ride horses, and because Nancy wanted so much to please him, she had been taking horseback riding lessons back home in the United States. So she told Tats, our Japanese promoter, that she wanted to go riding, if at all possible, while in Tokyo. Known for being the guy that could procure anything for anybody, Tats made a few phone calls and sure enough arranged for Nancy and me to go riding at the one place in all of Tokyo where there were actually horses—the racetrack.

Because property in Tokyo was so expensive, there were no ranches or other places for horses. Just the richest of the rich were able to own and keep a horse, which was almost always at the local racetrack. The only horses there were racehorses, plus a few older jumpers, etc.

Soon thereafter, Nancy and I were down at the track, ready to ride a couple of thoroughbreds, one of which was a retired Olympic champion jumper, which thrilled the inexperienced Nancy. Unfortunately, it was also dreary outside with light rain falling. In my view, having done a fair amount of riding over the years, it didn't look like a very good day to put on the spurs, so to speak. But Nancy couldn't be deterred. Dressed to kill in a beautiful custom-made, tan-colored English jumping outfit, she looked simply beautiful. As for me, well, I was a little more down to earth in my jeans and tennis shoes.

After being driven to the track and taken to our horses, Nancy proudly told me how she had been taking western-style riding lessons back home so she could ride with "Bobby" at his ranch. But a thoroughbred is not the regular *cowboy* kind of horse that Hopalong Cassidy or Roy Rogers used to be seen riding up on the silver screen during the Saturday after-noon picture show. First of all, they are about twice as big as an Arabian or American quarter horse, and at least twice as temperamental. Second, these horses only run at racetracks; that's all they do for exercise and it's all they know. Thoroughbreds don't mosey; they fly.

So, as we got on our horses and trotted out onto the track, the first thing Nancy's mount did was bolt and start galloping at breakneck speed. Taken by surprise, Nancy didn't have a prayer of reining in her horse. I was behind her and all I could see was Nancy's rear bouncing up and down out of the English saddle, higher and higher as the horse sped away. I was really scared for her because it was obvious that she was not going to stay aboard for long. I tried catching up to help rein in her horse, and I was definitely getting closer as we rounded the first turn and into the backstretch. But there was a pathway that cut across the infield, designed as a shortcut back to the stables and all the horses knew it well. As hers approached the path, it started pulling to the left while Nancy leaned with all her might to the right, desperately trying to make it go straight.

Except that the horse was winning the battle—a thousand pounds of determined equine versus a one-hundred-pound woman is hardly a fair fight. All of a sudden, Nancy went flying off the tail end of the animal high into the air where she did a three-quarter somersault and landed flat on her back on the muddy track. As for the now rider-less racehorse, it never broke stride and disappeared down the path.

While racing up to where Nancy lay sprawled on the track, I worried that she had been seriously injured since she wasn't moving. The fall looked horrific. As I jumped off of my horse and ran up to her, I could immediately see that she was covered in mud, her new riding outfit had been ruined, her makeup and hair were now destroyed, and tears were streaming down her face. I quickly asked if she was okay (maybe not the most intelligent question to ask a diva at that moment) and whether she could move.

Fortunately, Nancy was unhurt. Of course, she was so embarrassed and angry that she probably would have gotten up even if every bone in her body had been broken. So I helped her to her feet and watched as several people came running toward us from the stables. Everybody had seen what happened, making the whole incident that much worse.

Luckily, the only thing damaged was Nancy's pride. She was practically boiling as we walked back to the stables; nobody dared to say a word, except that they were all so sorry. After she cleaned herself up, we drove back to the hotel where her embarrassment was magnified because she had to walk through the lobby in front of everybody.

From there, I didn't see Nancy for the rest of the day. Later that evening, we got in the car at the appointed time and drove to the performance in silence. I could see that she was still mad. But in spite of the day's events, the show, as always, went on and we had a wonderful performance. That's the mark of a true professional. The great Nancy Wilson would never in a million years let her personal life interfere with making sure her audience got exactly what they came for.

One of my other forays into the outdoors on this wonderful trip with Nancy Wilson was unfortunately even more distressing, this time in the Philippines. We had a couple of days of rest after playing at Clark Field there (the US airbase) and then took off to play a show at Subic Bay (the US naval base). As usual, we all piled into some limos, cars, and a van and out of the city we drove. The road through the jungle was not good. There were lots of potholes, areas with just gravel, and generally it was a pretty bumpy ride. I was in the van this time around, and the driver explained that the monsoon season had just ended, leaving the roads heavily damaged from the hard rains.

After a couple of hours, our driver noticed that the water temperature gauge indicated that the van's engine was running hot. It wasn't boiling over, but he was concerned. We were now out in the middle of nowhere, and all I saw on each side of the road was dense jungle, the occasional bamboo hut, and a few water buffalo grazing on the grass that grew alongside the highway—hardly a hospitable environment within which to be having any kind of car trouble.

Eventually spotting what appeared to be a general store and a one-pump gas station, we pulled over. There were some children playing close by, and the driver decided to stop and check the water. The kids came running up to the van and were jumping around, laughing with big toothy smiles. and I rolled down my window to talk with them. One of the others in the back of the van opened the sliding door on the side next to where our drummer was sitting.

Our driver got out of his seat and leaned over the radiator cover that was located right in the middle of the floor just behind the driver's and front passenger's seats. He lifted off the cover and we could all see the radiator and other miscellaneous engine parts. Though the temperature gauge indicated trouble, the radiator cap wasn't bubbling or emitting any steam. So the driver decided to play it safe and pour some water in anyway.

As he carefully began unscrewing the cap, with a loud *boom*, the radiator suddenly blew up in his face. Boiling fluid exploded out of the hole like a hydrogen bomb had gone off, instantly blowing the driver all the way to the rear of the van. The superheated contents also hit our drummer in his face, chest, and arms, and I flew out of the side window and landed on the ground between all the now-screaming kids.

While laying there in a daze, I watched as the drummer leaped from the van and ran screaming into the tall grass nearby. He stumbled and fell, begging for someone to help him. Somebody from the now-stopped car in front of us fortunately rushed to his aide. In the meantime, I climbed to my feet and woozily walked over to the open side door of the van and looked in. What I saw made me sick: the driver was sitting there in silent shock, staring blankly. The skin on his face, neck, and arms looked as though it had been peeled off by a blowtorch. I spoke to him but he did not hear me.

Meanwhile, someone outside the truck was yelling at anybody and everybody to find some ice. Though our drummer sustained a variety of first-, second-, and a few small third-degree burns, the driver was in much worse shape. The promoter went into the store and brought out ice and rags to help the driver, who, while being treated, didn't say anything; he just sat there in an eerie silence.

We all talked and tried to figure out what to do, but there was no phone and so no way to get any help. The promoter said he would drive the van, which somehow still ran after refilling the radiator. So back on the road we went to finish our trek to Subic Bay. The road on the way, of course, was in terrible shape and every time we hit a bump or pothole our drummer would moan in pain. But the driver just sat in his semi-comatose state, never uttering a sound. I cannot imagine what internal torture he must have been going through.

It was already getting dark by the time we finally reached the base, and when we pulled up to the guard gate, the promoter had the sentry radio ahead to the medics. In short order, there arrived several military vehicles and an ambulance. The medics got the driver and our drummer out of the van, into the ambulance, and off into the night.

Nancy and I, along with the rest of our small group, were taken to the Subic Bay Officers' Club where we washed up, changed clothes, and then had something to eat. To our great relief, word came back that our drummer had been treated and, although in great pain, would, in fact, be able to play the show with us. His injuries were less serious than previously thought. After treatment and a lot of bandaging, sure enough he bravely walked into the club and joined us onstage. His hands and arms were bandaged and his face looked like he had a really bad sunburn, but the guy was a real trooper. He just wasn't going to let Nancy down.

Our driver was not as fortunate, however. We never saw him again, but we heard through the grapevine that he had been transported by helicopter back to a hospital in Manila to undergo treatment and would likely be okay.

Somehow—miraculously, really—we also managed to put on one of our best shows that night, no doubt lifted by heavy levels of adrenalin and our sheer gratitude at just being alive. And through the whole ordeal, Nancy remained just as gracious, helpful, and poised as she could be. It made me admire her all the more.

After returning to the United States from my amazing musical journey through Asia with Nancy Wilson, I took a little time back in Los Angeles to regroup, check my messages, dry-clean my tuxes, say hello to a few friends, and then Nancy and I were off again, this time to New York. She would be headlining a run of dates at the legendary Apollo Theatre and had signed on to do two shows a day, with three on the weekends.

Every concert we did was packed to the rafters, too. Of course, when we arrived for our first and only rehearsal, the guys in the sixteen-piece, all-black, NYC-based house band were more than a little surprised to see that Nancy had brought along a young white kid to lead them. And for a while, I felt as though I was running a gauntlet.

It seemed that those band members had been playing at the Apollo forever and had backed the biggest acts in show business, from Diana Ross to Ray Charles. And, believe me, they were in no way used to seeing a white boy pop up on that stage, especially one about half their average age. So, for a while, I felt a bit like an alien.

But when I counted down the first piece and Nancy started singing and didn't wait for anybody, their ears and their attention level picked up fast because we were not waiting around for any among them to play catch up. Also, Nancy's charts still had not been recopied and were not easy to read. So when the guys started asking questions about them, I answered in a language that they understood perfectly, especially when I pointed out some of the mistakes they were making here and there or not phrasing as marked. That definitely got their attention.

Finally, I gained a little respect from the musicians when I started playing the piano solos between her verses. And the band certainly had my admiration when I heard the way they played as a unit. It was an instant groove from the downbeat on. Man, they knew how to swing! And what a great pleasure to hear Nancy's music being played the way it was supposed to, especially after a month in Asia performing with guys who could only dream about laying it down like the Apollo Theatre cats.

Though other recording commitments would prevent me from playing more dates with Nancy after our appearance at the Apollo, I will always remember the time we spent together as being some of the richest of my musical life.

Thank you, Ms. Wilson, for giving me that wonderful opportunity to work and play with you. It was indeed a pleasure.

TWENTY
Jim Nabors

During the late 1960s, Columbia Records asked me to play piano on an album by none other than Jim Nabors, the actor who portrayed the title character on the popular *Gomer Pyle, U.S.M.C.* TV series. Jim was a very friendly, polite guy. I remember watching him come into the recording studio and introduce himself to all the musicians in the band, of which there were at least a couple of dozen. Not every star did that.

It was amazing to hear Jim sing, too, because when he talked, he had a Southern accent and was best known for the thin, nasally, high-pitched Gomer Pyle voice he used on TV. But when Jim sang, he sounded like an operatic baritone with a British accent. The transformation was so astounding that the producers of Jim's TV series sometimes had storylines written especially to showcase his marvelous voice. Nabors loved opera and listened to it incessantly from the time he was a kid. He told me that he used to practice at home by singing along with his parents' old 78-RPM opera records. By imitating their different voices, in his own homegrown way, Jim developed a wonderfully deep and powerful singing voice.

For whatever reason, Jim took a particular liking to me, perhaps because I told him I was classically trained and he loved that kind of music. Or maybe it was because I took an active interest in his records and chose to listen to the playbacks in the control room instead of going outside to chat with the other musicians during our breaks in the studio. Some theorized that it was because I was *young and handsome.* I have never liked that innuendo, by the way. I can say from personal experience that whatever has been written or said about Jim Nabors and his sexual preferences, he was never anything but kind and courteous around me. He never once made a pass. He was just a great friend.

Interestingly, too, Jim never spent his money ostentatiously, as do so many other celebrities. Though he earned mountains of cash from being a major TV star, for the longest time Jim lived quite simply and happily in a little house up in the hills of Studio City. I knew him for about two years before he finally decided to move to a mansion in Bel-Air, and he only did that so he would have enough room for his ailing mother and her helpers to come live with him. Of course, Jim did allow himself the luxury of eventually buying a Rolls Royce, and I took several rides in that car, which was like being in a luxury yacht on wheels.

Jim loved to throw parties at his little house, and everybody from the lowliest to the loftiest was invited. I attended a lot of cocktail parties and dinners up there and it was always something special. I met some of the most interesting and talented folks on the planet at his house because everybody loved Jim Nabors and wanted to be on his guest list.

One party that really stands out in my mind is the one where Marilyn Horne, the mezzo-soprano, and Beverly Sills, the coloratura soprano, were in attendance at the same time. Because Jim loved opera so much, he had become good friends over the years with these two world-renowned divas. To use a sports metaphor, that is akin to inviting two heavyweight world champion boxers like Mike Tyson and Evander Holyfield to the same party and expecting them to get along. However, the two women loved each other and were actually great friends. The best part for me came when Jim asked me to play some requests from the audience.

After I tickled the keys for a while, somebody asked Marilyn to sing a song. So she sat down next to me on the piano bench and asked if I knew a particular gospel song (which I did). She then gave me her key and there I was, all of a sudden, playing with the great Marilyn Horne. Who ever gets to do something like that? Not many, that's for sure.

It was amazing to listen to Marilyn's voice, too, especially at such ultra-close proximity.

She had more power in her vocal cords than the grand piano I was playing. It was electrifying. And it only got better from there.

Next, Jim asked Beverly Sills to sing something, so she hopped up, told me her key, and then stood at the end of the piano and belted out some Broadway show tune as I accompanied her. The guests were in a trance and applauded and whistled when she finished. To top it off, the *girls* decided to sing something together. I think it was "You Are My Sunshine"—the Ray Charles version—and the house simply rocked from that moment on. Of course, Jim got his licks in, too. He eventually joined in with his two singing guests and we were all up there in the front of the room doing our thing until about two in the morning. It was truly a night to remember.

Though I had a lot of memorable moments with Jim Nabors, one of the most unusual and enjoyable was the night we flew to San Francisco. We had just finished one of his recording sessions, and he told me that he wanted to hang out but was in a hurry because he had to fly up to San Francisco to see a comedian friend of his perform in a club there. So Jim asked if I wanted to go with him, all expenses paid. He said he had a room reserved at the St. Francis Hotel with two large beds, so if I wanted to, I could go with him to have a fun night out in San Francisco.

Naturally, I thought it over for a moment. I am not an idiot; I knew that Jim didn't have a girlfriend. I had heard all the rumors, too. Who hadn't? But he had never shown any interest in me other than just wanting to have a friend. So I decided to trust our friendship and said yes.

We hopped into his Rolls and drove down to the airport. He parked his car, bought an extra ticket for me, and off we flew into the beautiful blue California skies, headed for an evening on the town.

Landing around dinnertime, we hailed a taxi and drove directly to the St. Francis, where we dropped off his bags and then headed to a great Italian place where the owner greeted Jim like a long-lost family member.

It seemed like wherever I went with Jim, he knew everybody and everyone loved him.

After a great dinner, we grabbed another taxi and went to the comedy club where his friend was performing. He was a young comedian, just starting his career, and of course was thrilled when Jim walked in to see his show. Afterward, the three of us chatted over some wine and finally Jim and I made our way back to the hotel. He told me that he was planning on seeing a good lady friend of his the next morning for a late breakfast at her house and then we would fly back to Los Angeles.

Once we got to our room, Jim took his toiletries and went into the bathroom, after which he came out dressed in a full set of pajamas. He tossed me one of his clean t-shirts to sleep in, and we both hit the hay in our separate beds. The next morning Jim looked at me and observed that I wasn't really dressed appropriately for the place we were going. I was still wearing the same casual clothes from the day before when I had played on his recording session. He thought about it for a moment and then went to his closet and pulled out one of his beautiful sports jackets and asked me to put it on. Jim was a bigger guy than me by about two inches and twenty pounds, so the garment hung off my shoulders. I looked kind of like a street urchin out of *Oliver Twist* or something. But Jim decided it would have to do, and down the elevator we went to grab a taxi.

We ended up at the magnificent home of a wealthy and influential San Francisco society matron who was one of Jim's close friends. After we rang the doorbell, a butler answered, who then summoned her. She gave Jim a big hug and then he proceeded to introduce me. I knew I looked ridiculous standing there in jeans, a t-shirt, and a sports jacket two sizes too big. But after looking me up and down she held out her hand, gave a welcoming smile, and said it was a pleasure to meet me. Though she may have been appalled on the inside, she never said a word about my mismatched appearance.

After passing a couple of hours there with Jim's friend, we said our farewells and then he and I headed back to the airport where we caught a plane back to Los Angeles. He dropped me off at the Columbia Records recording studio on Sunset where I had left my car and that was the end of my big overnight trip to San Francisco with Jim Nabors.

Jim and I remained good friends until he eventually moved to Hawaii in the early '70s. The Hilton Hotel chain built a big theatre-in-the-round just for him, and he signed a multi-year deal with them to sing there several times a week. Because of that, he and I gradually lost contact.

All I can say about it now is that Jim Nabors was always a spectacular friend to me. Sadly, he passed away just as this book was going to press. May you forever rest in peace, Jim.

TWENTY-ONE

Elvis and Me

W hen I first heard "Hound Dog" on the radio during the summer of 1956, I was thirteen-and-a-half-years old and living in my mother's little two-bedroom, one-bath house in Studio City. I was well on my way to being out of control, too—always trying to comb my hair into a ducktail in an attempt to look tough, yet failing badly because of my curls, which wouldn't stay down no matter how much grease I used. Come to think of it, I'm not really sure how tough I was, either.

If someone had asked me back then if I thought I would ever meet Elvis Presley—much less work with him someday—I would have laughed in his or her face. Elvis was a giant rock-and-roll star, and I was just an awestruck kid. Not only that, his style of music was so different from what I had been taught all my life that it was like night and day. I was classically trained; Elvis lived and breathed rock-and-roll, R&B, gospel, and country. Nevertheless, I was drawn to the King like a moth to the flame.

My godfather, Sam Katzman, a prolific Hollywood producer going back to the 1930s, specialized in making really cheap movies and a whole lot of money in the process. Quality was never his concern, only profit. With my parents being close to Sam and his wife, Hortense (or "Horti," as her friends called her), my dad always asked Sam to give him a part in some of his B-movie productions, which occasionally happened. My father, trying to promote me too, also got Sam to put me into some of these films.

At nineteen, in December of 1961, I appeared on screen in my first movie for Sam, a teen feature called *Twist Around The Clock*. The silly plot revolved around the latest dance craze of the same name then popularized by singer Chubby Checker, who also had a starring role. Sam told me that I could be in the onstage band faking along to the prerecorded music tracks that the singing stars were in turn lip-syncing to. With no lines, I did not speak, however. Instead, I simply played the role of the piano player, enthusiastically jamming along while the singers did their thing. For that, my godfather paid me the union extra scale of about thirty dollars per day.

Always attempting to think big, I told Sam that I could actually supply the whole band because I had been playing with the guys from the Hollywood Argyles, a group that recently scored a number-one hit single "Alley-Oop." Of course, that was only half-true; I actually only knew the guys who went on the road *pretending* to be the Hollywood Argyles, not the studio band that recorded the hit itself. But my godfather didn't need to know about that little discrepancy. As can be imagined, he was thrilled to get a *famous* band to play for scale. And I received an extra day of work out of it, working as a dancer in a scene where a bunch of teenagers swiveled their torsos off doing the twist. I had never done it before, and let me tell you after six hours of contorting to Chubby Checker's hit "The Twist," my ribs ached for a week. In 1964, Sam signed on to produce the Elvis Presley movie *Kissin' Cousins* and I got him to hire me once again to be an extra. Though I begged my godfather to let me act and have some speaking lines this time around, he turned me down and relegated me once again to being a musical extra.

But the good news was this was going to be an honest-to-God Elvis Presley movie, not just some no-name grindhouse flick. Better yet, Sam put me in Elvis's on-screen band to play the banjo. The costumer gave me some stupid-looking hillbilly outfit and I followed Elvis down the road while strumming away, even though I had no idea how to play the instrument. I met Elvis for the first time on the day of the shoot and thereafter hung out on the set with him and his regular group of guy friends, including Red

West (Elvis's bodyguard and a noted stuntman) and Charlie Hodge. They liked to sit down during the breaks and sing together in three-part harmony. Though I was a piano player, there unfortunately was no keyboard handy. So I just listened to them sing and chat, which blew me away. Being musicians, we all got along great. Can you imagine hanging out with Elvis while having a private, front row seat like that?

Elvis made two films that year, the other being *Viva Las Vegas*. And once again, I got the call to play in his movie band. Elvis's co-star was the beautiful Ann-Margret, and let me tell you she was stunning. I talked with her two or three times during the shoot, but for some reason I never could get a real conversation going. Believe me, I tried. It made me wonder if she was just not very talkative or if she was saving her attention purely for Elvis. Only later did I learn through the grapevine that the two had engaged in a passionate (and highly secret) on-set affair.

One day, Elvis, Red, and Charlie decided to sing an old standard called "My Heart Cries For You." They worked at getting it just perfect, with every swoop of their voice and all their vibratos in the same tempo and pitch. It was beautiful. While standing there listening, it gave me an idea. Knowing it to be far-fetched and exceedingly presumptuous on my part, I nonetheless said to them, "You sound so great doing this you really should put it down on tape." They all laughed and told me that they did it just for fun. But I pushed the matter a little bit and told them I thought it should be recorded and I would be happy to put up the money for the studio time.

After talking it over among themselves, Elvis said he'd do it if the other guys wanted to. Charlie Hodge, in particular, was really hot for the idea. So I set up some studio time at Sunset Sound on Sunset Boulevard in Hollywood for the following weekend. On the appointed day, I went to the studio and waited for them to show up, with an eager engineer by my side and tape ready to roll. About an hour past the appointed time, I started to get nervous with no one in sight. Shortly thereafter, however, Charlie walked in with his guitar, and I knew everything was going to be great.

Except it wasn't.

When I asked him where Elvis and Red were, he told me that Elvis was busy and couldn't make it, so Red wasn't coming, either. But Charlie reassured me that it wouldn't be a problem because he knew all three parts and he could sing them himself. All I had to do was record his first vocal pass and then he would overdub the other two on top of that. Which was fine for Charlie, but not for me. I was crushed.

Though I knew it had been a long shot when I suggested that we record the three of them together, I was still really disappointed. I guess Elvis had better things to do, like getting it on with Ann-Margret. Of course, I couldn't really blame him for that, especially since I had tried my best to do the same. So I dutifully recorded Charlie, and while his performance was okay, nothing ever came of it. There was no point in releasing a single under the name of Charlie Hodge.

Several years later, in 1969, I ran into Elvis again. He was busy forming a band for his new, long-term Las Vegas performance residency at the International Hilton Hotel. Famed country guitarist (and Elvis's good friend) James Burton called me up to see if I wanted to come down to the rehearsal studio and play a couple of tunes with Elvis. They were apparently looking for a piano player to join them in Vegas and thought I might be a good fit. I asked James how much the job paid and he said Elvis didn't care; he would pay whatever I wanted. So I thought about it for a moment and told him, "Three thousand dollars a week, plus expenses." Without a pause he said that was fine. When I hung up the phone, my first thought was that I should have asked for more dough, that I had just undersold myself. But, hey, it was Elvis.

So we set a time and I drove down to the studio. Sure enough, there was Elvis, as magnetic and engaging as ever. But as he and I shook hands and said hello, he gave me an odd look. He said he couldn't recall where he had met me before, but knew my face. I reminded him that I had been his fake guitar/banjo player in two of his movies. That's what had thrown him off; he thought I really *was* a guitar player, because every time he saw me I had a guitar in my hands. It didn't occur to him that he had never heard me play it. Nor did he have any idea that I was in actuality a world-class pianist.

Anyway, we had a good laugh and then ripped into a couple of his better-known hits, including "Blue Suede Shoes." I played some solo stuff on the grand piano and we rocked the place, with everybody in the room clapping along. Afterward, I said goodbye to Elvis, with James telling me they would be in touch soon with the verdict on my audition.

A week or so went by and when I didn't hear anything from Burton, I gave him a call. He told me that he was sorry he had not gotten back to me and that Elvis had already hired a piano player named Glen Dee Hardin. Apparently, Elvis liked my playing just fine, but felt more at ease with Glen Dee, who was a down-home country boy from Texas.

Ever curious, I inquired as to how much Elvis was paying Hardin and James said, "Eight hundred a week." I was flabbergasted at the low amount. He then told me that nobody was getting more than a grand a week for the job, anyway. So I asked straight out why he had even contacted me to begin with. Being a fellow session player, James Burton knew full well that I could make more than twice that much money by staying in town and just doing my regular recording dates. But he just kind of mumbled something into the receiver, never really giving me a satisfactory answer.

A couple of years later, I did visit with Elvis one last time. I was in Las Vegas on vacation and he was performing at the Hilton. So I called Charlie Hodge and he got me some great seats for the show. Afterward, my date and I went backstage and spent time with Elvis, Charlie, and some of Elvis's so-called "Memphis Mafia" buddies. Elvis was as charming, funny, and gracious as ever. There was no sign, either, of the drug abuse and huge weight gain that would later kill him.

In 1971, at least, Elvis remained the undisputed King, a guy who could mesmerize his audience like no other performer. And in that moment, I was thirteen all over again. He was still my idol.

TWENTY-TWO

Streisand

My first encounter with the great Barbra Streisand came while I played on one of her late '60s movie soundtracks, *Funny Girl*. And though she had a reputation for being difficult to work with, I never found that to be the case. We had an easy working relationship, but I did see on a couple of occasions why some might have found her a bit challenging to be around.

It wasn't that Barbra had a chip on her shoulder or looked to pick fights. On the contrary, it was because she knew exactly what she wanted. And when musicians or arrangers didn't deliver, she was very vocal about pointing out their errors. She didn't mince words. But why should she? Barbra Streisand had a great ear. So if someone did something wrong, it was his (or her) fault for making the mistake, not Barbra's for pointing it out. Fortunately, I never made any misjudgments when working for her, so I didn't incur her wrath.

The *Funny Girl* recording session took place on a soundstage at Columbia Pictures in Hollywood, which was also the filming location. Not told ahead of time as to which movie I would be playing for, it was much like any other job in that regard. I often didn't know anything about what to expect until I walked in the door and sat down behind the piano. Of course, movie sessions were always more complicated than regular rock-and-roll (and other) recording dates because the arrangers painstakingly wrote out everything note for note, not to mention that the tempos tended to vary, too, so you had to stay on your toes and follow the conductor carefully. It was more of a challenge, but I thrived on the experience exactly because of that.

Fortunately, my sight-reading skills were honed to a razor's edge by that time (1968) and I usually aced any charts they put in front of me. That is not to say that it was simple or I never made an error. I did have some difficulty with a few parts, but I learned early on to employ the oldest axiom among studio musicians, probably from the prolific Wrecking Crew guitarist Tommy Tedesco, who said, "When in doubt, lay out." That meant that if you had any question about what you were doing, don't guess and don't fake it. Just skip that note or phrase. With all the surrounding instrumentation, your absence will likely go unnoticed, at least for a few seconds.

There were several moments here and there in my studio career when I did exactly that. There was so much chaos going on in those movie studio sessions that if I did stop playing for a moment to catch up or because I was lost, nobody ever noticed. Another thing Tommy or maybe Hal Blaine told me was, "Never say anything if you make a mistake. If they don't hear it on the playback, they will never hear it. So don't volunteer, just keep quiet."

That rule was golden for me. On several occasions, I saw what happened when some newbie stood up at the end of a take, or even worse, raised his hand in the *middle* of everything to announce that he had played a wrong note. Guys like that were crucified on the spot, not only by the arranger and producer, but also by the other musicians because the music had to be cued all over again and everyone had to start over. With time being money, it was a quick way not to be asked back. Not to mention that it was tedious.

Speaking of errors, on the day of the first recording session with Barbra on *Funny Girl*, she was standing in the control room behind the glass listening to all of us play the music. We were recording the instruments for one of the songs that she was going to be performing on after we were done (known as an overdub). There came a part in the song where Barbra would be singing a high part that, vocally speaking, would be the most dramatic moment for her, and the arranger failed to take that into consideration when writing his arrangement. He made the mistake of building the orchestra parts up and getting us to play louder and louder to the point where it would be covering Barbra's vocal at the most dramatic point in the song.

Being extremely experienced, Barbra heard the problem immediately and got on the talkback system to tell the arranger that he had to change the parts because his music was covering up her vocal. In turn, he was not happy about this and in his arrogance (or ignorance) made the mistake of arguing back with her that he knew what he was doing and it would all be fine.

Well, that's all Barbra needed to hear. She came storming out of the control booth, walked right up to the guy in front of the whole orchestra and read him the riot act.

"I'm the star and the only reason you are even working here today. So change the parts now, or go home and I'll get someone else that knows what they are doing."

You could have heard a pin drop. And you should have seen the poor guy. I almost felt sorry for him in a way. He looked ashen and probably thought his whole career had just blown up in his face.

Yes, Barbra had humiliated him in front of the whole crew. But the arranger brought it on himself. She was completely right; he was so in love with his own music that he forgot he was writing an accompaniment to a singer—and then dared to argue about it with the star of the picture, no less. Streisand really put him in his place, that's for sure.

We all took our ten-minute break (and then some) while the arranger and the copyists madly scrambled to fix the arrangement to suit Barbra, which was no easy task. The guy was writing for a forty-piece orchestra with the star of the picture standing over him, demanding that he play the parts for her so she could hear them before the copyists wrote them out for all of us to play. I remember we got some good overtime pay that day because of his bungle.

But as demanding as she could be, there was another side to Barbra Streisand. Off the clock, when things didn't need to be absolutely perfect, she could be quite engaging.

In the spring of 1969, soon-to-be-famous record producer Richard Perry asked me to fly to New York City with him to meet with Barbra and arrange all the new songs she was going to sing on her new album *Stoney End*. Perry (along with lots of producers in town) knew about my arranging skills, something the other Wrecking Crew studio musicians, for the most part, didn't possess. So I was a double threat in terms of employment; I could play any piano, organ, or harpsichord music thrown at me *and* arrange all the parts for the other musicians. All the years I spent studying and my very fortunate gift of perfect pitch had really paid off in that regard.

Richard and I were friends, too. I had played on some of the records he produced and I also hung out with him in his home. He liked to have company at his house, and we had the same interests, primarily music and girls (perhaps not in that order). So when Richard got the job of producing Barbra's first pop/rock-and-roll album, he was naturally very excited. Up to that point, she had only recorded songs that older folks liked, so this was a totally new direction for her. She was a huge star already, of course, but more tilted toward the Broadway musical crowd than teenagers or even people her own age.

In talking with Barbra, it became clear to me that in some ways she felt like she had missed out on her childhood. That is to say, while her contemporaries were digging rock and roll and listening to the Beatles or the Stones or the Animals, she was singing in Broadway musicals. Although she became famous doing it, she didn't have any young fans because of the type of records she made. So she felt sort of left out by her own generation, and this new album that we were going to make was her first attempt at really reaching that audience. But because it was a departure for her style-wise, she was afraid it might not work.

After Richard and I landed in New York, we checked into the hotel and then headed right over to Barbra's apartment. We rang the bell and she answered the door herself. Richard then made the introductions; though it turned out they weren't necessary since Barbra recognized me from the previous sessions I had worked on for her, so that put both of us at ease. Richard, however, remained noticeably nervous, which was understandable. This was the biggest assignment he had been given up to that point in his career.

We sat in the living room, had some refreshments, and got down to work. I played the tunes for her and determined the keys that worked best for her. Then we discussed the arrangements (i.e. which instruments would be used, what would be played, etc.) and various session details, which all went like clockwork. At one point I asked her if I could use the restroom and she showed me to the guest bath. Her opulent apartment was beautifully furnished with antiques everywhere, and when I looked in the bathroom, I saw that she had a nineteenth century French commode made out of fine mahogany. It was actually a beautiful piece of furniture that she had someone modify to fit completely over her porcelain toilet. I commented that I felt like royalty and we had a good laugh together.

After that, we all said our goodnights and then Richard and I went back to our hotel, where I busily went to work for the next couple of days writing all the charts for the upcoming recording sessions that Richard had planned there in New York. Up to that point, I had never recorded anything outside of Los Angeles, so it was exciting, although a bit nerve wracking, to be thrown into a room with a completely new set of East Coast faces. The guys in L.A. were much more easygoing and helpful, and Richard was not having a smooth time with all these new players, so things proceeded slowly. We ultimately didn't get all the songs recorded, but we did at least get a bunch of them on tape and headed home a few days later where we did a few more sessions in order to get all the rest in the can that were on the list.

Though I'm proud of my work for Barbra, the project unfortunately did not end well in terms of my relationship with Richard Perry. Following a disagreement between us regarding my payment that I'd rather not go into here, Perry subsequently left out all of my arranging credits on both Barbra's *Stoney End* album and her next release *Barbra Joan Streisand*. The thirteen tracks I had arranged were spread out over the two albums. The only credit he did give me was for being the pianist, which was unavoidable because I was already on the session's union contracts. So much for being good friends.

Though I never worked for Perry again, I did see Barbra from time to time in Malibu where we both lived. There was a new sushi restaurant that opened overlooking Point Dume beach, and it became quite the rage for a while. One night, both Barbra and I were coincidentally dining there. When I noticed her, I walked over and said hello and accidently caught her with her mouth full of a sushi roll. It was quite comical because she tried to introduce me to her friends at the table but couldn't because she was chewing and swallowing at the same time. It didn't come out clearly, and everybody started laughing at the same time. But she quickly recovered her composure, and the introductions were made in good order. We then toasted to great sushi and great music. It was an unexpectedly fun time, something I'll never forget.

TWENTY-THREE
Conducting and Arranging

G oing back to when I was a baby in my crib, I used to revel in watching my father practice his violin. But Dad also did something that I saw and learned from, yet didn't know would ever come in handy: the art of conducting an orchestra.

My dad loved to listen to concertos and symphonies in our living room, and he would conduct the orchestra while listening to the records. I watched him do this several times a week for the first thirteen years of my life. It was like taking conducting lessons from one of the best symphony conductors in the world. What a music student might not learn until college, I was being shown firsthand as a young child.

Though it may sound hard to believe, by the time I was twelve, I could conduct a symphony orchestra just as well as my father, even though I had never taken an actual lesson in my life. It was just like breathing to me. This unique skill would come in incredibly handy starting in my early twenties.

As I became established as a studio musician, I was, of course, acutely aware of how much we were earning for our services. During the '60s, union scale was about sixty-five dollars for a basic three-hour session. Even better, the arranger/conductor of the session not only made double that as the leader of the session, but would also be paid about three hundred dollars per arrangement. Since we almost always recorded four songs per session, it put the arranger's total take at somewhere around thirteen hundred and fifty dollars (twelve hundred for the four arrangements and one hundred and fifty for the leader's scale for the same three hours). That was huge money back then.

I don't have to tell you that it didn't take me long to start thinking about how I could possibly get an arranging and/or conducting job. So I started looking at the arrangements on the conductor's podium when everybody else took their ten-minute rest breaks each hour. While the rest of the players were outside smoking cigarettes, I stood on the podium studying what the arranger had written on the score paper. With my perfect pitch, I could always hear all the notes that the musicians were playing and then I could look at the arrangements and see how the arrangers were writing it all down on the paper. Most of the time, it was so simple it surprised me. The only problem was how to get a record producer to give me the chance to arrange some music for a recording date. The answer was easy; just ask one of them, but with the condition that if they didn't like what I wrote they wouldn't have to pay me anything.

Jimmy Bowen, the hot young producer for singing stars such as Dean Martin, Keely Smith, and Frank Sinatra, was one of the first to give me a chance. I started off by writing just the rhythm parts on some of his B-side songs, and little by little, I started making some headway in the world of arranging. I then started working for more and more people, with Johnny Mathis asking me to become his musical director in 1968 and the great Nancy Wilson asked me to do the same for her in 1969.

Within a space of two years, I had two major credits to my name. Then, in 1971, Sonny Bono asked me to take over the musical reins on his behalf because, as he confided to me, he and Cher had a second chance at a really big career comeback. He said they had been offered a TV show called *The Sonny & Cher Comedy Hour* on CBS. Sonny further related that he needed someone who could handle all of his musical needs for not only the new show, but also their live act and in the recording studio—a person who was classically trained, but also steeped in rock and roll. In other words, somebody with his feet firmly planted in both worlds. I was, of course, tremendously excited by this new assignment and totally ready. It was a huge and highly lucrative opportunity for me.

For the next two-and-a-half years, I wrote music, conducted bands and orchestras all over the country, and produced albums for Sonny and Cher. I was on constant call and found myself up to my ears with assignments needed by them. They were constantly adding new songs to their show that I then had to write arrangements for. Sometimes, at the last minute, Cher would grow tired of the current arrangement of one of her set musical pieces. So she would ask me to rewrite it for her in a slightly different tempo or style, which I then had to do in a hurry.

One song, in particular, "God Bless the Child"—Cher's favorite—is something I must have changed at least five times for her in a space of two years. Not only that, but even when I wasn't currently working with Sonny and Cher, it seemed that every singer that hired me *also* wanted to sing that song. Crazy! All in all, I must have arranged "God Bless the Child" about a dozen times for different acts.

Looking back, I think the high point, for me, of working with Sonny and Cher came when they accepted an offer to perform with the Houston Symphony Orchestra. Sonny told me we were going to do their whole act with the symphony, so it had to be completely rearranged specifically for those performances. The orchestra had about a hundred musicians, and I had never before written for or conducted a full symphony orchestra. But I figured if my world-famous father could do it, so could I.

So, I took a couple of lessons from a well-known orchestrator, and off I went into the world of writing for symphonies. I only had about a month to prepare everything for the show, but I somehow got myself ready and got it all done on time.

On the big night, there I was, standing on the stage in front of the orchestra with a hundred sets of eyes staring back at me, all waiting for the downbeat, while Sonny and Cher stood waiting for me to start the music. I raised my arms, nodded to our rhythm section, and off we went for better or worse into a previously unknown musical universe. We opened the show with Sonny and Cher's most recent hit record "All I Ever Need Is You" and then closed with a special arrangement of the Beatles' "Hey Jude."

Sonny had asked me to write a big, dramatic instrumental overture using the theme of "Hey Jude" for the grand finale, which I did. But when our little five-piece rhythm section heard the orchestra come blasting in behind them with the first thunderous notes of the overture I had written, they almost jumped out of their chairs. Nothing had prepared them for the sound of that booming orchestra behind them.

We rolled through the "Hey Jude" overture and then I brought the orchestral volume back down to double pianissimo (extra soft), and when we settled into a kind of rolling vamp, Cher put the microphone to her lips and began to sing, "Hey Jude, don't make it bad..."

By the time of the song's ending vamp with the famous "Na, na na, na na na na, na na na na, hey Jude," the orchestra had started to build again from very soft toward a mighty crescendo, with each repeat of the chant getting louder and louder. We finally hit the last chord of "Hey Jude" and held it until the trumpeters were out of breath. I then cut the band off with a ferocious wave of my arm.

For a moment, the auditorium fell silent, the audience stunned. It was as if they couldn't quite comprehend what they had just heard. I think most of the ticketholders had expected to see a nice little show with Sonny and Cher doing their little comedy routine and maybe singing a few cute songs, just like on TV. But no one in attendance could have possibly dreamed they'd be witnessing this Johann-Strauss-like cosmic fireworks show. But one by one, the crowd started to applaud, then stood and cheered. It was something to behold, let me tell you. Not only did we have our standing ovation for the evening, it turned out to be one of the most memorable shows I ever performed with Sonny and Cher—or anyone else.

TWENTY-FOUR

A Cowboy's Work Is Never Done

By 1969, the music duo of Sonny and Cher had lost their glow and the hit records were gone. Needing to survive, they knuckled down and played smaller venues, among them the Playboy Clubs. Hugh Hefner signed them on for a five-year contract that really helped the pair survive the lean years. Because of this, Sonny and Cher were forced to reinvent their act. Just singing the old songs would no longer cut it. What they came up with contained a lot of sly, dry, comedic repartee between the two, most notably about Sonny's lack of height and other characteristics. He was a great target for Cher's slings and arrows, and in 1971, they emerged victorious with their own summer TV series entitled *The Sonny and Cher Comedy Hour.* This was a major turning point for them, so Sonny asked me to become their musical director. He told me how he had blown their first taste of fame during the mid-'60s by living too lavish a lifestyle. They spent millions and saved nothing. Now, with their second shot at stardom staring them in the face, Sonny and Cher weren't going to let it happen again.

Sonny told me he picked me to be his music guy because he wanted to make sure that he got the best possible person to take care of all their musical needs. In that regard, I was his first and only choice. Also, the pay was going to be commensurate with the position, which was really music to my ears.

Sonny and I had a great relationship during the time he, Cher, and I worked together, and I can't thank him enough for all he did for me. That being said, as I mentioned in an earlier chapter, there were a lot of disappointments along the way, the main one being that he promised to help me launch my solo career and that never happened. Perhaps in the end, it really was my fault because I didn't give him enough to work with. The problem may have been that what I put forth was usually too musically complicated for most people's taste. I needed to learn to write a simple song with a catchy hook that would stick in people's minds. But I just couldn't seem to write simple enough to catch a hit.

In 1971, Sonny and Cher were working on a new album called *All I Ever Need Is You* when Sonny asked me to come up to their house one day to help him flesh out one of his tunes. He had an idea for the verse and the hook of the song, but didn't have a bridge. He wanted me to creatively fill in the blanks. So, I wrote the bridge and some other parts, arranged the whole thing, and we subsequently ended up with a unique song called "A Cowboy's Work Is Never Done." Released in 1972, it shot to number eight on the Billboard Hot 100 singles chart.

Since I had written half the song with Sonny, I naturally asked him for fifty percent of the songwriting credit, too. I didn't think this would be an issue. After all, fair is fair, right? But Sonny saw it differently. He told me that for "political reasons" he didn't want to give me that credit, but would make it up to me. How, he didn't say. But I certainly didn't want to argue the point with him because he was now supplying my main source of income. Plus, I was their musical director, a prestigious position that carried a lot of résumé value.

In retrospect, what I think Sonny meant by "political reasons" was that he figured the song we wrote together might end up being his only real production contribution to the album and he didn't want to dilute his credit by telling anybody that I co-wrote the song with him, including Snuff Garrett, the project's main producer. This is certainly not a new story in the record and songwriting businesses. It's done all the time. Except in this instance, it was happening to me.

Because I didn't see any practical way to force the issue without hurting myself, I just sucked it up and told Sonny that I understood. I suppose all the other benefits I received from working with Sonny and Cher made up for me being aced out on "A Cowboy's Work Is Never Done." But it still stings when I think about it. Sonny didn't need the whole songwriting credit. He was already a huge star. Me? I really could have used that credit in so many ways, but that's life. Get over it, and move on.

Sonny and Cher really kept me busy from 1971 through 1974 during their TV series' three-year run. I was constantly meeting with Sonny and writing musical arrangements for both Cher solo and for Sonny and Cher as a duo. Further, after each season concluded, we then toured all summer, playing county fairs and concerts across the country. And when we weren't filming the show or flying somewhere, we were usually playing month-long engagements in Las Vegas, two shows a night, six nights a week. It was hectic, to say the least.

Because *The Sonny and Cher Comedy Hour* was such a ratings smash, we were all treated like rock stars when on tour. We traveled in ultimate style, too. Sonny chartered Hugh Hefner's private and luxurious "Big Bunny" stretch DC-9 plane, with a bevy of Hef's gorgeous bunnies thrown in for good measure. As you might imagine, I was in cottontail heaven. There were three shifts of four girls with one alternate, and each of these shift groups could not fly for more than seven consecutive days, so the girls were *always* alternating.

As it turned out, I was the most eligible among everybody onboard because Sonny was married to Cher (obviously), Denis Pregnolato, Sonny's personal manager and also our tour manager, had a wife back home, and the boys in the band were literally just teenagers (more on that later). The bunnies were all in their mid-'20s, so bedding a bunch of high schoolers wasn't really high on their menu (even though they were great musicians). But I was.

Now in my early thirties and in my prime, I became the focus of most all the girls. These air bunnies were Hef's personal favorites, too, and for good reason—he handpicked them for their beauty, charm, intelligence, and personality. It was every heterosexual male's fantasy, and I more or less had my choice. That is to say, I really did have to select just one of them for each leg of our journeys because, for the most part, the girls didn't like to share (darn it). So it was a delightful yet frustrating dilemma for me because I could only be with one bunny at a time each week until they rotated their shifts; then it was musical chairs all over again.

Britt Elder seemed to be the *bunny mother* of all the girls, and she and Michelle Speitz were always up for a *good time*. Lieko English and Maynelle Thomas were both spectacular girls, too, as were basically all of them. They told me that traveling with Sonny and Cher was a welcome change for them and a lot more fun than most of the flights they did with the older corporate types that usually rode on the plane. The girls also really loved to party when they were off duty, and we usually invited them to come to the concerts with us. Afterward, when we all returned to the hotel, there was generally a lot of carousing, and I can say with much gratitude that I never lacked for female companionship. For me, it was indeed an unforgettably great time.

Sonny, Cher, and I had worked side by side from their start in 1965 as Caesar and Cleo all the way through their TV show years in the early '70s—until the very day they split up, in fact. Actually, I stayed on even after that, but it was clear that they were not going to stay together and it was getting very uncomfortable being around the two of them. For example, on Big Bunny they wouldn't even sit near each other. Sonny would be at one end with Cher at the other. I could see that there was going to be a breakup soon, and I didn't want to be there when it happened.

Not knowing how to get out of the situation gracefully, I came up with the idea to ask for a large raise while we were in working in Vegas. Denis Pregnolato came back to me with a much smaller counteroffer that was easy for me to refuse. With that, I was able to quit under the pretense that I wasn't getting the money I felt I deserved.

Then it happened. Before I could officially leave Sonny and Cher's employ, Jeff Porcaro, our drummer, came running up to me in the hotel lobby one day, his adrenaline pumping, repeating over and over, "The shit has really hit the fan." He then told me that Sonny and Cher had just had a huge fight and that we might be done for good.

According to Jeff, unbeknownst to each other, Cher had been sleeping with Bill Hamm, our guitar player, and Sonny had been sleeping with Bill's girlfriend while using Porcaro's room as their liaison destination. Apparently, Sonny and Cher accidentally ran into each other in a hotel hallway coming and going from their respective illicit encounters and then had an explosive argument on the spot for all to hear. Cher left in a huff and flew back to Los Angeles, forcing the cancellation of that night's performance. I figured that most likely the whole engagement was going to be cancelled, and it was. It was an ugly mess.

Of course, that did not please the hotel management at all, and Sonny and Cher made up for those cancelled performances sometime later.

Thinking back about the next time we appeared there, Sonny and Cher came out on stage and performed all the same songs and jokes, all right, except now the two were staring daggers at each other. Every joke Cher told at the expense of Sonny was no longer delivered in a humorous way. She let fly through clenched teeth, and there was no smile on her face when she delivered them. They barely kept it together in front of the audience, and when it came time to sing "I Got You Babe" at the end, it was really embarrassing.

Things became a little saner after that show, at least onstage. The two forced themselves to play nice, and we all somehow managed to complete the rest of our multi-week run. And then that was that, the end of Sonny and Cher.

On an interesting musical side note, after Sonny and Cher split up in 1974, David Paich (the keyboardist I had hired to take my place), along with our drummer, Jeff Porcaro, and our sensational bass player, David Hungate, went on to form the Grammy-winning band Toto in 1978. In fact, Jeff, who would become one of the greatest session drummers in all of rock and roll, often told people that I had hired him for his very first professional gig.

Of course, the three were all only seventeen or eighteen when they worked for me in the early '70s. Because of this, they used to affectionately call me "Daddy Rubes." It's amusing now when I look back at how I always thought of myself as being the youngest guy in the studio with the Wrecking Crew (which I was) and then not long after that suddenly becoming the elder statesman at the age of only thirty-three alongside the three future Toto guys. Time flies, I guess, especially in the music biz.

TWENTY-FIVE

My Other Family

As far as I knew, when I was a child I had only one sibling, David, my younger brother. David and I were just regular kids, at least I thought so. Aside from the differences of me having a girl's first name, curly hair, and being a piano prodigy (David was subjected to none of that), we got along pretty much like any other pair of brothers at a young age. Everything went along fine until our parents decided to divorce when I was thirteen. Being unhappy with the split, I began running wild with friends while gradually hanging around with my brother less and less.

David and I lived together with our mother until I turned sixteen. That's when my relationship with him basically ended. Mom decided to move back east with David to Asbury Park, New Jersey (Bruce Springsteen's famous future stomping grounds), but I refused to go there with them. New Jersey seemed like another planet to me. Plus, I wanted to build my music career and Los Angeles was where the action was.

My mother immediately went crazy, though. And her constant drinking didn't help matters. Threatening me, she said that if I didn't go with her she would have me locked up in the Los Angeles County Juvenile Detention facility. During an epic, face-to-face screaming match between the two of us I yelled, "Fine, you have legal custody of me and can do whatever you want. But no matter what, I'm not going with you." And I meant it.

Ultimately, Mom backed down and gave in, but only grudgingly. I ended up moving in with my dad in Beverly Hills, much to her eternal ire.

She hated my father so much after the divorce that she couldn't bear to let him *win* anything more, including me.

We were a completely divided family from that point on. Their move not only put an emotional distance between us, but also three thousand miles of interstate highway, something that served to cement our demise as far as ever being physically near each other was concerned. David, under the influence of only our mother, and I, under the influence of only our father, were caught in a bicoastal system of parentage that guaranteed we would become strangers to each other, which is exactly what happened. David dutifully went to college, earned a teaching degree, married his high school sweetheart, had kids, became a teacher and a soccer referee, and has led what I consider to be a totally normal middle-class life. And I applaud him for that. I'm proud of my brother.

On the other hand, for better or worse, I did everything the opposite. I did not go to college, nor did I ever marry or have kids. It was the risky music business all the way for me. David was and is a great guy, but because we rarely communicated, he was never aware of all the things I had done, mistakes I had made, and musical milestones I had achieved.

To this day, David is continually surprised about my adventures. And when he boasts to his friends about something I may have done, they pepper him with questions that he invariably cannot answer. So David writes to ask if I know some celebrity or played with a particular group or played on some hit record, etc. It's sort of like he is a fan from a faraway place.

There was one thing, however, that neither of us knew about and that was our father's other life, his *other* family. Our father (and our mother) kept this a total secret from us. Dad was officially married four times. From these matrimonial unions came two children with his first wife (which, as I said, I knew nothing about), then David and me from wife number three. My question: does every man have a secret family that he fails to tell his regular family about? Or is this just something only Arnold Schwarzenegger and my father had in common?

How did I learn about all this? Well, it happened one day while I was recording the music for one of "The Sonny and Cher Comedy Hour" episodes. All the guys in the show's band were downstairs in the pre-recording room at CBS's Television City studios in Hollywood when on one of the breaks, Ollie Mitchell, the trumpet player and one of my really good friends, casually walked up to me and said, "Hey, Michel, guess what? I've got a date with your niece tonight."

Sure that he was confused or more likely pulling my leg, I replied, "Ollie, I don't have a niece. I just have my brother, David." But Ollie was both insistent and incredulous. He seemed serious.

"No, Michel, you not only have a niece, but you also have another brother and sister. Don't you know them?"

From there we got into a conversation that was surreal, with Ollie telling me about this family that I supposedly had that I didn't know anything about, yet they knew all about me. Knowing Ollie as well as I did, I found this tale to be wildly comical. After all, if I had another brother and sister, and incidentally a niece that was old enough to be dating Ollie, I would certainly know about them, wouldn't I? It had to be one of Ollie's latest pranks. He was known for that kind of thing. But this time he wasn't giving up. He kept saying that I had another family and that he had been dating my niece. More so, she wanted to know if I would like to come over with Ollie and meet her that very night.

On the off chance that Ollie's crazy story might somehow have a grain of truth to it, I decided that I had to find out what was going on. With my head spinning, I agreed to go with him to a little bungalow in Santa Monica. When we knocked on the door, a lively, pretty woman greeted us. She kissed Ollie on the cheek and he introduced her to me by saying, "Michel, this is your niece, Toni." I then politely shook her hand in some sort of state of disbelief.

After we stepped inside and had a seat in the small living room, Toni patiently explained that she was the daughter of my half-brother, who was named Jan Jr., but for some inexplicable reason everybody in his family called him "Bobby." As in Bobby *Rubini*.

Toni also told me that I had a half-sister, her aunt, named Tonia who lived nearby. She then showed me an old black and white photo, circa 1920, that depicted two little kids, Tonia and Bobby, sitting on some garden steps looking up at a very debonair man who was leaning over and playing the violin for them. I immediately recognized it to be my father, which shocked me into silence. How could he have kept such a thing secret?

Gathering my nerve, I phoned him from Toni's house and said, after taking a deep breath, "Guess where I am, dad—your *granddaughter's* house!"

You could have heard a pin drop.

After a brief silence, all my father could summon in reply was, "Stay away from those people, they're bad. I will tell you about it some other time." And that was it.

After I hung up the phone, Toni asked if I would like to go see my half-brother (her father, Bobby). Apparently, he lived just fifteen minutes away in Santa Monica Canyon. The next thing I knew, there I was shaking *his* hand, which was equally mind-blowing. He was about twenty-five years my senior and I didn't know what to say or do. How does one act when being introduced to the previously unknown and estranged other half of their family? Fortunately, Bobby and his lovely wife, Babe, made it easy. They couldn't have been more welcoming to me. Yet, I was still reeling. Obviously, my father had some reason, valid or not, for never telling me about his first family.

This was all too strange; my father had acknowledged knowing Tonia and Bobby, all right, though he didn't volunteer anything about them other than to say they were "bad" people. But clearly they were not. I could see that for myself. It just didn't add up.

Over time, I finally learned the backstory from Bobby that something really bad did happen when he and Tonia were little children. It had to do with a nasty divorce between my dad and his first wife, who evidently coerced Tonia into falsely telling the police that my (our) father had molested her when she was about four. Given Dad's sterling reputation as a world-renowned violinist, the story made for some particularly salacious newspaper articles and the divorce proceedings grew even more ugly. That scheme to dishonor and defame our father subsequently caused him to completely disown not only his first wife but their two children, as well. In his own mind, Dad blamed them all. That's why he never mentioned his other family to me.

As it turned out, I went on to have a wonderful relationship with my half-brother and half-sister for many years before Bobby sadly passed away. Tonia is still with us and sharp as a tack at the very young age of a hundred. Their presence in my life was a real gift. And I'm happy to report that my niece, Toni, and I remain in contact to this day.

In the early '80s, my girlfriend at the time, Adele Yoshioka—a beautiful and talented actress and dancer—somehow managed to reconcile the whole family, including my father. Bobby and Tonia came to a concert that dad and I were giving, and afterward they came backstage with their respective spouses. Tears flowed freely in between all the smiles and hugs; it might be the most emotional moment of my life.

And the best part? My dad was finally able to see and accept his first children again, along with his first granddaughter, which meant the world to him and them (and me). Bobby, Tonia, Toni, and my father all enjoyed many years of newly discovered love and companionship amongst each other until dad finally passed away in late 1989 at the ripe old age of ninety-six.

TWENTY-SIX

Nilsson

H arry Nilsson was unique. Period. There is simply no other way to put it.

Around 1969, when I got the call to play on my first Nilsson recording session, I didn't even know who he was. A couple of the other guys there told me what they knew about him, that Harry was a pal with the Beatles and also the Fab Four's favorite musician. All of which naturally made me wonder why.

After Harry and I were finally introduced and chatted for a bit, I came away impressed with his deep knowledge of music history and his passion for singing. And his personality was so much fun that I found myself really liking the guy straight off. I could see why the Beatles dug him and his music so much. Consequently, over a short period of time, Harry and I became really good friends and I played on a lot of his stuff. He had a lot of hits too, including, "Everybody's Talkin'," "Without You," "Jump Into The Fire," "Coconut," "Me and My Arrow," and "I Guess the Lord Must Be in New York City." Harry also wrote "One," which turned Three Dog Night into stars. For a while Nilsson had the golden touch. He was a talented, driven man.

However, my friendship with Harry went way beyond the studio. I wasn't his closest friend, but we did have a lot in common in terms of music, humor, and a well-developed appreciation of the fairer sex. We got along famously and hung out after recording dates and, on occasion, we would meet for lunch at the local diner. Once, by sheer coincidence, the two of us even ended up together in Hawaii. What an adventure that was.

We both found ourselves on the island of Maui in a place called Hasegawa's General Store in Hana. Now, the odds of me running into Harry in such a random, remote locale like that are probably somewhere around a million to one, I would say. Hasegawa's is a quirky little place in a very small beach town on an outer island where folks can buy a loaf of bread, a bottle of wine, and maybe a wind-up hula doll to take home to the grandkids. It's pretty isolated. I stopped there because I was low on film for my expensive new camera (remember film?).

While paying my bill, I heard someone shout, "Rubini, Rubini." At first I thought it was my friend Tony who had come on vacation with me, so I turned in the direction of the voice. But, instead, it was Harry Nilsson, of all people, walking toward me from the back of the store. You could have knocked me over with a feather. *How in the world did he get here?* I wondered.

Harry and I talked for a few minutes outside, and then he invited Tony and me to stop by his nearby vacation rental. But before we followed Harry back to his place, he wanted to get high. That was typical Harry, all right. He told us that he had some acid, but couldn't let his wife find out because she definitely wouldn't understand. If we wanted to, he almost begged, we could have some, too, and then he wouldn't be alone in his "condition." Being the hospitable types, Tony and I dutifully ingested a couple of LSD tabs along with Harry and then we made the four-minute drive back to his villa overlooking the ocean.

With a wary look, Harry's wife Diane greeted us with some obviously mixed feelings. With her husband forever working and being in the limelight back home in Los Angeles, for once she wanted to just have him all to herself, which was completely understandable. Compounding matters, and likely causing some jealousy, our little group also included a gorgeous black girl in her early twenties who called herself Maui Belle. Yes, that was her name, Maui Belle, at least on the island. Sometime later, I found out that her real name was Sharon Mack. Tony and I had befriended her earlier during our trip, and she subsequently decided to tag along with us and be our island guide for the duration.

Sharon had cut her hair to about a quarter of an inch, had a gleaming toothpaste-model smile, and curves in all the right places. Constantly lubricating herself all over with coconut oil, she looked like a shiny black pearl fresh out of the oyster shell. Furthering her allure, all she wore was a loose-knit, crocheted mini-bikini and a pair of sandals.

While Harry, Tony, and I all visited outside on the veranda, with the clearly none-too-pleased Diane sitting next to us, Belle decided to up the eye-candy ante. Seductively positioning herself about fifteen feet away on a beach towel, she proceeded to languorously rub the coco oil all over her body, including under her bikini top. A crowbar couldn't have pried Harry's eyes away from that picture, let me tell you—a fact that didn't go unnoticed by his wife, who being pregnant at the time, probably felt less than able to compete.

As the acid started to kick in, Harry began to tell us about this idea he had been working on. It was a story about a little boy born without a point on his head. Now, ordinarily, that would be a good thing, right? But in this case, poor little Oblio (the kid's name) was born into a family where everybody else *had* pointed heads. Also, his family lived in a small village where all the other neighbors had points on their heads, too. As you can probably guess, everybody in town made fun of Oblio because of his lack of a point. The poor kid had just one friend in the whole world: his loyal dog, Arrow, who loved him no matter what.

Harry, who was in the process of writing this story, wanted to make a movie or maybe a TV series out of it. But he hadn't finished the complete storyline yet, plus there were still songs to be composed for it. Even through the haze of the acid (or maybe because of it) I thought, *Wow! This is sure a great little tale.* Little did I know that later on, once we finished our mutual Hawaiian vacations and had gone back to our regularly scheduled lives on the mainland, Harry would not only make his vision a reality, but would call me to play on the soundtrack, too, for what would become an animated TV special on ABC called *The Point*.

But let's get back to Hawaii for a moment, shall we? With the acid really kicking in, Harry asked us if we would like to go swimming at a black sand beach that he and Diane had recently discovered nearby. It sounded like fun, so we all trekked over there through a small jungle path and emerged onto one of the most beautiful beaches I had ever seen. The contrast of the black sand, the green of the jungle, and the turquoise water proved to be breathtaking. Of course, I was on acid and was just about peaking by that time, so the colors were insanely intense and everything felt surreal. The black sand seemed so friendly and inviting, we even stuck our heads into it like ostriches and discovered that, even though our faces were submerged, we could still breathe. OK, I knew we were definitely stoned now because nobody sticks their head in the sand and inhales just for fun (unless you are on acid, of course).

I'm sure that Diane knew something was going on with us, but we weren't going to admit anything (we didn't want to get Harry in trouble), so she just sat there in a state of pregnant aggravation, wishing we would all just disappear. Harry, Tony, Maui Belle, and I all soon jumped into the ocean to wash the black sand off our faces and out of our swimming suits. Through it all, Harry was still obviously mesmerized by Maui Belle; he just couldn't take his eyes off of her. She knew it, too, as she casually shed her bikini top and then started backstroking and diving through the water in front of us like an Olympic synchronized swimmer. I took some shots with my Nikonos underwater camera of all of us in the water, including of Belle performing her semi-nude antics—photos that I still have to this day and enjoy so much. They bring back many wonderful memories of that day.

Following our Hawaiian adventure, I didn't see Harry too much for a while because he went to England to record his incredible *Nilsson*

Schmilsson album and I became busy with my own projects. One day, perhaps close to a year later, Harry called me out of the blue and asked me to join him at the Hotel Bel-Air's bar that evening. So I rounded up a date, and off we went after dark to visit with Harry.

After parking the car, as my female friend and I strolled up to the path to the bar, we passed a lovely pond that happened to be the home to several families of ducks and a couple of white swans. The ducks were very tame, and just as a joke, I decided to pick up one of the ducklings and take it into the bar with me. I was going to present it to Harry as a little gift.

Putting it in my pocket so the customers wouldn't see anything, we then met up with Harry, where we talked and joked around like no time had passed since our time in Hawaii. After about a dozen or so drinks, just before saying goodbye to Harry, I remembered about the poor little creature, took it out, and surreptitiously dropped it into the side pocket of Harry's jacket. I thought for sure he would feel it right away, but he didn't seem to.

With a few more minutes of unsuccessfully waiting for Harry to discover his new *pet*, I said my farewells and tottered back to the car with my date. That was the last time I ever saw old Harry. Some bad times came upon him both financially and health-wise in later years, and he finally died of a massive heart attack in 1994 at the young age of only fifty-two. I felt a huge loss when I heard the news, just as I have since for many of my other friends from the '60s and '70s.

It's tough being a rock-and-roller; it's certainly not an occupation for the faint of heart. Many among our ranks don't live all that long. The clichéd culprits of too much smoking, drinking, and drug-taking tend to make sure of that. But the gifted Harry Nilsson never stopped composing and recording, even as the quality of his life diminished over time. He was true to his love of music to the end. And I, for one, will always miss him.

TWENTY-SEVEN

Girls, Girls, Girls

D uring the '60s and '70s, my life and career developed at such a star-
tling pace that along with it came introductions to some of the most
influential people in show business, from recording artists to record company presidents to scores of beautiful women. Of course, not all of these
nice ladies were the kind you'd necessarily want to take home to meet your
mother.

At the age of twenty, in 1963, I met the madam—no, let's change that
and say the *owner*—of a rather sleazy operation in Hollywood known
as the Hollywood Model Studio. This was a business that provided nude
and semi-nude models for amateur photographers. Terri, the owner, had
rented a rundown 1930s clapboard house on Santa Monica Boulevard and
then decorated each of the several rooms in different motifs. Accordingly,
a customer could come in and say that he wanted to photograph a woman
in the "Hawaiian" room or the "Japanese" room. Terri would also rent a
camera to the men if they didn't have one. She would even toss in the film
for a few extra bucks. As you can see, this wasn't exactly a regular stop
among photography professionals. I would say that only about ten percent
of the customers ever even had their film developed. They just wanted to
get into a room with a nude woman and do whatever the *models* would let
them get away with.

During that time, when I was not on the road with the Marketts, I
would stay with Terri in her rented house/place of business. While there,
it was like putting a fox in the proverbial hen house; I played around with

every girl I could get my hands on, even though I was technically Terri's boyfriend. Dale, my partner in crime and co-leader of the band, was also going with one of the models, a really sweet and sexy but not overly intelligent Midwestern girl named Star. So, the four of us hung out a lot. And I must say that Terri and Star were a couple of the most fun but screwed up girls I have ever met.

For example, at the end of our time together as I tried to ease myself out of the picture, a distraught Terri tried to commit suicide by shooting herself in the heart with a pistol. But she somehow managed to mess that up by missing her heart altogether, instead blowing a hole all the way through her body that never hit anything vital. Thankfully, Terri merely wound up with one of her breasts swollen about twice the size of the other and a couple of entrance and exit scars to show for her effort.

Dale, on the other hand, managed to get Star *in a family way*. Which was more amazing to Star than to any of the rest of us because she had been whoring around for about six years without any sort of birth control and had never gotten pregnant. Of course, when Dale found out about the pregnancy, he skipped town and immediately went back home to Texas. Though we were close friends, I never saw him again until he surprised me by showing up at my father's funeral some twenty years later.

After my questionable experiences at the Hollywood Model Studio, I decided to start hanging out with a little higher class of women. That's around the time I met little Terry Fischer of The Murmaids, a popular '60s girl group. Remember "Popsicles and Icicles"? That was their big hit record and Terry was one of the three female lead singers. I met her while she was singing on demo records at Gold Star one day. Many a romance started in that recording studio. All the boys who panted for her and all the girls who wanted to be her out there in listener land had no idea how passionate little Terry was about her music *and* other things. But I knew. Oh, did I know. As they say, the best presents often come in small packages.

By the early '60s, the first female black background singers in Los Angeles started making major changes in the sound of the hit records of the day, especially regarding rock and roll. Previously, all the studio background singers were white, so when the black girls came on the scene, it was really a major change of sound and style. Rhythm and Blues was going pop. Phil Spector used a little known group called the Blossoms that was composed of three African-American girls—Darlene Love, Fanita James, and Jean King—on almost all of his recordings.

Jean King and I first met when I was called to play on a demo record for some unknown songwriter and she was the lead singer. There was only a piano, bass, and drums on the session. When Jean walked through the door, she instantly caught my attention and I evidently caught hers. She was dark, sultry, and had eyes that seemed to penetrate right through to the back of my head. Jean also had a look about her that said this was no lady to fool around with. She had been around the block and knew how to get home without any help from anybody.

We started to rehearse the song, and I noted that she just picked up the music and started singing the notes, which meant that not only could she sing but she could also read music. Her voice was magical, a cross between the breathiness of Julie London and the strength of Etta James. It was both delicate and full-bodied at the same time.

When we finished the demo, I asked for her phone number, saying that I would love to use her on some demos of my own sometime. She looked at me with a half-smile that said she knew I was lying and also knew what I really wanted. I couldn't hide anything from her; she was way too smart for me. But she gave me her number anyway. Jean told me much later that she loved the way I played the piano and my dark curly hair. She saw the way I looked at her that first day and it turned her on.

Jean didn't mince words, ever, and I loved that about her. There was something in her smile, too, that was particularly lovely. It was a slow, half-smile that said she knew what was going on, had been there, and was okay with it, whatever it was. Jean knew how to handle any man; none of them were ever going to treat her poorly and get away with it.

We started dating and the first thing Jean told me was that nobody, and she meant nobody, could know that we were seeing each other. It would have to be our secret. She was not about to lose any work because some racist record producer might object to her dating a white guy. It was one of the oddest things I have ever done in my life. Jean was so wonderful and so beautiful that I wanted to be with her every minute of every day; I didn't care who knew. I wanted to shout it from the rooftops. Yet, here I was, unable to tell *anybody* that I was seeing her. Every time I saw Jean singing on a session she all but ignored me. The most she permitted me to do was to subtly nod her way and/or say "hello" and just walk on by.

But one person figured it out first thing; it was Earl Palmer, my favorite drummer. Earl, a much older black man from New Orleans who had a groove behind the kit like no other (he had played on most of Fats Domino's and Sam Cooke's hit records, among countless others), was always perceptive. Once, on a session over at TTG Studios in Hollywood, Earl happened to notice Jean and I trading looks. When I sat down at the piano, Earl leaned over and said to me with a glint in his eye, "Uh, huh. You and her are doin' it. I know that look, Rubini."

I started to deny it, but he just shut me up.

"It's okay, man. I've been there, too. Your little secret is safe with me."

On another occasion, while working at Gold Star, I used the lavatory where I had the misfortune of picking up the crabs. Yes, I got the crabs and didn't even know it. All I knew is that I just starting itching and I didn't know why. That night I went up to Jean's house to spend the night with her, like usual, and I told her that something was wrong. I thought maybe I had a rash or something. In that no-nonsense voice of hers, she simply said, "Pull down your drawers and get up on the bed."

That sort of shocked me, especially with the tone in her voice, but I did as I was told and pulled down my trousers and my underwear and got in position. I had no idea what to expect, but what she did next shocked even me. Jean walked over to the bed, grabbed my legs, and then sort of threw them up in the air. "Keep 'em up there," she commanded.

So there I was, lying on her bed with my legs over my head like a baby getting his diaper changed. With that, Jean got down on her knees and spread my legs even further, pushed my privates over to one side, and started picking around in my pubic hair. A few seconds later, before I had time to object, she said, "Yep, just like I thought. You've got the crabs."

Putting me in the shower, she told me to lather up with some kind of medicated body shampoo she had on hand. While I dutifully scrubbed away, Jean went back into the bedroom and stripped the bed. I'm certain that I heard her mutter something like, "Men are more trouble than they're worth."

But Jean was one of the most down-to-earth women I have ever known, and we had some wonderful times together before we finally parted. One especially interesting night came when I went with her and the other two Blossoms to a show they were doing in South-Central L.A., shortly after the Watts Riots there. The show was put on at a local high school, and the three girls and I rode down together in a big four-door sedan. I was Jean's date for the night, which came as a surprise for Fanita and Darlene because Jean had never told them that we were seriously seeing each other. Jean really meant it when she said to keep it a secret.

As the conversation went back and forth between the girls while we got closer to the venue, Jean suddenly turned to me and said, "Okay, now you have to get down on the floor of the car and stay down there until I tell you that you can get up."

Confused, I asked why, to which she relayed that if anybody saw the three Blossoms with a white guy there could be trouble. Tensions were still high in the all-black neighborhood, after all. So I rather naively asked, "What sort of trouble would we be in if somebody does see us together?"

to which Jean replied, without missing a beat, "What do you mean, *we*, white boy?"

Darlene and Fanita had a big laugh at that remark, and I knew Jean had a great sense of humor. But she was only giving me that half-smile of hers, so I figured she might be serious. So there I was, crouched down on the floor of the car for the next fifteen minutes until we parked at the back of the auditorium, with me worrying all the while whether I would even survive the night. Taking no chances, I jumped out of the vehicle and dashed inside the stage door. The show was a big hit, however, and I'm happy to announce that we all got back home in one piece. Though Jean never did tell me if she was joking.

Along with meeting and dating various models, singers, and actresses (like Raquel Welch and Joanna Moore, etc.), I also ended up having a steamy affair with none other than the beautiful and multitalented Lynda Carter, Miss World-USA in 1972. You may best remember her from TV as the star of ABC's *Wonder Woman*—and a *wonder* woman she certainly was.

In 1972, Sonny and Cher were starring at the Sahara Hotel in Las Vegas and I was their musical director. We were booked for a month, two sold-out shows a night, six nights a week. Onstage, Sonny always wore his Elvis lookalike jumpsuits and Cher always wore one of her custom-made Bob Mackie evening gowns. The piano and I were center stage just behind them, with the orchestra seated just behind me. I alternated between wearing a black custom-tailored tuxedo, a separate version made from light-blue denim, and a custom leather jacket with complimentary silk trousers designed especially for me by Suzy Creamcheese, one of the top boutiques in Las Vegas at the time. I was dressed to die for if you were a female audience member. Both Sonny and Cher would turn to me several times during the show and good-naturedly make me the brunt of one of their jokes. And they always introduced me to the audience about midpoint in the most flattering way.

Lynda Carter happened to attend one night and, as I would learn after the show, had seen me waving my arms while conducting the orchestra, which caught her eye. She asked to be brought backstage afterward, ostensibly to meet Sonny and Cher. But as it turned out, Lynda was much more interested in getting to know *me*. As I entered S & C's dressing room, I saw them talking with Lynda and Sonny quickly motioned me over. Lynda told me that she had really enjoyed my performance, especially all the wonderful music I had written for Sonny and Cher. As I would find out later, Lynda was a talented singer, and before becoming Miss World-USA, she had made her living singing in clubs and lounges from Las Vegas to San Francisco. So she knew plenty about the subject.

As Lynda Carter and I stepped toward each other to shake hands, I could see a twinkle in her eye and I instantly felt blood rush up my spine. This was one of the most beautiful women I had ever seen. When our hands touched, it was positively electric. Everything except Lynda suddenly went dim; Sonny and Cher faded into the background. I think it was Sonny who finally quipped something about how he and I could talk about the show later because my mind was obviously somewhere else.

We all chatted for a few more minutes, and then Lynda bid Sonny and Cher good night, explaining that she had to get up early the next morning for some kind of function. She then asked me if I would be willing to accompany her back to her hotel suite so she wouldn't be bothered by anybody along the way. As Lynda and I walked out of the dressing room, I swear I was blushing from head to toe. That's how incredible she was.

Before we knew it, we were at her door. She didn't want to go in, and I didn't want her to, either. But I knew I had to let her go. Something special was happening between us and I didn't want to ruin it by making a cheap pass. I gave her a quick peck on the cheek, and then, after looking into each other's eyes, we pressed our lips together in a much more passionate kiss. And in that moment, I was sunk. I was a ship going down in the ocean of Lynda Carter's smell and caress. There was no saving me.

Lynda and I saw each other off and on for a fairly long time. When possible, I would fly to wherever she was working and stay with her in her hotel. That led to some really intense romantic feelings, and with the added adventure of seeing each other in strange towns and hotel rooms, it really heated things up.

Sometimes, when her schedule permitted, Lynda would visit me in my new digs in Malibu. I had recently moved back there and was renting a guesthouse on Malibu Road, right on the beach. A young lawyer and his rich wife owned the property and lived in the main house. They were well past the honeymoon stage of their relationship, and my impression was that they were not romantically involved much at the time. I, on the other hand, being a bachelor and not really tied down, invited female friends over all the time to stay the night. The lawyer's wife was not happy about this because she saw her husband's wandering eye whenever a female showed up on my doorstep. That led to some tension between the couple and me.

Likely at his wife's urging, the lawyer finally came over one time and told me that I would have to keep my drapes drawn because they could see in my living room, where clothing tended to be optional. I accepted this rule because I wanted to stay where I was. But the pair's tolerance for my living situation wouldn't last long.

Both the lawyer and his wife were gone one day when Lynda came over. She brought her tiny string bikini and planned on getting some sun on her spectacular body. As she went out onto the deck, she laid down a big beach towel, took off her top, and began rubbing suntan lotion on every inch of her gorgeous body. While I watched from inside the living room, thoroughly enjoying the view, both the lawyer and his wife (who was holding their baby) suddenly came tromping down the stairway and onto the shared deck. There, at their feet, was Lynda, lying between them and the entrance door to their house. The lawyer's eyes were transfixed, as you might imagine, and his gasping wife almost had a heart attack. I knew on the spot that my time in that guesthouse was over.

Sure enough, later that night, I got a letter pushed under my door that gave me a week to vacate the premises or else there would be legal action taken against me. It was the only time I have ever been evicted. Though I really couldn't argue with the lawyer because I saw how angry and embarrassed his wife had become. She was definitely not Wonder Woman, and Lynda was, in *every* respect.

During the 1970s, in between Lynda Carter and others, I began going out with some of Hugh Hefner's (*Playboy* magazine founder) favorite bunnies, in particular the girls he chose to be the attendants on his personal Bunny Jet. If that wasn't enough to fill my dating plate, while working on *The Sonny and Cher Comedy Hour* around that time, I met a guy named Earl Miller who was one of *Penthouse* magazine's principal photographers. Earl and I quickly determined that we had certain interests in common, principally women. If I had to name the one profession that could get a person laid more often than being a musician, it would have to be Earl's job. It was phenomenal.

Penthouse routinely sent young women who wanted to be centerfolds to Earl's house in the Hollywood Hills and had him do test-photo sessions with them. After he did the tests, he would send the film back to *Penthouse* so they could choose which models they wanted to include in the magazine.

Basically, the girls would come over to Earl's place, have a few drinks or whatever to help them relax, then get completely naked. They would lay back on a bed in all their glory while Earl shot about three or four rolls of film of them in every kind of provocative pose. Because these beautiful women of every description desperately wanted to be the next centerfold, they were usually more than willing to do whatever it took to get the job. Of course, Earl never promised anything other than to make them look as good as he could in the photos. But they thought they might have a better chance if he really liked them, so the models all worked toward that end.

Earl got more action than anybody I have ever met. He also liked to have little parties at his house, to which he would invite some of his favorite

Penthouse pets. Earl often asked me to attend these sensual revelries, as well, something I was *very* happy to do. In terms of female companionship, the 1970s were very, very good to me. Thanks, Earl!

TWENTY-EIGHT
Play it Simple, Stupid

One of the most difficult things a studio musician has to learn is to play simple. The guys who are unable to master this basic lesson never do make it in the studios. It goes against every grain of learning and ego and wanting to express oneself as an artist. I have been trying to learn this lesson ever since I first started playing popular piano and, for that matter, I'm still working on it. The biggest criticism I have of myself as a player is that I play too many meaningless notes for my own good. It's something in my brain that just takes over and my fingers seem to do things that I don't want them to do.

During the heart of my session days in the '60s and '70s, producers and arrangers commonly asked me to play piano or organ solos, which almost always made me a little nervous. This meant I was going to be heard soloing in front of the band for those few seconds and whatever I played would be indelibly stamped onto vinyl forever. I was more accustomed to just being part of the rhythm section, where my playing usually sat sort of mixed in somewhere between two or three guitars, the bass, and the drums. So, for a solo, it had to be perfect.

Every record has a style, be it pop or rock or blues. So, whenever it came time for my solo, of course I had to play it in the same style as the arrangement. I couldn't very well play a classical-style solo in the middle of a jazz tune. Which means I had to be exceptionally proficient at playing any and every possible kind of music. The trick was to make the producer or arranger think that whatever style I was playing was my first love, so it had to be convincing.

Of course, I had listened to a lot of music over the years in just about every style there was, so my ability to be genre-appropriate was never an issue. In particular, I was especially adept at playing what we used to call "classical shuck." That's sort of an imitation classical-sounding piano style that I would then use to sound like a concerto soloist on a pop record. Perhaps my most famous example of this is on Frank Sinatra's Grammy-winning recording of "Strangers In The Night" from 1966. If you fire up the song on iTunes or YouTube, you'll see what I mean.

When the orchestra comes sweeping in to play the bridge—just as Frank stops singing—you can clearly hear me there playing the melody while sounding like a concert pianist. This happens just before Frank comes back in and the orchestra modulates up a half-tone for the ending of the song. While recording, I actually played the whole six-bar bridge section merged in with the strings, but Frank's producer, Jimmy Bowen, decided afterward during the mixing process that it would be more dramatic to have the piano stand out over the last two bars of the bridge. Bowen must have known what he was doing because the record returned Sinatra to number one both on the album and singles charts, creating one of the most famous comebacks in popular music history.

One other piano solo, however, almost ended my career, at least in my own mind. When we were first introduced, and to my very good fortune, the great arranger Don Costa (for Frank Sinatra, Sammy Davis, Jr., Petula Clark, etc.) told me that he loved the way I played piano and was one of my biggest fans (imagine that!).

After Don permanently moved from New York to Los Angeles in the early 1970s, he started calling me for almost all of his sessions. I was also *his* biggest musical fan because I had heard his arrangements for Sinatra and other greats for years and absolutely loved his style and the way he wrote, especially for strings. The richness of his music and the depth of his harmonic sense have rarely been touched by any other arranger.

At MGM's recording studio on Fairfax in West Hollywood (most movie studios owned one, along with a record label, back in the day), Don brought me in to record three or four songs with a big orchestral ensemble. On one of the tunes, sort of a mid-tempo pop composition, he wanted a piano solo in the middle. Except that Don didn't notate anything on the charts as to specifically how the solo should be played. Instead, he just put the words "piano solo" on top of a series of empty bars on the sheet music, along with the chords to be played underneath.

I listened to the song once through and then dreamed up something unique that I thought would be a perfect solo. When the time came for me to do my thing, I played what I thought to be quite stylish and showy.

However, at the end of the take, instead of applauding my incomparable efforts and then throwing me a victory parade on nearby Melrose Avenue, Don said something over the talkback about wanting the solo to be a little simpler and that we should do another take. I immediately froze in terror at those words. Remember what I said earlier about "play it simple"?

So we did another take, and this time, I simplified my solo significantly. But at the end, Don once again stopped the tape. He said in a polite yet somewhat brusque way that I was not playing what he wanted and could I *please* just make it simpler? I began to panic and burst out in a cold sweat. Now I knew I was way off base. My three pals Beethoven, Tchaikovsky, and Rachmaninoff were suddenly of no help.

Deciding that honesty was the best policy, I finally said, "Don, I don't really know what you want. I'm playing as simple as I can without it sounding stupid."

"Just play a Carole King solo and everything will be fine," he replied, stopping me in my tracks.

Huh? That made no sense at all.

"I don't know what a Carole King solo is. She never plays them," I offered.

"Exactly," Don said, smiling. "Just play it like it isn't a solo, and everything will be fine."

While thinking over what Costa had just said, I took a moment to try to remember everything I had ever heard Carole King play on her records, which wasn't much. Maybe "I Feel The Earth Move" and a few others.

When the spot for the solo came up again on the next take, I just played some mindless King-like straight eighth-note chords, basically amounting to what a first-year music student could probably do.

At the end of the take, Don came out of the booth, sat down next to me at the piano, and said, "That was perfect, Michel, exactly what I wanted."

Let me tell you, I barely dodged the bullet of death that day. Don fortunately continued to call me as long as he was working, so I guess whatever it was I played must have been passable. And the big lesson I learned from him, despite all my years of classical training?

For God's sake, Rubini, play it simple, stupid!

TWENTY-NINE
Malibu in the Seventies

O ver time, many people have remarked to me about what a wonderful life I have had and how exciting it must have been to have known and hung out with so many famous people. And that is all true. I've had amazing good fortune and a whole lot of fun. But just like everybody else, I have also had my share of ups and downs, with plenty to worry about along the way.

Take insecurity, for example; that unpleasant emotion is the very definition of being a musician. We don't have regular jobs, we never know where our next paycheck is coming from, and there is no job security whatsoever. Then, when we do work, we're sure that it's going to be the last job we'll ever have—and not without cause, either. I've had plenty of slow times that seemed to last almost forever, forcing me to make many hard decisions in order to save my finances. Everyone has taken advantage of me from business managers to promoters to business partners. I have lost small fortunes to coked-up stockbrokers, including one in particular that worked for E.F. Hutton in their Malibu office.

At various points, I have been forced to sell my homes to survive, too, all of which has probably taken years off of my life in terms of the stress. So it has not been all fun and games for me by a long shot.

In the '70s, I went up and I went down like a yo-yo, both emotionally and financially. Good parts of that decade came in 1971 when Sonny and Cher hired me to be their musical director, arranger, and producer, and another came in 1976 when Berry Gordy, Jr., the legendary CEO of Motown, signed me to a deal as a recording artist, songwriter, and record producer. Bad times were the spaces in between and after that when I didn't know what was going to become of me.

Here's a good example. In 1973, I bought a wonderful home in Malibu overlooking the ocean on two acres of land, but at one point had to move out because I found myself almost broke. Had I not quickly rented it to one of the sons of an oil sheik from Saudi Arabia for the whole summer, I would have lost it. I then moved into a little guesthouse overlooking the Pacific on Point Dume. Whenever I went to buy groceries, I had to pass right by my real home, something that really stung. But it was a good lesson for me. At the time I was too much like my father for my own good: champagne tastes on a beer income.

One time, I even had to ask my evil stepmother (my father's fourth wife) for a personal loan just to carry me until I could sell one of my houses. (Remember, I was a child by his third wife). Otherwise, I was going to lose all of them. That was a bitter pill to swallow, let me tell you. Her name was Helen Pabst, who was a multi-millionaire by way of the Pabst Brewing fortune, and yet she made me sign a loan document to secure the loan. When it came to money, that old lady was all business, family or not. Furthermore, she gave me only half of what I needed, so then I was forced to go to my half-brother and ask for the rest. Talk about humiliation. What a difference between them, though. I offered to sign a loan document for him, just as my stepmother had demanded, but to my huge surprise, my half-brother simply pulled out a wad of cash and said, "Here, take what you need." He didn't ask for any signatures or collateral. He told me to just pay him back whenever I could. That's the difference between real family and someone who in reality wishes you didn't exist.

Conversely, a good time in the '70s happened when the brilliant (and I do mean brilliant) and lovely Suzanne de Passe, the executive vice president of Motown Records, stepped into my life. I very much fell in love with her, and we spent several wonderful years together.

Of course, a bad time came not long after when the then-president of Motown, a very unpleasant guy named Barney Ales, accosted Suzanne in his office. She told me that he had been drinking and threw her up against the wall. However, she managed to get away and ran out of the room to her office where I was waiting. She immediately filled me in about what had happened and I, of course, went crazy and started for the door to get revenge. She grabbed me by my arm and said, "Don't you dare leave this office. I will take care of it." So, I listened to her and stopped what was going to be a quick example of Barney's head meeting my fist.

Afterward, Ales cut all promotional funding for my records and productions, presumably so that Suzanne would look bad if they didn't sell. She ran Motown's creative division and was responsible for all my projects. Fortunately, Ales eventually left the company, which was fine by me, except that it happened after the damage had been done. I had departed Motown sometime before then because it had become clear that I was never going to have a hit record as long as I was signed to that label. The corporate infighting, particularly in relation to Ales, had taken its toll on me.

But Suzanne was the winner in the long run. I remember the day she called me to jubilantly announce that Barney Ales was gone. All I could say in response was that I was truly happy for her, which I was. She would soon become the president of Motown Productions, and it couldn't have happened to a better person. But, at the same moment, I couldn't help but also think, *Wow, wouldn't it have been nice if this had all happened before I left the label?* Oh, well.

I was very fortunate that years earlier I had been given the sage advice to invest in real estate whenever possible. With the world's population ever growing, the value of houses always goes up. Unlike a lot of my musician friends and acquaintances during this period, whenever I got my hands on a chunk of money from royalties or playing in the studios, I invested it in real estate. I bought a house whenever I could afford the down payment, instead of snorting it up my nose like so many others in the '70s. That's not to say I didn't ever do a line of coke here or there, but I never got hung up on drugs like some of my friends. In that sense I was very lucky.

Thankfully, my financial position strengthened over the years, and by the time I retired in 2003, I already owned several high-end rental properties that I had scrimped and saved to buy and that now provide me with a very satisfactory income stream for my later years.

Though I really loved my home in Malibu, and might well have stayed forever, it wasn't just the financial strain from my up-and-down income flow as a musician that made me move. There were increasing problems with Malibu itself during the '70s that made me leave. It was no longer the place that I had grown up in.

When I was young during the late '40s and early '50s, Malibu was pristine. The word "smog" hadn't even been coined yet, let alone any of it ever floating our way from nearby Los Angeles. More so, Malibu Creek was pure, Malibu Lagoon was full of birds and fish, and there was no traffic on the Pacific Coast Highway, the main arterial that runs right through the center of Malibu itself. But by the '60s and into the '70s, Malibu had changed.

At the time I bought my house in Malibu, I could ride my horse down to Little Dume Beach. There were trails that ran across the backside of people's properties, and I and other riders used those trails freely and frequently. But the state began to make trouble for all the homeowners by trying to reclaim any land that was not fenced, so everybody put up chain-link fences and thereby cut off my access to the beach. So riding in the surf, which I dearly loved to do, was over with. I would have to take my and my horse's life in my hands and cross Pacific Coast Highway and ride in the hills instead.

By then, too, the traffic on the Pacific Coast Highway had been getting so bad that on weekends it took me almost an hour to go from my house to the grocery store, which was only about two miles away. I finally had to start shopping on Friday evenings and then just barricade myself back inside my house for the rest of the weekend. With thousands of people driving to Point Dume and elsewhere on PCH (which ran right in front of my house), it made leaving my place just about impossible to do from Saturday mornings through Sunday nights.

But the thing that permanently ended my love affair with the Malibu I once knew came when two of my friends and I all got staph infections at the same time while swimming at Little Dume Beach. We never learned if the staph had traveled north from the water at polluted Santa Monica Bay or south from the sewage runoff from Oxnard or Ventura.

In any case, I wound up in the hospital with my leg swollen to about twice its normal size. It was so painful I couldn't walk. The friendly doctor told me I was lucky that it hadn't spread anywhere else and he would be happy to lance the boil for me. He said it was going to explode whether he stuck the knife in it or not. To me, the thought of someone cutting into my already throbbing leg was more than I could stand. So the doc sent me off with a bottle of antibiotics and some pain pills and wished me luck.

Sure enough, however, about a day later, the inflamed area ruptured like Mount Vesuvius and pus poured out for the next forty-eight hours. It sounds disgusting, I know, but what a relief it was when it finally burst open, almost better than sex.

Thinking it was all over, I soon returned to my regular life. But after another week, I noticed that my lower stomach and hip area started showing the same symptoms; it was starting all over again. The antibiotic had suppressed the infection, all right, but it didn't kill it. Now the staph was back with a vengeance, except this time, it wasn't just in my leg; it was right next to my private parts, and that was no joke. I was really scared.

So I got into my car and raced back to the hospital where that same friendly doctor asked me if I was now ready for him to stick the knife in. This time I said "Yes." He then pulled out his trusty scalpel and sliced right down the middle of the boil that was growing by the minute. Though I thought I might faint, it actually proved to be a relief. I stayed in the hospital all that day, finally heading home with even stronger medicine and more pain pills. Luckily, this time the infection gave up.

When back on my feet, I decided to have a serious talk with myself about Malibu. It no longer featured open land, country living, and clean beaches. Instead, it had become a traffic-clogged, celebrity-filled little town with a polluted ocean and no place for horses.

No, this wasn't the Malibu that I had grown up in; the dream was over. The staph infection had been the breaking point. I put my home on the market and soon sold it to the Oscar-winning actor, Louis Gossett, Jr. And though I have visited Malibu many times since, I remain happy with my decision. If I've learned anything during my life, it's that everything changes. Like it or not.

THIRTY

Leon Russell

D uring the early 1970s, I sort of felt displaced.

I knew that my days of working as a studio musician were coming to an end. It was obvious to me, although it was not apparent to a lot of the other musicians, at least not as soon as it was to me. Self-contained groups were now making a lot more records, as opposed to during the '60s when almost everything was being made using studio players. The first session musicians to really feel the pain were the string players: the violinists, the viola players, and the cellists. Synthesizers were becoming better and played up to sixteen voices (sounds) at a time, not to mention that programming them was becoming easier. So, record and film producers started employing this equipment to augment or replace the string sections all together. I felt very bad for the old-school guys who were losing their livelihoods to technology.

My father was a world-famous violinist, so I had a special place in my heart for all these wonderful players who were so ill prepared to make a living in the brave new world of electronic music. They didn't comprehend what was happening to them until it was too late. So many of them were living in the past, and as the calls for recording sessions started to dwindle in a downward spiral, they were left with their mortgages to pay, families to feed, and no way to make a living. The Musicians Union (Local 47) was unfortunately of no help to them, either, because the board of directors there was more out of touch with what was happening in the real world than the musicians they were trying to help.

As an illustration, around 1975, Michael Boddicker (a fellow key-boardist, best known for his synthesizer work) and I were invited to attend a special meeting of the board at the Local 47 office building on Vine Street in Hollywood in order to answer two pressing questions: 1) Are synthe-sizers here to stay or are they just a passing fad? And 2) Are synthesizers good enough to take work away from established string players? I couldn't believe my ears. These questions should have been asked a decade before! The union officials had no idea what synthesizers were doing to the indus-try. They were nice old men, of course, but they should have been put out to pasture about ten years earlier.

With an arsenal of synthesizers in my own collection of musical instru-ments, I not only played them on sessions, but I also rented my synths out to the labels for other keyboard players to use. I was one of the worst offenders in regard to replacing string sections on records. Yes, I felt ter-rible about it, but I also had to eat, and it had become clear to me that if I wasn't prepared for the future, then I wasn't going to have one, either. So I accepted synthesizer work, but not because I liked it; I didn't. I knew I was taking food out of other people's mouths and that has never sat well with me.

During the '70s, I was working some, but the era just didn't have the spirit of the '60s. I felt a kind of desperation in the air. It affected me just as much as the other musicians. Nobody was working as much as they used to. It was feast or famine. There were times when I really didn't know how I was going to continue. I actually had a lot of success in the '70s, but when in those moments between jobs, I felt like I was just alone out in space somewhere floating around, not tied to anything or anyone.

One of those times occurred when I left Sonny and Cher. I quit the job as their musical director in 1974 when their TV series ended, because I felt that my role with them was going nowhere. If I had stayed any lon-ger, I would've become a person with only one job: working for Sonny. Which meant I would have had to follow Sonny wherever he went and no matter what he decided to do. He was an unpredictable guy, too. If Sonny suddenly decided to quit the business (which he eventually did after I departed), I would have been stuck. In my line of work as a session musician at the time, you had to always keep your hand in the game with the producers and arrangers around town or else other eager musicians would take your place in the studios. And I had already been with Sonny and Cher on basically a full-time basis for far too long in that regard. But I had stayed for more than just the steady, high-profile gig with them. Sonny had promised me for years that he would jumpstart my career so that I could become a successful recording act, too. But he never followed through. Unfortunately, he was just too preoccupied with his own ambitions to ever give me the help I needed in order to catch attention and become a star in my own right.

After I left Sonny and Cher, I stepped out into a space where I felt totally alone. It was like I had to start all over again. I wanted so much to be a successful recording artist so I wouldn't have to be a slave to anybody else's whims. If I could release a piano-based, instrumental hit record like Roger Williams did with "Autumn Leaves," my future would be secured— not just financially, but emotionally as well. It doesn't take more than one or two really big songs to become established. It would have allowed me to play shows all over the world, even maybe do three months in Vegas every year after I got a little long in the tooth. But it was not to be.

Various sessions did come my way during the mid-'70s, but nothing significant. I scored some commercials, but could not get a real foothold there either. I was good at it and I did some major national commercials for Coke, Chevrolet, Brach's candy, and quite a few others, but it was really unfulfilling as far as music goes. Imagine having to write a piece of music that would only last 29.5 seconds from the beginning to the end of the echo fade every day for a living. It was akin to being a ball boy for a basketball team. You get to touch the balls during warm-ups but are never allowed to play in the real game. That's how I felt. I yearned to write something major, to really show what I could do. Cars and candy may have paid the bills, but, creatively, I was dying inside. Cutting commercials was mindless as far as I was concerned. Though, of course, the advertising guys who hired me acted as though they were producing *Gone With The Wind* or something. What planet did they grow up on? I could talk about commercials all day long, but let me give you just one example of why I stopped trying to develop that kind of work into a career.

One day, I was arranging a thirty-second commercial for Brach's candy and in doing so had hired my old girlfriend, Jean King (a black woman, God forbid), to sing the jingle. It was all of about five or six words, something like "Brach's candy, you'll love it!"

In trying to imagine how the message of the jingle should best be delivered, I told Jean to sing the words like a blond high school cheerleader and she did a perfect job. We had just finished doing the vocal when the account guy from the advertising agency that Brach's had hired showed up. Mr. Self-important listened to the vocal and said, "Great sound, Brach's will be thrilled." And then a moment later Jean stepped out of the vocal booth, and the guy saw her for the first time. He sort of froze in place and then asked to hear the track again. After I played it for him, he took me aside and told me that the vocal was good but it sounded too "colored." He wanted me to redo it with a white girl. *What?* I couldn't believe what I was hearing.

Though I objected, he was paying the bills and he held his ground. So I hired Julie Rinker (a white girl, by golly) and scheduled a session with her. The ad agency guy showed up and watched Julie sing the same little vocal, which left him very pleased. He said that would be much better. So this racist asshole liked the first vocal until he saw who the singer was. What made the difference? The color of somebody's skin. You can see why I didn't like doing commercials.

In between doing commercials and whatever other jobs came my way during this time, I also met a very talented Southern rock guitarist named Wayne Perkins. He was a great picker, and we hit it off really well. Because of this, I decided to write a new album of material and record it with Wayne. He was a good singer and had a way with lyrics, so I decided to put my energy into making something happen with him. It seemed to me like we had a real shot at doing something special as a duo. Over a period of a few weeks, we wrote a few songs and came up with ideas for several others. Wayne was from a very poor Southern family and they were depending on him to send them money every month. So I helped him out and gave him money as we went along because I needed us to stay together and get our album done.

One day, Wayne told me that he had to return home because of a family problem. He suggested that I go with him back to Alabama and continue working there. He told me he had a good studio and knew a lot of great musicians, so I paid for our tickets and off we flew to Alabama. He introduced me to his family, and they were charming and welcoming of me. They lived in a small country house surrounded by the most beautiful forest of maple, pine, and other trees I had ever seen. He had one sister that took a liking to me, and she showed me around by taking some walks together in the forest around his house. It was a lovely place.

A couple of days after we arrived, Wayne told me he had a session all set up for us at the local studio. So we went there as scheduled, but the other musicians never appeared. Wayne started making excuses for his friends, but clearly something was wrong. He suggested that we lay down some tracks by ourselves and he could overdub bass afterward. But that was not an option. We were supposed to be doing a session with a live band, not laying down individual tracks. I never got a satisfactory reason from Wayne as to why the other players didn't show up. The trip turned out to be just time wasted for me, and I returned home very unhappy. Little did I know it was a harbinger of more to come.

When Wayne finally returned to Los Angles a few weeks later, we started recording the album again. At about this point, in early 1976, he received a phone call from Leon Russell. Leon wanted Wayne to play with him on his upcoming tour, and of course, Wayne couldn't turn it down. I asked him what was going to happen with us, so he put Leon on the phone with me. Leon, whom I knew from the old days in the studios when we played together on Phil Spector and other sessions, asked if I would come to Tulsa (where Leon lived) along with Wayne. Leon said that when they weren't rehearsing for the tour, Wayne and I could continue writing and working on our album in his (Leon's) professional studio there. Leon also thought that I might be able to help him out with other productions, too—sort of give them an idea of what a real Hollywood record producer would do in the studio.

It sounded like a great offer. I could continue working with Wayne and also maybe produce some music for Leon in Tulsa. So off Wayne and I went, where we wound up living in Leon's house for about a month. Which sounds great on paper but didn't work out so well in real, because Wayne basically slept all day and was out all night. I could never get him out of bed.

So instead of writing new music with Wayne, I had nothing to do but go running, which I did. Everyday, I would get up early, cook breakfast for myself, and then leave the house for a long jog down to the Arkansas River. I would follow the river along its banks for about twenty or thirty minutes, then turn up one of the side streets and head back to the house. I was definitely getting my running chops together, but my piano chops were going down, down, down.

Leon was a very nice host, but I didn't see him much either. He was a very private guy, and it was a big house. About the only time I saw him was in the middle of the night because he had a habit of coming down to his kitchen around 1:00 or 2:00 a.m. to make himself a tuna sandwich, though we did go out a few times to a couple of the clubs there in Tulsa, especially where the Gap Band was playing. They were recording at the time in Leon's studio, and he eventually asked me to give them a few pointers about how to record faster. But with me being an outsider and a city slicker in their eyes, they didn't take too well to my advice.

That I ended up at Leon Russell's house to begin with was truly ironic. Back in Los Angeles, I had been seeing one of Leon's old flames, backup singer and songwriter Donna Washburn. Donna had written a lyric, really more of a poem, which summed up her feelings for Leon. When she and I first met, she showed me the lyric and I then wrote the music for it. It was a lovely song called "You Don't Love Me Today," which was recorded by Marjorie McCoy on her 1971 album *The Other Side*. I also arranged the track for Marjorie and played piano on the session. Having told Donna that I was going to Tulsa to stay with Leon, she begged me to sing the song to him when I got there. It was a crazy idea, but I promised I would do it just for her.

On the first night in Tulsa, after unpacking and freshening up, I walked downstairs to the living room of Leon's monstrous mansion where he warmly greeted me. Though he had by then grown long white hair and wore sunglasses even indoors, he was still the same old Leon underneath it all. We talked shop for a while, with him bringing me up to date on what he had been doing. Finally, I summoned the courage and said to him that I had been writing music with Donna and that she wanted me to sing a song to him that she and I had co-authored. I could see some hesitation/confusion in Leon's eyes as he contemplated what he might be about to hear, but he gave me the green light nonetheless.

So I sat down at Leon's grand piano and started playing and singing the love-gone-wrong lyric that Donna had torn out of her heart about him. You can't imagine how strange it was; there I was, sitting at Leon Russell's piano, singing a tortured love song to him *about* him, written by his old girlfriend who I was currently seeing. How is that for an only-in-show-business moment? It was both embarrassing and hilarious all at the same time. Thinking back, it's a wonder Leon didn't ask me to pack my bags and get out right then and there.

Amazingly, I stayed with Leon in Tulsa for almost a whole month, which was a lot longer than I had expected. Wayne eventually left with

Leon to go on tour, leaving me with nothing to do but either wait for them to return or go back to L.A.. I chose the latter.

After several weeks, Wayne finally showed up at my doorstep and we commenced the recording of our album project only to be interrupted yet again. This time Wayne told me that he had just received an invitation to go to England and audition for the Rolling Stones as the replacement guitarist for Mick Taylor, who had recently left the band. The Stones were in the middle of cutting their *Black and Blue* album and were trying out various guitarists on various songs. In other words, it was the chance of a lifetime.

Wayne's only problem was that he had no money; he claimed he sent most of it to his family. More likely, it went up his nose. Nevertheless, though I was very frustrated about our album never getting done, I wanted only the best for Wayne, and so I asked him how much he needed to make the trip. He figured it to be about two thousand dollars, which I gave him—but not as a loan. I had discovered long before that loans never get paid back and you just lose your friends, because every time they look at you, they are reminded that they owe you money. Inevitably, resentment subconsciously builds up until it undermines your whole friendship—you end up not only losing your money, but your friend as well. Better to just offer it as a gift.

With that in mind, I told Wayne he would never have to pay me back. Hopefully something good would come from it, and if it didn't, then he was always welcome to return and finish recording with me. So Wayne flew off to England where the Stones used him on a few album tracks, but that was it. He didn't become the Stones' next lead guitar player. From there, Wayne Perkins returned to Alabama, and I never saw him again. He just went home, and that was the end of our collaboration. Just as I feared, I not only lost my money, but I also lost my friend.

There was one other initially promising but ultimately horrendous event that happened during this period for me in the mid-'70s. The one and only Jerry Lee Lewis had actually recorded a song that I had written with my friend Ric Marlow titled, "Only Love Can Get You in My Door." Released on his album, *Country Class*, in 1976, Jerry Lee unfortunately absolutely butchered the tune. He really fell in love with it and wanted to make a real production out of it. So instead of just following the simple country two-beat demo that we sent him, Jerry Lee made an overwrought concerto out of the song. He turned a simple, two-minute possible hit into the second longest track on the album, timing in at a very long 4 min 22 seconds.

As you might imagine, I was really excited at first when I was informed that "The Killer" was going to record my song. He was one of my idols growing up. But when I heard the final result, I just dropped my head in sorrow. In my view, Jerry Lee must have been high on speed or something. The recording speaks for itself. To me, he just trashed it.

Two or three years after the Jerry Lee Lewis debacle, I got a call from Dick Clark's people asking me to play on one of the *American Bandstand* anniversary specials. And guess whom I was scheduled to play with? Yep, none other than Jerry Lee himself. It was me on the organ, my old Wrecking Crew pal Jerry Cole on guitar, Jim Keltner on drums, and a couple of other really great studio players. We were assigned to be Jerry Lee's backup band because the producers didn't want to pay for all of his regular guys to fly to Burbank from Tennessee.

After being introduced to Jerry Lee, I told him who I was and that he had recorded one of my songs. When I mentioned the title, his eyes just lit up. He said, "Goddamn, boy, I love that song. If you have any others like it, send 'em to me." As I smiled and said, "Sure, that'd be great," all I could think was that I never wanted Jerry Lee Lewis to record any of my songs ever again.

On the *American Bandstand* reunion show, Jerry Lee was going to sing just one of his hits, "Whole Lotta Shakin' Goin' On," and so we started to rehearse it with him before airtime. Of course, the guys in the band and I knew the tune inside and out because we had all been raised on Jerry Lee

Lewis's hits back in the late '50s. But as we started playing, it immediately became clear that Jerry Lee was rushing the beat. He kept speeding up and getting way ahead of the rest of us. The tune fell apart in about twenty seconds. We all stopped, and Jerry Lee looked at us and asked what was wrong. Trying to be polite, we told him that nothing was wrong; we simply got a bad start.

So we started again, and once more the same thing happened. It was like Jerry Lee was on meth or something. This was particularly bad because Jim Keltner, our drummer, was and is probably the most laid-back, in-the-pocket drummer in the world. He is the only drummer I know that actually slows down while playing fills in the turnarounds. So between Jerry Lee and Keltner, it was like two opposite forces pushing each other away.

Jim was not happy, and he was about one step away from packing up his drumsticks and leaving, which would have been a disaster. I saw the tension in Keltner's eyes, so I walked over to him and said, "Let me talk to Jerry Lee for a minute. Don't do anything rash."

Trying to be as diplomatic as I could, I then told Jerry Lee that we were having a little trouble adjusting to his style because he was pushing the beat. In that regard, I let him know that we had a couple of choices: we could either follow him wherever he went with the tempo, or we could lay down a solid beat and then he would have to follow us. It didn't make any difference to any of us as to which way Jerry Lee wanted to go; we just had to agree on something definite.

Jerry Lee thought about what I had explained for a moment and then said that he would follow us. So we started the tune again, and this time Jerry Lee listened to us. Though he still rushed the time, at least when he got about a half-beat ahead, he would then slow his piano-playing speed and try to fit with the band. It was obviously the best he was able to do.

Finally, it was Jerry Lee's turn to perform live on the show and we just tried to put his chronically out-of-tempo piano playing and vocals out of our minds by laying down as solid of a beat as possible. The combination sounded terrible to me, but the audience loved it. So who cares? Everybody got paid, we avoided a disaster, and I got to meet the man who, in my opinion, absolutely ruined one of my best songs.

THIRTY-ONE

South America

In the mid-'70s, when Leon Russell finally left to go on tour and Wayne Perkins went with him, they left me with nothing to do. As I mentioned in a previous chapter, they wanted me to wait in Leon's house in Tulsa until they got back so Wayne and I could start writing again. But it was too much. I found myself doing nothing but eating, watching TV, and jogging around town. I learned just about every residential street close to the river, and I was starting to say hello to the birds in the trees as I passed by them. This was not a good situation for me.

Feeling sorry for myself, I thought about my situation and decided that maybe it was the perfect time to do something I had always dreamed of, which was going to the Galápagos Islands, home of the giant tortoises, and also exploring the jungles of South America. I have always had a somewhat overdeveloped affection for exotic animals, having owned everything from a boa constrictor to a baby Malayan sun bear to a wolf, coyote, fox, and even a tamandua (a South American medium-sized anteater).

So I figured it to be the perfect time to really satiate my appetite for this affliction and perhaps get it out of my system for good. I had such a large menagerie at my home in Tarzana that I had to hire a houseboy to care for my little zoo while I worked to support it. I sometimes felt that I related better to animals than to humans, and that was not helpful in trying to advance my career, but at least animals didn't let me down like the humans did. Maybe I would have been better off as a zookeeper like my good friend, Aaron Krieger, who I used to trade snakes with at the Griffith Park Zoo in Los Angeles when I was about fourteen.

After returning to Los Angeles from Leon's house in Tulsa, I told some friends about my planned trip and they suggested that I go to Buenos Aires, Argentina. Once I saw where it was on the map (it's just about the southernmost city in the world at the very bottom of South America), I decided to fly there first and then work my way northward. Another friend said that since I was going all that way, I should definitely not miss Rio de Janeiro, so I added that to be the second stop on my little trip. Somebody else added that I should definitely go to Machu Picchu in Peru, too, that I couldn't very well afford not to see the Incan ruins as long as I was in South America. So that made the list, as well. Not long after, I bought a one-way ticket for Argentina and off I went.

If you're wondering ahead of time as to whether I did indeed get to experience South America in all its most primitive and captivating glory— was it the eye-popping adventure of a lifetime I had so desperately hoped for?—the answer is an unequivocal "yes." And then some.

From going eye to eye with a pair of sinister, hungry-looking caiman (South American alligators) deep within the Amazon Basin to having an angry horde of Ecuadorian army ants go crazy with their powerful jaws on my arm when I accidentally blocked their passage to getting stuck in quicksand, only to be rescued at the last minute by an Indian guide (not to mention watching a tribal woman squat, urinate *through* her skirt, and then get up and walk away as if nothing had happened)—yes, my trip to South America was truly unforgettable.

But not only because of my almost daily run-ins with various indigenous species or the indescribably gorgeous mountains, rivers, and jungles the continent is known for. No, as usual, it also had to do just as much with the women I met along the way—and one in particular—that really put my travels over the top.

Upon landing in Buenos Aires at the beginning of my trip, I expected to see the jungle all around me when I deplaned. Not so, as it turned out. It was just flat countryside with the airport located about a two-hour taxi ride from the city itself, depending on traffic. Passing by a wasteland of old factory buildings and junkyards, I didn't see one tree on the way into town. Now I was really confused— where was the jungle?

Finally arriving at the hotel I had reserved in the middle of the city, I quickly realized that Buenos Aires was nothing but a sterile, massive city with nary a vine or wild animal to be found. As obvious as that may sound, I was nonetheless stunned. Whenever I looked at a globe or a world map back home, it always showed South America being solid green from the north all the way down to the bottom. So I just figured the whole continent was one big jungle. That's how naïve I was.

After leaving Buenos Aires and visiting the breathtaking Iguazú Falls, which makes Niagara Falls look like a tiny dripping faucet in comparison, I made my way to fabled Rio de Janeiro, hungry to explore its infamous nightlife. I asked the young assistant manager at my hotel about where I might go to hear some real Brazilian music and find some friendly senoritas and told him that I could use a guide. He saw this as a great opportunity and told me he spoke several languages and that he knew all the best places in town. If I would pay for everything—the drinks, taxis, and tips—then he would present the Rio that you only read about in novels. It sounded great to me; now I had my own personal guide.

Meeting up that evening after he got off work, my new friend, Otto (of all things) and I grabbed a taxi and off we went into the night. Short and a bit bald, but not unattractive I suppose, Otto was very intelligent, speaking several languages that he had learned on his own. But he was also poor. He reminded me a little bit of the invisible sidekick, a type of guy girls never notice, so for him to be hanging out with this tall, rich (by his standards), and groovy American musician guy was a really great deal for him. He could take me to all the places that he could never normally afford to go anywhere near.

After we had a great meal in our stomachs at a fabulous local cafe Otto knew about, it was time to hit the clubs. Otto decided to take me to one of his favorite haunts, a gaudy strip club that looked like it had been imported straight out of the pre-Castro Havana of the late '50s. Small and reeking of the whiskey that had undoubtedly permanently soaked into the floorboards over the years, it had a bunch of small tables with dirty white tablecloths on them and a raised stage surrounded by a bar. Music was blasting, but it wasn't samba like I had hoped to hear, but instead some combination of salsa, rock, and bump and grind music. There were *hostesses* all over the place, too, dressed in cheap, imitation-silk evening dresses sitting and flirting with the male customers. One of them seemed to know Otto, and they chatted loudly to each other and, after a small bribe, we were seated at a table with a good view of the stage.

We had no more than ordered our drinks before the lights went down, the spotlight came up, and the mega show began. It was a sort of Vegas showgirls type of dance number, but the girls, all six of them, could hardly dance. Their costumes were terrible, and none of them could kick higher than their knees. It was quite funny, but the audience was really into it. The music was so loud that it rattled my brain, but Otto wasn't having any problem with it; I guess that's because he spoke the language and I didn't. I looked around the room and I saw girls sitting alone at the bar staring at me. They had all spotted me when I first walked in because I stuck out like a sore thumb, a head higher than anybody else there and a full beard plastered on my face. As my eyes wandered from one to the other, they all gave me their toothiest smiles.

A few moments later, one of them came out of the shadows and plopped right into Otto's lap and gave him a big wet kiss. She and Otto spoke for a moment and then he introduced her to me as his girlfriend. He told me that they had been seeing each other for some time and that they were very much in love. This was really a surprise. He asked if he could buy her a drink and I said, "Of course." In a split second there was a waitress at our table ready to take her order, sort of like it had been preplanned. Naturally, I went along for the ride.

Meanwhile, the music continued to blast away with the girls lip-syncing along to some silly salsa song while provocatively wiggling their backsides to the audience. Another hostess came walking up to the table and wanted to sit with me, but I didn't want the company. I just wanted to watch this whole spectacle. So she went away, and after a short time, another one came over and tried the same thing. I politely declined by putting my hand up in a "no thank you" gesture and she left too. Then Otto told me that I really should pick a girl to sit with me because his girlfriend wouldn't be able to stay if I didn't. It suddenly became apparent to me that his *girlfriend* wasn't just hanging out; she *worked* there.

Otto's gal pal was a hostess, not a bank teller or a secretary. This shed a new light on the situation because I realized that maybe he thought the girl loved him. He loved her, but it was clearly a business arrangement, at least on her end. She wouldn't have been sitting there if he and I weren't willing to buy drinks and spend money. So I looked around the room and tried to find one girl who didn't look like a shark stalking its prey.

Finally spotting a young lady who appeared sort of innocent (ha!) and whose makeup wasn't quite as heavy as that of the other girls, I pointed her out to Otto. He then told his girlfriend and she went over to talk with the girl for a moment, who got very excited to be picked over the others. The two came back and the girl sat down next to me, whereupon I asked if she would like something to drink. Of course, she didn't understand one syllable I spoke. No matter, the waitress was there in the blink of an eye with my date's drink in hand.

So there I was, sitting in a Rio club with my new friend Otto and two hostesses, watching the worst stage show I had ever seen through a cloud of cigarette smoke with music blasting my brain to shreds and people shouting and screaming with delight. Everybody was having a great time, including me, in some weird way.

It was now about two or three in the morning, and over the noise of the music, Otto told me his girlfriend wanted to spend the night with him but she couldn't go with him unless she got paid. Surprise—the chick was a hooker!

Suddenly, I found myself caught in a peculiar situation. If I didn't pay for Otto's girlfriend to have sex with him, then he wouldn't get laid. I could see that he was really hot for this girl, but I sure didn't want to go to some hotel with him and sit in the lobby while he went upstairs for an hour or two. So I decided to also pay for the girl sitting next to me, who was looking at me with longing eyes that said, "Don't leave me here; take me, take me, please!"

As a matter of record (and pride), I would like to state here and now that I was always the guy who never paid for sex. Ever. That was for other people. My philosophy was that if I couldn't get a girl without paying, then I didn't deserve her to begin with. And up to that point in my life that was true; I had never paid for sex. Of course, I routinely paid for a lot of dinners, movies, plays, and gifts. But there never had been a time when I needed to slap down a wad of cash on a nightstand in order to get it on with somebody. So for the first time in my life, I not only paid for a hooker, I paid for two.

After leaving the club, Otto hailed us a taxi, we all piled into a miniature car of some sort, and, after some conversation, wound up at another hotel. We walked in, and I paid for two separate rooms. Otto and his love went off to theirs to enjoy a night of bliss in each other's arms. I, on the other hand, headed to my/our room filled with trepidation. For one thing, I didn't know what to expect. There I was, thirty-two years old and feeling like a virginal school kid, scared to death and not knowing how to act. My girl, however, had no such problem. Evidently, this hotel was well known to the girls back at the club.

As cliché as it may sound, our room actually had a round bed in it and a mirror on the ceiling, like something out of a cheap Russ Meyers sexploitation flick from the '60s. The place didn't smell too bad, and it looked as though it had been recently cleaned, maybe within the last week. So at least there was that.

But I was still having a lot of confusing feelings. Yes, I was strangely excited, though, quite honestly, also scared. I had never been with a prostitute before, and maybe I wasn't such a great lover. How would I do in such a situation? To compound matters, I wasn't really attracted to this girl, though she seemed to be into it. Of course, that was just her act, I'm sure. More than likely, she would have much rather been back at the bar drinking martinis with her fellow hostesses. But sex for pay was her job, and she was making the best of it.

In getting down to business with the Brazilian hooker, I tried to do everything right, but it all went embarrassingly wrong. I simply couldn't perform. The whole situation seemed so ridiculous that I just didn't feel at all turned on. After a few hours of nothing on my end, Otto and his girl mercifully knocked on our door and said it was time to go. They both looked surprisingly happy and content. I guess love comes in all shapes, sizes, and prices. At about 5:00 a.m., Otto and I hailed a taxi and dropped the girls at their apartment building. From there, I went back to my own hotel room and gratefully fell face first on my bed. What a night.

While having lunch alone the next day at the café in my hotel, I noticed a young dark-haired woman in a business suit sitting alone at a table nearby. As I watched her for a while, I noticed that nobody came to join her. She saw me looking at her and smiled ever so slightly in a shy sort of way, which is all it took. Did I ever mention that I'm a sucker for that kind of thing? I have a definite weakness for gentle, innocent women.

Having nothing to lose at this point, with my only other option being to go back to the strip club with Otto and pay for another night with the girls, I got up and walked over to this striking young woman. After introducing myself, I felt like an idiot, especially when she replied, "I don't speak English" in Portuguese. It had never even occurred to me that every single Brazilian wasn't automatically conversant in my native tongue. The arrogance or ignorance of a typical American tourist, I guess.

Yet this creature was so beautiful, so classy, and most crucially, so by herself, I then came up with the brilliant idea to ask the waiter to translate for me and called him over. Through him I was able to tell her who I was, where I came from, and other basic information. She listened intently and said in return that her name was Maria and that she was a recruitment executive on a business trip for a large Brazilian bank located in São Paulo. She seemed awfully young to be in such a powerful position, but then who was I to judge?

What I did know for sure was that she was gorgeous and she was smiling at me. I asked her to join me at my table, but she invited me instead to dine with her, which I did. We sat and ate, with me all the while pulling out my Portuguese/English translation book and making a fool out of myself while madly thumbing through it. Through it all, Maria remained so polite and tolerant, instantly captivating me with her charm.

After I paid for our lunches, I somehow convinced her to go with me to find a translator so we could have a real conversation. We wound up in a local bilingual travel agent's office where I found out that Maria lived in São Paulo, didn't have a boyfriend, and was actually attracted to me in return. Always leading with my heart, I began falling for her fast.

We then met again that evening for dinner and subsequently strolled back arm-in-arm to our hotel where I had plans for a night of love, lust, and romance. Maria's room was on the eighth floor and mine was on the sixth. In my mind, either would do. So we got into the elevator and asked the operator to take us to floor number eight. He pushed the handle and up we went, the air thick with anticipation.

When we got to Maria's floor, she got out and I started to follow, but the operator suddenly, albeit politely, stopped me with a hand on my arm. He waved a finger indicating that I couldn't get off. Maria was standing there outside the elevator with a smile on her face as I stood inside looking back at her. I tried to get off again, but once more the operator stopped me, a little firmer this time. It seemed the hotel had a rule that guests could not visit each other in their rooms. It was crazy.

With my new love Maria watching and waiting, I told her to hold on, that I would somehow return to her. It was almost Shakespearean in its poignancy. I'm sure she didn't understand, or maybe she did, but it didn't make any difference. I was now on a mission.

After verifying with the front desk that I could not, in fact, visit Maria in her room, it left me stunned. Wasn't this Brazil, supposedly the land of the barely-there string bikinis and lots of free love? But never fear; I had a plan. I let the elevator operator take me to the sixth floor (my floor) where I got off and very conspicuously went to my room. The operator watched me as I turned the key in the lock and entered. Waiting a couple of minutes, I then left the room and hoofed it up the staircase to the eighth floor where I knew Maria would be waiting for me. Except that just as I stepped into the hallway, the elevator operator was standing there waiting for me, too. The conniving little bugger had outguessed me. He very nicely put up his finger again and waggled, "No, no, no!"

By now incensed, I really couldn't believe what was happening. The whole thing was becoming preposterous. And then I got mad. Cussing under my breath, I went back to my room to ponder my next move. Just two floors above was a girl who I imagined to be languorously waiting for me to knock softly on her door, only to then make mad, passionate love to her all night long. I was not going to be denied.

Figuring that the elevator operator would probably be waiting for me to make another move, I decided to wait him out. Two could play his little game. I looked at my watch and decided that in thirty minutes, I would make another break for it.

As I sat there in my room watching the minutes slowly tick by, a multitude of contradictory thoughts flashed through my mind. Should I or shouldn't I? How long do I really have to wait? Does Maria really want me or will she scream if I appear at her door? But by now I was obsessed. There was no turning back.

Finally, after exactly thirty minutes, I took a deep breath, carefully opened my door, and peeked out. Excellent. The coast was clear. Evidently, the nosy little elevator operator had decided that I was in for the night—a big mistake on his part.

Like the stealthiest of cat burglars, I tiptoed my way back up the two flights of stairs to the eighth floor. But just before entering the hallway, I decided to peek around the corner. And it was a good thing I did. For there sat the crafty elevator operator, this time having set up a chair in the hallway across from Maria's room. The guy was standing guard!

He didn't see me, but it was now clear that any nocturnal plans Maria and I may have had for that night weren't going to happen. I was certainly not going to climb out on the window ledge high above the street and then somehow mountaineer my way into her room. My ardor did have its limits.

Bursting with anger and frustration, I slowly made my way down the stairs and back to my room. I subsequently spent the rest of the night tossing and turning, wondering what I could do next to get this girl. When dawn finally came, I returned to the restaurant in hopes of somehow seeing Maria. Sure enough, shortly thereafter, in she came. We looked at each other and I'm certain she wanted me as much as I wanted her; it was that electric.

After breakfast, we once again went to the travel agent to translate between the two of us. We professed our love for each other then and there, with Maria asking me to come to São Paulo because she had to leave that very day. She was not on vacation. So we arranged for her to get me a hotel room where she could visit me, preferably without a sneaky elevator operator. With the reason for our hastily planned rendezvous hardly a mystery, the travel agent became quite flushed by the end of our conversation.

Waiting a day, I then flew to São Paulo to be with my new love. I took a taxi to my hotel and late that afternoon Maria came to me, just as I had dreamed. Hesitantly, she entered the room; she clearly had some questions on her mind, but couldn't really ask me because of the language barrier. Sensing her nervousness, I tried my best to reassure her nonverbally. I wanted her to know that my feelings were real.

Finally, after time spent hugging and kissing, we were out of our clothes. Maria was beautiful, more so than I had even imagined. Grabbing my camera, I indicated that I wanted to photograph her; amazingly enough, she consented. So I placed her in front of the curtained window and took several black and white photos of her silhouetted against the afternoon light. Maria was so willing and secure with me that I felt like I was Van Gogh painting his masterpiece. She was a natural nude model and here we were, together at last.

Putting the camera away, I then led Maria to bed. It was heaven on earth. She was so passionate, so warm, and so . . . virginal! I was stunned. The sheets had bloodspots all over them when we finished making love and she was crying. My God, I had no idea. Though I never expected this, it did make sense. Brazil was a heavily Catholic country, and from what I could gather, she had been saving herself for her husband to be. Which now seemed to be me. I understood just enough Portuguese to realize what was happening. This was a really serious thing for her to do. For me, not quite as much, although I had been caught up in the moment and was completely smitten with her.

From there, we spoke our different languages and a lot got lost in translation. At some point, she asked me if she could wear the turquoise necklace that had been around my neck for most of my trip. Of course, I said yes. I then took it off and gently fastened it around her neck. It looked just beautiful on her. It was a hand-tooled Navajo piece that I bought on tour with Sonny and Cher. So besides being gorgeous, just like Maria, it had a special significance for me as a remembrance of my time with them. In fact, I'm wearing it on the cover of this book.

Maria and I then spent the night together in each other's arms, and the next morning, she returned to work. I had a plane to catch to cross the country to Quito, Ecuador, where I planned to sail to the Galápagos Islands, which were, in fact, the main goal of my whole trip to South America.

Before parting in front of the hotel, we exchanged addresses and phone numbers. Our plan was to speak again as soon as I got home. It was clear that Maria wanted to marry me and be my wife in America. On my part, I had become so emotionally involved that I temporarily lost my mind—the notion of a future with her actually seemed like a good idea to me. True, we didn't even know each other, nor did we speak the same language. Plus, every meaningful conversation between us had come through an interpreter. But love, or at least infatuation, can be a powerful thing.

After a heartfelt goodbye between us, as Maria rode off in a taxi into the São Paulo traffic, I suddenly noticed that she still had my necklace on. I didn't mean to give it to her *permanently*; I just intended to let her wear it while we were together. For her, I think it was almost like an engagement ring or something. That was her hope. Yet, at the same time, I knew deep inside that I would never marry her, no matter how strong our connection had been.

Yes, I know how terrible that sounds; I never said I was a saint. I always tried to be a good man, but I failed miserably in that area. There were just too many attractive females out there, and I had too many opportunities. When I think back on all the wonderful women I carelessly tossed aside in my youth, I am embarrassed to admit it. I didn't deserve them, and they really didn't deserve the likes of me. They were lucky I left them. I must say, however, that not all of them were perfect, either. Many were just looking for a free ride in the fast lane of life, and I was their driver.

After leaving Maria so that I could go off to swim with the fur seals and play with the tortoises on the Galápagos Islands—and almost fly home with a wild baby Margay cat (similar to an ocelot) hidden in my pants—my wonderful trip was finally coming to its conclusion. The next day, I flew to Guatemala City and then, after spending a night there and having a few more adventures off in the jungles, it was back to Los Angeles with about thirty rolls of film to develop and enough memories to last a lifetime.

Since Maria had my turquoise necklace, I made a mental note to try to get it back once I got home. But as often happens with *summer* romances, neither of us followed up on that or anything else. Perhaps we both thought better of the idea after some time and reflection. The intensity of our short time together could never be sustained in the long run nor would we likely ever overcome what was essentially an insurmountable language barrier. And I think we both secretly knew that.

Once back from my trip, all I had as a remembrance of the lovely Maria were two black and white photos of a hauntingly beautiful girl. Tony Bennett may have left his heart in San Francisco. But I left mine, if only fleetingly, in São Paulo.

THIRTY-TWO

Duos

During the mid-'70s, I recorded two albums with the popular singing duo of Kenny Loggins and Jim Messina: *So Fine*, released in 1975 and *Native Sons*, released in 1976. In particular, I enjoyed working with Jimmy. With the pair known best for such hits as "Your Mama Don't Dance," "Angry Eyes," and "Be Free," Jim Messina was firmly in charge of all production. In that capacity, he knew exactly what he wanted and I knew I had to get it right—and fast. He was not going to wait around for any slow learners.

For me, the music was simple, but for the horn section, not so much. They insisted on writing all their own arrangements, and they were definitely not professional arrangers. The guys stayed up half the nights figuring out what they were going to play the next day. And then if it didn't work when Jimmy heard it, they had to immediately rewrite the parts in the studio while everybody else waited around. I think the horn players were insecure for some reason and were trying to write parts that were unique in order to stand out and not be just another horn section. Jimmy gave them a lot of latitude, because he could have hired any of the great arrangers that were working at that time and be guaranteed of a superior job with no problems. But he wanted to give his boys a chance.

A pleasant circumstance existed for me because Jimmy Messina lived in the town of Ojai, a beautiful artistic and agricultural enclave located around eighty miles north of Los Angeles, where he owned a beautiful ranch and recording studio complex. I had been to Ojai a couple of times before to hear the esteemed philosopher, Jiddu Krishnamurti, speak. So I knew the place fairly well. And, as an added bonus, Messina's property was only about an hour north of my home in Malibu, right up Highway 101, with the always-beautiful Pacific Ocean sparkling on my left. So it was not only a great job, but also a delightful drive.

As a side note, I must confess that Krishnamurti's book *Freedom from the Known* had a profound effect on my perception of the world and in some ways changed my life. After reading it many times over, I actually contacted the publisher directly and ordered twenty copies. Over the years, I gave every one of them to friends and others that I thought would find it interesting with the proviso that they return the book after reading it. But I never received one copy back. I guess that once read, the book was hard to let go of. That was OK though. I never expected anyone to return it after reading, anyway. It's just that sort of book.

One image that especially stands out in my mind while working with Loggins and Messina, aside from Kenny's fantastic vocal abilities, is the infamous redwood hot tub that Jimmy had installed. That hot tub was one of the best features on the property, at least as far as I was concerned, because that's where Lynda Carter and I spent many long and luxurious clothing-optional hours when she came up to visit me.

Lynda and I had been lovers on and off for several years, and she had just recently won the lead role in the TV series *Wonder Woman*. She was really busy shooting in Hollywood, so it was no easy task to get her to come all the way up to Jimmy's ranch. I think the deal-clincher came when I told her I was recording with Loggins and Messina. Being a big fan of theirs, that piqued her interest to the point where she couldn't refuse.

However, having the voluptuous, raven-haired Lynda there was not the best political move I could have made. I thought Kenny and Jimmy would be happy to meet her, and indeed they were. But I hadn't thought it completely through regarding what Jimmy's wife, Jenny Sullivan (the daughter of actor Barry Sullivan), might think about the former Miss World-USA

(Lynda) staying overnight in what was her territory. I think Jenny wasn't feeling too glamorous around then because she was working hard helping Jimmy with the logistics of feeding everybody at the ranch and pretty much running the place while he recorded. So having Lynda show up and command the attention of literally every male on the ranch didn't make me the most popular guy with her.

Kenny, though, was very cool about it; he was used to beautiful women in his life, so no problem there. And Jimmy was madly in love with Jenny. However, I do remember that Jimmy did wander out to the barn late one evening to visit with us while we were soaking in the hot tub. He ogled and charmed the clearly topless Lynda, who in turn enjoyed the conversation and attention. Everybody ran around naked in those days, anyway. We were pretty much all just one step removed from being hippies in some ways. It was the wild and free '70s—what can I say?

While up at the ranch, Jenny Messina prepared all the meals for everybody, so we ate breakfast, lunch, and dinner together in the dining room. The table was set up like an old-fashioned ranch house, and everybody sat at a long dining table where we passed the food up and down. It was a lot of fun, and I could almost make believe I was a cowboy in the Old West, just like in the black-and-white movies of my youth. Not to mention that Kenny and Jimmy were really nice, in addition to being great talents. And I loved the ranch-style atmosphere because it reminded me of our neighbor's place in Malibu where I spent so much time as a kid.

One other incident I experienced with Loggins and Messina had nothing to do with music and everything to do with pain. On a particular trip to record with them in Jimmy's studio, I brought along my favorite pet at the time, a beautiful scarlet macaw (a large red, yellow, and blue South American parrot). I thought maybe the laid-back, animal-loving Kenny and Jimmy would get a kick out of seeing him. But when I introduced my bird to Jimmy, it promptly hopped onto his arm, but lost its footing and chomped down on his arm with his powerful beak, causing a major gash and plenty of blood to flow. That was not good. Literally biting the hand that fed *me* was not the introduction I had envisioned for my brightly colored avian companion. While Jimmy went to get some much-needed first aid, I put the macaw back in his cage and whisked him out of the room.

My prized pet wasn't supposed to do such things (he never bit me), but he must have been getting old and cranky. Or maybe he just didn't want to share me with anyone. Pets, even wild ones, can be like that.

Not too long after the incident with Jimmy Messina, my feathery friend bit my mother on the foot while she was visiting me, and this time he did it on purpose. The bird was on the floor on the far side of my living room, and when he saw my mother, he waddled over, leaned in, and clamped down on her instep. My mother screamed in terror, and I once again had to grab the bird and stash him in his cage. With blood everywhere, I should have learned my lesson then and there and gotten rid of him. But it would take one more attack before I finally got the message.

Suzanne de Passe had come out to the house one day, and when I showed her the macaw, she asked if she could hold it. With some trepidation I said, "Of course." But when I tried to transfer the bird from my arm to hers, it reached out and bit *her* forearm, just like with Messina. That did it. The bird had to go. I had to sell it.

So I put an ad in the local newspaper, and in no time, a man responded. Fortunately, my macaw took to him immediately, standing on the guy's arm like he had been doing it for a lifetime. They were going to get along just fine. My bird's new owner also let me know that macaws tend to prefer the sex of the person who regularly feeds them, so that made sense as to why he went after my Mom and Suzanne (though not Jimmy—hmm...).

As the buyer walked out my front door holding the bird, it looked back at me and started speaking the only word it had ever learned (from me saying it to him whenever I left the house).

"Bye-bye, bye-bye, bye-bye," he repeated over and over in his cackling macaw voice.

And then he was gone.

It was terribly sad. He was my little buddy, after all.

But I at least experienced a measure of comfort in knowing that I had found him a good home—*and* that my friends, family, and employers would now be safe, which included another famous musical duo that I would soon come to find myself working for.

As in many professions, every move and decision made in the music business is one that offers the potential for a great step forward or perhaps a giant step sideways or even backward. Even choosing the style of music that you want to play can mean the difference between being a full-time musician and paying your bills or always needing two jobs (or more) just to exist.

For instance, through the years, I have met so many players who simply refused to play popular music. These musicians devoted their lives to playing only jazz while looking down on every other style, never bothering to find the fun in what they considered to be less sophisticated genres like rock, blues, or country—in the process, literally robbing themselves of a successful career in music.

Some of the most talented players I've ever heard never played jazz. So it's not about what style we play; it's about how good we can play in any style. And two of the best all-around musicians I ever had the pleasure of performing with were Jimmy Seals and Darrell "Dash" Crofts, better known as the hit-making 1970s singing duo of Seals and Crofts.

Being huge stars, Seals and Crofts could have hired anybody they wanted to play keyboards for them. Twelve Billboard Hot 100 hit singles, including "Hummingbird," "Summer Breeze," and "Diamond Girl," will give you that kind of clout. It just so happened that they had heard some of my work and chose me. Flattered though I was to get the call, I nevertheless had to consider whether it would be a good move on my part. Their situation was complicated (and would inevitably lead to the breakup of their band).

After I returned from my big adventure in South America, I badly needed a job, which is never good for the psyche of a musician. Being a musician is both a job and a passion, and when I was between jobs, it seemed that my whole world stopped spinning. It wasn't just the lack of a paycheck; I felt like I was missing my whole life. Intellectually, I knew that something was coming just around the corner, but that didn't help me emotionally. Every time I finished a session, I felt like I was being bucked off a horse and I didn't know how I would land. Would it be just a bruise or would I break my neck?

However, nobody bets on a horse that refuses to run, so I started writing the songs that would eventually wind up being on the *Dunn & Rubini* album. At least I could focus on that while waiting for session work from others. But before I got too far along, I received a call from Marcia Day, Seals and Crofts' manager.

Marcia told me that Jimmy and Dash were preparing for a new tour and asked if I would consider going on the road with them. She knew that studio musicians were notoriously reluctant about going on tour because of the possibility of losing clients to other musicians while out of town. Indeed, there were a long line of hopefuls and wannabes salivating at the opportunity of grabbing a session from the A-list guys; it was sort of like a pack of young wolves standing back and waiting their turn to eat until after the leader ate his fill.

However, losing my place to others was not my worry. I hesitated a bit before saying yes only because I knew it would slow the progress of my album. Marcia offered me all types of incentives while letting me know that the *boys* really wanted me as their keyboardist and de facto music director. In particular, Jimmy expressed great respect for my work and reputation. There was a lot of money involved, too, and Seals and Crofts' recording studios would be open to me, as well. It seemed like it could be a good move on my part. So I signed on. As it turned out, Jimmy and Dash even wound up singing background vocals on my *Dunn & Rubini* album. Who would have guessed a nice gift like that was going to happen?

But, as is often the case in music, when I started rehearsals with Seals and Crofts, it soon became apparent that this was going to be more of a challenge than expected. First, Jimmy was not happy with the existing drummer. On the other hand, Dash was much more easygoing and wasn't bothered like Jimmy was. Instead, what upset Dash had to do with Jimmy going nuts trying to cope with the situation.

After thinking things over, I suggested the possibility of getting Jeff Porcaro (the future Toto founder and drummer) for them. Sonny Bono and I had given the teenage Jeff his first professional gig back in 1973 with Sonny and Cher, so I knew him well. Porcaro also had played on a bunch of Seals and Crofts' early-to-mid-'70s albums, so Jimmy and Dash were well acquainted with his skills. Though in high demand in recording studios, when I told Jeff the generous dollar amount being offered, he jumped at the chance to join us on tour.

Shortly thereafter, we went into rehearsals and I memorized their show fast. It was an easy one to play, and when we got into the groove, it was a lot of fun. But there were other problems bubbling under the surface.

Both Seals and Crofts were married and their families came with them everywhere, including Marcia (who was also Dash's mother-in-law). So it was a restrictive atmosphere in that regard. As a single guy, I had no compunction about enjoying a romantic rendezvous after any given show with whichever pretty lady came my way. I think that caused some consternation with Jimmy and Dash, because while I was having a great time, they were feeling sort of locked up. They would see me with a hot girl at most every tour stop and, at a distance, I got some concerned looks. But what's a young piano player in a world-famous pop group supposed to do while on the road? Read a book?

Jimmy also had a terrible time with the onstage sound system on most nights and could not seem to get his soundman to adjust the stage speakers to suit him. They tried earphones, but that didn't work either. In fact, several different speaker setups were demoed but nothing satisfied Jimmy. Part of that was because he drank Southern Comfort to *medicinally* calm himself before the shows, which I watched him do. So his nerves were being rattled by his perceived problems with the sound system, which caused him to drink, which only served to impair him further. It was a circle of grief, and Jimmy was slowly losing it.

Once, Seals actually stopped a show right in the middle of a song because he said he couldn't hear himself. He screamed at his soundman, who was standing just offstage, and then froze when he noticed that the audience seemed mystified as to why the music had ended. Jimmy quickly apologized and we all finished. But at the conclusion of that concert, Jimmy marched down into the under-stage dressing room and right in front of me smashed his guitar against the mirrored wall in a fit of rage. In tears, he told me that nobody understood his problem. I did my best to talk it through with him and got him somewhat calmed down. Marcia then came in and worked her magic, which got us through the incident. But Jimmy now had one less guitar and an unabated fondness for Southern Comfort.

This drinking also created another problem. Both Jimmy and Dash were of the Baha'i Faith and Jimmy, in particular, had difficulty living up at least one of the standards of that religion because the rules dictated that followers were not allowed to drink. Jimmy had a hard time with that one.

While working with Seals and Crofts, I played many different types of venues, some of them quite small by rock-concert standards and some of them really large. In the smaller venues, such as high school gymnasiums, there existed no proper permanent stage set-ups, so our roadies had to construct them out of metal frames and wooden platforms. The crew would then set up all the band's amplifiers and other sound equipment, plus all the stage lighting, on these temporary structures. The lights themselves were strung high above us on metal towers that were basically just four-legged frames shaped like barstools, only much taller (usually about twenty feet in the air).

One night, a leg on one of the main lighting stands happened to be placed precariously on the edge of one of the wooden stage platforms that we all sat and stood on. A little more than halfway through the concert, with us happily rocking away, the vibrations from the intense volume of the music gradually caused the improperly placed lighting tower to shift. It finally slipped into a crack where two of the platforms were joined and began to topple. I looked up just in time, to see it tipping right toward Jeff Porcaro, who was too busy playing his drums to notice. It was like seeing an earthquake in slow motion.

At first I didn't know exactly what the lighting tower was doing. But then my brain calculated the trajectory, and I realized in that split second that Jeff was in mortal danger. I immediately stopped playing mid-song and ran around the side of my piano screaming at Jeff to get his attention. At the last moment, he saw me running toward him while pointing up to the lights as they were coming down. Jeff sort of simultaneously jumped and fell backward off his drum throne just as the whole thing came crashing down right onto his kit. Had it hit him, he surely would have been severely injured or even killed.

As you might imagine, the show came to a screeching halt as Jimmy and Dash turned around to see what I was yelling about and why the keyboards and drums had gone silent. Some girls in the audience were screaming, and the crew rushed over to see if Jeff was okay. Fortunately, he only had a couple of bruises from falling. So aside from being in shock from realizing that he had almost been crushed to death, he was fine.

Thankfully, we all came through the horrifying incident unscathed, with the exception of a few bumps and bruises on Jeff's derrière. Jimmy and Dash made an announcement that everybody was fine and we would continue the show just as soon as the roadies could get the mess cleaned up. Once Jeff was able to reconstruct most of his kit, we started the song over to a huge round of applause and everyone breathed a big sigh of relief, including those in the audience that saw it all go down.

Sadly, that tour was to be one of the last times I ever saw Jeff Porcaro. Not too long after the Seals and Crofts tour, Jeff and his band, Toto, became huge stars in late 1978. He then unexpectedly passed away from a heart attack in 1992 at the age of only thirty-eight after spraying some insecticide in his yard. Apparently, his family history included weak hearts.

But I will always remember Jeff Porcaro as someone who was a bundle of laughs, a wonderful pal, and forever charismatic. Rest in peace, my dear friend. You were the best rock studio drummer of your era.

THIRTY-THREE

Dunn & Rubini

You know, it's funny, I don't remember exactly how I first met Don Dunn, but the introduction that likely came sometime in the early-to-mid-'70s would certainly prove to be fateful. Don had been the "Dunn" of a late 1960s pop/rock duo named Dunn and McCashen, best known for having written a song together that José Feliciano turned into a minor hit in 1968, called "Hitchcock Railway" (the same tune that Joe Cocker would later cover, becoming an FM AOR favorite throughout the '70s).

Although not soulful, Dunn was a pretty good singer and lyricist, so I proposed that we start a writing partnership. If we could come up with some strong material, I would produce (which means I would pay for) an album and try to get us a recording contract. If I couldn't sell our combined effort to a label, then Don wouldn't owe me anything. The risk would be all on me. And I was willing to bet a lot of money that I could produce something that might not only get us a deal, but also maybe even a hit record or two to boot.

Don didn't have any money to speak of, so I wound up supplementing his income and helping him survive while we worked on our material. He had binders full of unfinished lyrics, and I spent hours with him going through all his previously written ideas, punch lines, hooks, and titles. After what seemed like an eternity, we finally had about twenty songs ready to go. So I started buying studio time, hiring my musician friends, and producing our album-to-be. This was happening while at the same time I still

259

worked as a session musician, producer, arranger of commercials, and also the touring keyboardist with the hit singing duo, Seals and Crofts.

Since I didn't have the financial luxury of locking Dunn and myself up in a studio for six months straight with a set group of backup musicians, I had to use whoever I could find available in a particular timeframe. This led to a situation where I employed lots of different musicians on different songs. If you look at the credits on the final product, *Diggin' It*, from 1976, you'll see that there were about a dozen different guitar players, several bass players, a few drummers, and lots more. I could never get the same group of guys together for multiple dates.

Another reason for that was because I wanted to go into the studio whenever we had a finished song and get it down on tape. Perhaps if I would have had fifteen or so great songs all finished and ready to go early on, I could have scheduled a series of dates and gotten the album recorded both faster *and* with the same group of musicians. But Don's maddening, snail-like pace and inconsistency as a lyricist made that impossible. So we inched along, and over the period of about six months, we finally, some-how, finished the album.

Since the *Diggin' It* project was so very important to me and because I had put so much money into it, I felt that I needed something more to help sell it to a label. So I decided to make a video, which was a bit of a pioneering notion on my part. Remember, this was about five years before MTV came along and music videos were not the expected entities they became during the '80s. All of which left me in more or less uncharted creative waters.

After asking around, I found a cameraman that happened to be the boyfriend of my half-niece, Toni, who agreed to shoot a film of Don, me, and our band doing a live performance, although we would be just lip-syncing (miming) to the pre-recorded tracks. I looked high and low for an affordable venue where we could shoot this video and wound up renting the Fox Venice Theatre, an Art Deco house that had opened in 1951 to much fanfare, but had seen better days long before we got there.

Renting the place for one day, I then sent out invitations to everybody I knew and even to some I didn't know, inviting one and all to come on down for a big party and to be part of our film. We got almost a whole theatre-full of bodies in there that day, too, which was saying something. With a capacity of 1003 seats, it was like a real concert. And I provided food and drinks for everyone. I also hired five of the musicians who played on the album to recreate their roles as the stage band. As an aside, I got my good Malibu friend, Dennis Dragon, to play the drums that day. Dennis is Daryl Dragon's brother, who you may remember as being the male half of the hit-making '70s pop duo, Captain and Tennille.

We set up the playback system and on cue started singing to our pre-recorded tracks. The audience hooted and hollered as though we were big rock stars while we sang our hearts out and everyone had a total blast. There were close-up shots of me sweating, singing, and beating my hands on the piano keys. Our makeup lady even had the ingenious idea of putting rhinestones on all my fingers so that my hands would flash like diamonds in the spotlights. My hair had been all puffed up, too, so I had this big Afro hairstyle going on. The costumer (i.e. the makeup lady) also sewed a fancy silk tie-dyed shirt for me with no buttons on the front so my chest would be exposed.

Covered with what I would call "glam" makeup (think early David Bowie or maybe Marc Bolan from T. Rex), I was a rock idol that day, baby. Mick Jagger had nothing on me. After running through each song about two or three times to get all the necessary camera angles, we were there for about four hours filming and about four additional hours setting up and breaking down all the equipment. As exhilarating as it was, I was one beat puppy at the end of that day.

Afterward, it cost me about four grand more for the cameraman to cut the whole thing and then sync the video footage with the corresponding songs. That was a lot of money back then, but I was committed to making the project the best it could be. The guy also said it would be ready within two to three weeks, definitely no more than a month. He planned to cut it all together when he wasn't filming his other projects, which sounded reasonable to me.

As it turned out, I don't know who the bigger fool was, him or me. A month went by and the video editing wasn't even half done. He then made excuses, saying it was a lot more work than he thought it would be and naturally he needed more money, which I gave him. After that, a second month went by, then another. The budget doubled. It finally reached the point where I almost became violent with him, which did the trick. When the cameraman saw murder in my eyes, he got the message fast and finished all the editing in short order. And I was delighted; I finally had my biggest sales tool, my first music video!

Now that my/our album and video(s) were ready, I decided to send the results out to some of the major labels to see what response I might get. In the meantime, in a stroke of good fortune, I ran into one of the guitar players from our album over at Motown Records (where I was doing a session) who asked me if the project was done yet. At that very moment, who should step into the studio but Berry Gordy himself, the founder and Chairman of Motown. Since the microphones were still hot (i.e. on) out in the tracking room where we were, Mr. Gordy overheard my friend's question to me over the speaker in the control room.

When all the musicians, including me, took a break, Berry walked right up to my piano, sat down next to me on the bench, and introduced himself. It stunned me that the one and only Berry Gordy was now sitting next to me as if he were an old friend. Putting his arm around my shoulders, he proceeded to tell me how much he enjoyed listening to me play. Then he got down to business: he wanted to know if I was making an album. When I told him that I was, Berry asked if I had shown it to anybody. When I said no, he replied that he wanted me to bring it to him as soon as possible, before I took it anywhere else, which was a huge surprise for me. About the last place I would have ever thought about shopping my album would have been Motown. As far as I knew, their roster contained only black artists. And I was white.

At the end of the recording session (which was for a Diana Ross song), I decided to walk into the control room to find out just where I should bring my album when it was ready. Berry didn't give me his business card or any other way of contacting him.

Standing there behind the console was a tall, tawny beauty with a mane of wavy auburn hair who smiled at me and asked if she could be of help. I introduced myself and she said, "I know who you are," which was another surprise, since I had no idea who she was. Assuming she was *somebody*, given her obviously professional demeanor, I told her about my conversation with Mr. Gordy and asked if she knew where I should drop off my record. Without hesitating, she replied, "You bring it to me. I'm Suzanne de Passe. I'll see that it gets to Mr. Gordy." And that's how I met Suzanne, who would soon become one of the most influential and powerful women in show business.

Although I didn't know it at that moment, my relationship with Suzanne de Passe was going to become a long, passionate, and difficult one on both a romantic and professional level for several years to come. Suzanne was the type of woman who could take over a room just by entering it. All the men's eyes would turn toward her even if they had wives or girlfriends on their arms. She had a gorgeous smile, magnetic personality, and was smarter than any two rocket scientists put together.

Suzanne had been *discovered* by Berry when she was only about eighteen and quickly became his creative assistant, meaning that he put her in charge of handling all the creative matters—records, new acts, album covers, and songs that came directly to Berry's office. Additionally, she also oversaw superstar Diana Ross's many recordings, live shows, and television appearances. It would have been a lot to handle for anyone in Suzanne's position, but then again, she was never just *anyone*. Rising fast through the ranks to become the head of the whole creative division of Motown Records by the time I met her in 1976, Suzanne was a force to be reckoned with. She told me right then and there that if I made a deal with Motown, I would be making it with her.

As it turned out, Suzanne was a delight to work with and Motown did indeed buy my record. Not long after, Suzanne and I started seeing each other in much more than an artist/label kind of relationship. We became quite an item at Motown, which had its good and bad points. It was great for me to have an in-house champion, but it was bad in terms of the jealousies among other employees. Some felt I had only gotten my deal because I was dating the boss, which was infuriating because I only started dating her sometime after our deal was signed.

Once finished with *Diggin' It*, I presented the album and video to Motown. I met with Suzanne in her office, and she listened to some of the tracks and then rather abruptly said, "Leave this with me. I will be seeing Mr. Gordy soon, and we will discuss this and I will get back to you." I left the meeting wondering if I had made a good impression and if she liked what she heard. She was very pleasant and upbeat, but I couldn't read her. A few days later, her secretary called me and said, "Ms. de Passe would like to meet with you." I was, of course, nervously thrilled and chilled at the same time. What did it mean?

As our appointment began, Suzanne got right to the point.

"Here is the deal," she began, smiling. "We want to sign you, not only as an artist, but also as a writer and record producer. In short, we want you to work exclusively for us. We will release this album, with a commitment for a second album in the second year and pay you a quarter of a million dollars over the two years, with details to follow."

Of course, that sizable-sounding amount of money wasn't all profit, by any means. I had to pay myself back for all the costs of *Diggin' It* and the video, plus produce another album the next year. And then there was Don's fifty percent share of the deal, after expenses.

But it was still an unexpectedly generous offer, and I was beyond excited. My solo career, even if it was part of a duo, was finally happening, just like I had always dreamed. At first, Don was thrilled to see so much money, too, but unlike me, he was not good at budgeting. He now had cash to spend, and spend it he did. I don't know how much of it he blew on cocaine (pun intended), but besides getting himself a new car and some clothes, I never saw any improvement in his living condition. What I did see, however, was Don getting high most of the time.

It was exceedingly frustrating that Don and I were not able to write well together. But his drug use just made things worse. Way worse. He thought he was fine, of course. By the time we were writing for our next Motown album, *Round One*, the songs were getting harder and harder to come by. Then, Don really torpedoed any progress we might have been making on the night he attended a party I threw at my Malibu home. He got high as a kite, left the party unannounced, and crashed his new car about halfway over Malibu Canyon. Don not only totaled his vehicle, but also injured himself quite severely, enough so that he could not function at all for about two months. He finally got well enough to start writing again, but was high all the time then, too, and definitely in no way productive. It was just a disaster.

Finally, by early 1978, we somehow had enough songs to make it worthwhile to go into the studio again to cut album number two. After finishing the recording of all the instrumental tracks, we started to overdub (i.e. record) the vocals on top of them. And that's when the reality of Don's condition became apparent to one and all.

Singing lead one day in the studio, Don could barely even squeak out his vocal. After letting him adjust his headphones, I reset the volume levels to his liking, got him a glass of water, and we tried it again—still to no avail. The problem was twofold: not only could Don Dunn not sing, there was no life or attitude in his presentation. It was as if he had no interest or maybe didn't understand what we were doing. I tried everything I could to get him in the mood, but he was like a limp rag with no energy, no voice, no nothing. Having had months to prepare his vocals, he clearly hadn't done anything. It just made me sick. I really didn't know what to do, but I did know that I was not a lead singer and could not do the vocals by myself.

With my head spinning as I saw my cherished solo career dissolving before my eyes (and ears), I made a mix of the first song with Don's vocal on it and rushed it back to the Motown office to play it for Suzanne de Passe. In my mind, I saw the cancellation of our contract looming and maybe a lawsuit for damages, as well.

Suzanne, bless her heart, listened intently to Don's vocal performance and then sat back in deep thought for a moment. Nothing ever seemed to throw her.

"Stop worrying so much, Michel," she finally offered. "We'll work it out."

Yes, it was definitely bad news as far as Don was concerned, but Suzanne would take care of it. She was marvelous that way. When presented with a problem, she would think about it until she came up with a solution. She never let anyone or anything beat her down, and she definitely wasn't going to let Don Dunn be the cause of problems for me or her or Motown.

Suzanne ultimately came up with a plan that saved the album and me almost on the spot. There was a young singer/songwriter named Chuck Smith that had been angling to become a solo artist at Motown. Suzanne liked his voice and saw him as the perfect replacement for Don. So she brought Chuck in, we all had a meeting, and Suzanne promptly signed him to a recording contract. Chuck then joined our group and sang all the lead vocals that Don would have done if he hadn't been so strung out on coke and whatever else he was taking.

Suzanne also changed the group's name from "Dunn & Rubini" to "Friendly Enemies," an appropriate name given the situation we were in.

Her plan was to release this next album, *Round One*, and then when it came time to renew our contracts, she would keep me and maybe Chuck, but Don was done. That way I could move forward either with or without Chuck, depending on the success of the *Friendly Enemies* album, and I would no longer be connected to or dragged down by Don Dunn. Thank, God.

After the release of the *Round One* album, Don and I were officially through as a team. It was the sad end of what could have been a great rock career for both of us if he had just had the discipline to stay away from drugs. Though my two albums for Motown didn't sell as well as I had hoped, due mainly to a lack of marketing, I nevertheless went on to produce other Motown acts, write more commercials, and arrange lots of sessions for other artists.

Then, in 1980, came my biggest break yet: writing the score for my first feature film.

THIRTY-FOUR

Into the Eighties

S omewhere during the late-1960s is when I first met David Winters. We worked on a lot of TV shows together where I played piano and he danced and/or choreographed. His career was gaining momentum, and in 1970, he directed the Raquel Welch special that I had also been called to play on (what a coincidence!). We were both climbing the ladder of success and worked together fairly frequently. But in 1979, David Winters made an offer that would change my career forever.

He called me and asked to have a meeting. That's when he told me he was directing a new movie entitled *Racquet* and asked if I would be interested in composing the music for it. Though I had not yet written for a full-length feature film at this point, I had done a lot of commercials and I had also composed the music for an industrial film, so I basically knew the ins and outs. Better yet, David said it would be simple; it was mainly just rock-and-roll stuff and should be a piece of cake. So I told him I would be delighted.

David then asked if I could deliver the music for twenty-five thousand bucks, all in, and still make a profit. I thought about it and decided that I could. Even if I didn't make any money out of the project, I would at least have my first full-length feature film credit under my belt.

So I took the job and went to work. I stayed home and wrote the whole score in a month, which took a lot of concentration and imagination. We then booked the TTG Recording Studio in Hollywood, had two back-to-back recording sessions in one day, and the music was finished. I gave David the master tapes, he duly handed me a check, and the deal was done.

In addition to the pay, I found that I liked the whole setup; all I had to do was please one person, the movie's director. The music didn't have to be a hit, it didn't have to be run by quality control at the record company, it didn't have to be OK'd by the label's promotion men, and it didn't have to be accepted by the programming director at a radio station, and finally, it didn't have to be bought by a million people to be successful. This was something I could really get into. And into it I got.

After finishing *Racquet*, I wanted to do it again, but I was up against a lot of stiff competition. There were a lot of composers and only so many films being made each year. It was around that time that a friend told me about a new type of synthesizer called the Synclavier Digital Music System that could do anything except maybe fly to the moon. He thought I should see it because, as he said, "Someone with your talent could really make use of an instrument like that." He knew the West Coast sales representative, a man named Denny Jaeger, who wanted to meet me. So off to San Francisco I flew to meet Denny and see this new wonder machine.

Denny was very cordial, and he showed me the Synclavier housed in his small recording studio. After the demonstration, I was really impressed and thought that this could really be the key to scoring more films. I made a deal with Denny for us to work together by splitting any income fifty-fifty. I would do all the composing, and he would supply the Synclavier and the studio. Together, we then recorded a demo tape to showcase my composing skills and for Denny to have as a sales tool to sell more units.

Denny already had a lot of commercial clients coming to his studio, so we started working together right away. I had taken the demo and passed it on to several heads of music at the major film companies. When I told them that there were no musicians on the tape, that it was just me playing the Synclavier, they were amazed.

MGM's music department head, Harry Lojewski, was so impressed with the tape that he sent it on to the famous director, Tony Scott, who was in London at the time making the final cut of the film *The Hunger* starring Catherine Deneuve, David Bowie, and Susan Sarandon. Tony listened to the tape and fell in love with the music, so much so that he started cutting pieces of it into the film. By the time they were finished editing, they had filled up about half the picture with my music. Tony was then left in the position of finding somebody to finish the music for the film, and since he had already used so much of my music, he signed a contract with Denny and me to do just that.

By the time *The Hunger* came out, I was on a roll, now writing the music for a TV series called *The Powers of Matthew Star*. However, I was not getting along with Denny Jaeger. He was very controlling in his studio and had an idea of perfection that was out of touch with reality. He made the Synclavier sync everything together in order to keep everything in exact time. Which sounds great in the abstract, except that it was *too* perfect. No musician on the planet can keep perfect time all the way through a song and that is one of the biggest drawbacks of relying on a synthesizer to compose the music; they lack a human feel, often sounding robotic.

Denny and I had gotten to such a low point arguing over this issue that the fun had evaporated for me. So one day, after a particularly disagreeable spat between us about where a note should fall, I announced to Denny that I was through and going back to Los Angeles. He couldn't believe it at first, but finally got the message; our working relationship was over.

The Hunger quickly became a cult classic and generated a lot of work from producers and directors that saw it. They wanted me to score their films too. A well-known team of producers, Riff Markowitz and Lewis Chesler, were among those that saw it and decided that I just *had* to be the composer for their new HBO series, *The Hitchhiker*. Riff and Lewis became a couple of my biggest fans (and good friends) for years to come. That series, in turn, generated even more jobs for me, and on and on it went (including playing piano in the house band for many years during the '80s on the game shows *Name That Tune* and *Face the Music*). I was in one studio or another practically every day and night.

In addition to my personal projects, my studio also generated income from doing sound effects for TV shows, including the first two seasons of *Northern Exposure*. In fact, I was beginning to find it difficult to get into my studio to do the music for my *own* projects. Since the sound effect jobs were always done in the daytime, I became relegated to using the place late into the night. That was something I didn't count on and really didn't like. Many times I found myself sleeping on the couch in my control room. My engineer would arrive in the morning and wake me to get me out of there before the clients showed up for that day's work. I was starting to pay a pretty heavy price for the extra money the studio was generating.

In the middle of all the scoring work that came pouring in, I received a call one day in November of 1982 from my next-door neighbor in Hawaii, a fellow by the name of Merril Beck, who was a professor at Leeward College in Oahu. Merril looked after my home when I wasn't there, and he also parked his Jeep under my house so that the place would look like it was occupied all the time. He hardly ever called me, so it was a bit unusual when I picked the phone and he said, "Hi Michel, it's Merril. Have you heard about the hurricane we are having here?"

Unbeknownst to me, Hurricane Iwa had slammed into the Islands and my house took a direct hit. The winds were so strong that they blew my home right off its foundation and it fell onto Merril's Jeep. I was stunned, to say the least. With my head buried in work, I had little clue about the outside world. I told him I would come over as soon as possible, but I was under the gun to finish an episode of a series and I had to stay in the studio and finish it before I could do anything. I was going crazy; I had the producers waiting for the music and my house had just collapsed.

The minute I finished the episode and delivered the music, I flew over to Oahu only to find half my house sitting in the sand and the other half propped up by the roll bar in Merril's Jeep. The house was tilted at a 30-degree angle and all my furniture was smashed. I felt like I had just been sucker-punched by George Foreman. Fortunately, my insurance paid for nearly everything, and I literally remodeled my home out of the proceeds. I had taken a room at the Kuilima Hotel and stayed there for about two months while the repairs were being made.

Finally, after everything was back in order, I flew home to L.A. and went back to work on my own personal hamster wheel of music. I felt like I was doing the same thing over and over: working in the studio, going to the gym when I could, and then having the occasional date. At the time, I had very little personal life and felt lonely. Whenever I had some extra time on my hands, I would fly back over to my home on Sunset Beach in Hawaii and try to relax. Even there, I knew few people, so some nights I would just drive into Waikiki and cruise around in the car by myself. Female-wise, I had a few flings here and there, but nothing that developed into a real relationship. It was a hard time for me. I wanted a companion.

However, I did come to know one woman who was quite out of the ordinary. I met her at a party thrown by one of my few friends on the island, Ric Marlowe. Ric was a bon vivant musician/actor and lyricist best known for writing the words to the hit, "A Taste Of Honey." With the Beatles and everyone else recording it, that song generated so much income for Ric that he just lived the life of Riley on the island and supplemented his income by selling a little island ganja from time to time. For years, he rented a beach house near Koko Head crater and threw some of the wildest parties ever. As I mentioned earlier, he and I even wrote one song together called "Only Love Can Get You in My Door" that Jerry Lee Lewis recorded for his *Country Class* album in 1976.

Anyway, so there I was at Ric's house by myself one night during a party, and he introduced me to a half-Japanese, half-American young woman who wanted to meet me. Her name was Yuki Berenson (well, okay, not exactly—her real name has been changed here to protect the innocent) and she was charming, amazingly energetic, and beautiful. Apparently, she wanted to personally welcome me to Hawaii. I guess she could see that I was dateless and maybe felt sorry for me.

Yuki and I chatted for a while, and then she asked me to meet her the next day for lunch. She said that she wanted to prepare a real Japanese lunch for me, so I stayed overnight at Ric's, and the next day I rendez-voused with her, as requested. Yuki took me to a local Japanese food court (which I had never experienced before) and she picked out a number of delicacies and put them into a picnic basket she brought with her. She then drove me up into the mountains far above Honolulu through a botani-cal paradise and tropical rainforest, where she finally stopped at Tantilus Lookout, which is an extinct volcano crater that overlooks all of Honolulu and the vast Pacific for as far as you can see. I had never been there, and she wanted to show it to me.

We got out of the car, she grabbed her picnic basket and a bottle of Dom Perignon that she had stashed behind her seat, and guided me to a secluded spot. Things were getting better by the minute.

Without question, Yuki was the most interesting and complicated per-son I had ever met on the Island. There seemed to be layer after layer to her. After she spread a blanket and laid out all the food, I opened the champagne and we toasted the day and our meeting. After that, we ate and drank and just had a wonderful time getting to know each other. Once we finished and put all the food away, Yuki suddenly stood up and then languorously removed all of her clothes in front of me. Yes, that's right—she was now totally naked, with only the sunshine and blue sky as her backdrop. From there, stunning little Yuki proceeded to give me the kind of royal Hawaiian welcome that we mere mortals only read about in South Pacific novels.

After our glorious back-to-nature romantic tryst, Yuki and I contin-ued to see each other regularly and had a lot of fun, maybe too much. She seemed to be a really energetic girl with a lot of cash to spend, except she had no job. I thought perhaps she came from a rich family or something, but that proved to not be the case. As it turned out, Yuki was a coke dealer. But not just any coke dealer; she supplied the biggest dealer on the island with ounces at a time. She was way too paranoid to deal small amounts to friends or customers, so she only sold to this one guy. Where she got her supply, I'll never know. She simply told me that she was doing it temporarily, that she had sold it in her past life but had also become addicted and then stopped for a long time. But now she needed a little money so she was back at it again. Yuki told me I didn't need to worry about her because she would never become addicted.

Naturally, I was both nervous and skeptical. I didn't want anything to do with all this, but Yuki seemed to have her act together. As long as I wasn't involved in her business, I thought I could continue to date her. Except, that plan didn't work out too well because she started snorting again, with it getting the better of her little by little. She boiled it in her kitchen and then smoked the rocks. Yuki was a full-blown crack addict who went downhill really fast, faster than I could keep up with.

One day I came over and found her passed out on the bed with almost a kilo of coke on her desk and thousands of dollars just scattered around her. I couldn't wake her completely, but she was able to give me the name of the hospital she wanted to go to. So I dragged her to my car and took her there and dropped her off. She went into treatment (again), and I said a sad farewell to her.

Such was my short-lived island romance, originally so full of promise, yet torn apart by drug abuse. It was not at all what I had in mind from my island princess. But life goes on.

Following my Yuki experience, I moved forward to continue my film and TV composing career, all the way up until 2003, when I finally decided that twenty years in a windowless recording/production facility was enough. After all, how many more years did I have on the planet? I decided it was time to get some fresh air and enjoy the fruits of my labor.

THIRTY-FIVE

The Wrecking Crew

W e never had a name, at least at first.

Those of us in the Wrecking Crew, the small, elite group of now-famous session musicians that I played with and was part of in the Los Angeles recording studios during the '60s, never thought of ourselves as having any sort of official designation. That came later.

While it's true that I knew the guys I was working with day in and day out were the cream of the crop, many of them being the best rhythm and solo players in the world, we really never talked about names. It was always just the *guys*. Of course, we all knew that something special had happened to us, that we were all so very fortunate to be part of a select group of musicians that played on hit record after hit record. None among us took anything for granted, either. It went without saying that if we didn't perform up to expectations, it would end—somebody newer and better could easily replace us.

It would be easy for me to go on and on about how wonderful my time in the Wrecking Crew was. When I first started getting calls from producers to play alongside them, I was absolutely amazed at some of the faces I saw sitting across the room—famous players like guitarists Herb Ellis, Barney Kessel, and Tommy Tedesco; bassists Ray Brown, Lyle Ritz, and Joe Osborn; pianists Don Randi, Mike Melvoin, and Leon Russell; trumpet players Ollie Mitchell and Tony Terran; French horn player Bill Henshaw; percussionist Emil Richards; and the esteemed rock-and-roll drummers

Hal Blaine and Earl Palmer. These were all world-class musicians, and there I was, somehow, tossed into the mix with them.

Most of them have passed on from this earthly plane by now, and I can't express how saddened I am whenever I hear of another one going. It's like my old friends are leaving me one by one, and I can't do anything to stop it. It makes me think about my own mortality, because one of these days it will be my turn. But until then, I will continue to rock on.

My Wrecking Crew pals and I were all different types of personalities, too. But we had one thing in common; we strived to be the best in the world, twenty-four hours a day, while at the same time delivering whatever style of music we were called on to play one hundred percent perfectly on a moment's notice.

Some of my fellow Wrecking Crewers were quiet, several were extroverts, some were comedians, and still others were a bit crazy. Hal Blaine always had a serious look on his face, but he could deliver one-liners almost as well as Henny Youngman. On the other hand, Barney Kessel had one of the driest and funniest senses of humor I have ever heard. Howard Roberts always gave the floor to Barney, and practically never said anything during sessions except to occasionally whisper something into Barney's ear. They always sat next to each other, too.

Tony Terran made the occasional wisecrack, but the funniest thing about Tony was his compulsion to run to the payphone on every ten-minute break to call his stockbroker in order to check on his portfolio. Every time I stepped into the hallway, I would see Tony with his little book, desperately speaking to his stockbroker like the world was going to end. When it was time to go back inside the studio to play, I could see the pain on his face when hanging up the phone, as if he was somehow going to go broke in the next ten seconds.

Since the engineers almost always put the bass players next to the piano, I got to know them more quickly. Lyle Ritz, who played both stand-up and electric bass, used to tell me jokes between takes all the time. He was always quiet on the dates, but had a comedian's heart and timing. His humor was so dry and unexpected that he kept me doubled over in laughter.

Gene Cipriano, one of the coolest cats on the planet, and the guy who played the signature oboe part on Sonny and Cher's "I Got You Babe," would always greet me by saying, "Hey, Mike, you're out of sight!" Which always cracked me up.

There were others, too. Bill Henshaw—probably the best French horn player of all time and who recorded with all the greats, including Barbra Streisand, Peggy Lee, and, perhaps most famously, on the classic Richard Harris version of "MacArthur Park"—had such a warm personality. He was a dear friend of mine and always so polite. I loved seeing him on dates. When I started arranging and producing, I always called Bill first, hands down. He played things that were impossible for other guys to do. He also treated me like a son and taught me how to write for the horn.

Speaking of writing, Sid Sharp, the legendary concertmaster, taught me how to write for the string sections. The lovely Gayle Levant taught me how to write for the harp. Jim Horn always helped me with my horn arrangements so that I didn't make a fool out of myself. And last, but certainly not least, Earl Palmer showed me how to write an easy drum part, not like what they taught you at the Berklee School of Music at the time. Earl knew how to keep things simple and appropriate and always smoking.

Also, let's not forget about Glen Campbell. I first met him when producer Bob Keane hired Glen and me in Hollywood in the mid-'60s to help cut a series of hot rod-style rock-and-roll albums for Keane's small Del-Fi record label (all under fake group names, of course, as was the custom of the day). I was awestruck by how cool Glen was and how much fire he had under his fingers when playing his guitar, even though he couldn't read a note of music. He definitely had it all: good looks, personality, and major talent. It's easy to see why Glen became such a big star later in the decade. It was his destiny.

In short, I could go on and on about each of my Wrecking Crew friends. Suffice it to say, I remember everybody I played with, and he or she enriched my life beyond measure.

When I first started getting real sessions, not just demo records, I was the youngest guy in the room. Everyone was older than me, most by ten years or more. But, by the end of the '60s, I started noticing new faces showing up, and all of a sudden, I wasn't the new kid anymore. That was sort of a shock for me at first. Time marches on and it waits for no one, I guess.

As music evolved and new faces emerged by the dawn of the '70s, the Wrecking Crew members began to go their separate ways. A number of the guys were slowly being put out to pasture, yet they didn't know what to do about it. Some didn't even realize what was going on until it was too late and their studio work had dried up. The best players did continue to get calls for a while, but they quickly became few and far between, too. I saw it start to happen early on, and I worked very hard to ensure that this change would not negatively affect me in a financial way.

But I loved playing the sessions, nonetheless. I probably would have happily continued doing just that for the foreseeable future had it all remained just as it was in the glory days with my Wrecking Crew buddies and me, all playing and laughing and loving every minute of it.

For all those wonderful years, I thank everybody in the Wrecking Crew from the bottom of my heart. I wouldn't be writing this book without having had their presence in my life. But, you know, it's not over yet. Not by a long shot. There's a lot of music left in me. To paraphrase my old friends Sonny and Cher: the beat, does indeed, go on.

ACKNOWLEDGEMENTS

I would like to take these pages to pass along my sincere thanks to every-body who has helped me along my path. Sometimes we think that we are self-made, but that's not correct. Nobody is self-made, especially me. There have been many people who either dragged or pushed me down the road to becoming a better man.

So, thank you to

— My father and mother, who both saw that I had the innate talent to play the piano. But it was my mother who sat down next to me on the piano bench every day and made me practice. Her Norwegian knuckle sandwich in the small of my back is responsible for the great posture I have had all my life—plus a lot of bruises around L3 and L4. But never mind that...

— My brother, David Rubini, for always being so accepting of me.

— The asshole kids in school that beat me up all the time and who inadvertently taught me that there is no free lunch. You have to fight for your place in line, or you won't be in it.

— My first serious teacher, Herman Wasserman, who taught me one of the most valuable lessons in life: how to teach myself once he was gone. And gone he was when I turned just fourteen years old.

— Dale Hallcom, who at the time was the leader of the Marketts, and gave me my first real job in an actual touring rock-and-roll band. He also introduced me to Joe Saraceno who let me play on my first really serious studio sessions.

— The guys in what is now known as the Wrecking Crew, who helped me get ahead in the studios all the time. Don Randi and Mike Melvoin were two of the best friends I could have had during those years.

— My special buddy, Mike Post, who has been there since our early studio days together. He was even the best man at my first and very recent wedding. He is the consummate definition of a great friend.

— Adele Yoshioka, for the continued love, friendship, and wisdom.

— Producer/arranger Don Costa, arranger Gene Page, and producer Jimmy Bowen, who were all my biggest fans and helped me immeasurably.

— Johnny Mathis, Nancy Wilson, Barbra Streisand, and Sonny and Cher for putting their faith in me and giving me the opportunity to work with them; they could have hired anybody, but they chose me.

— Lester Sill, who gave me a huge opportunity at Screen Gems, which I totally blew. But he gracefully accepted my apology years later when we both wound up working at Motown Records.

— Every producer and director who put his or her faith in me to compose the music for all the TV shows and films I've scored over the years. I can only say thank you, thank you, and thank you!

— Suzanne de Passe, whose brilliance is utterly indescribable and who has been a shining light for me throughout the years, not to mention never holding a grudge against me for my bad behavior. When she attended the premier of the first major film I scored, *Manhunter*, she said, "I always knew you were going to make it big and here you are. I'm proud of you." Thank you, Suzanne, for everything. I hope I've lived up to your expectations.

— Kent Hartman, in regard to whom I have to say there really are no words to describe the help and support he has given me. Without Kent, I would never have written this book. He was the one who said I had to write it, and I believed him and went ahead. What a journey he has put me on.

— My lovely Cecilia, with whom the past eighteen years have flown by faster than I could have ever imagined. They have been the best of my life. I hope we have eighteen more.

ARTISTS FOR WHOM MICHEL RUBINI PLAYED KEYBOARDS AND/ OR ARRANGED (PARTIAL LIST):

Johnny Cash (movie only)

Jackson 5

Michael Jackson

Mel Carter

O'Jays

Righteous Brothers

Frank Sinatra

Don Costa

Mike Post

Jimmy Bowen

Sonny and Cher

Cher (solo)

Beach Boys

Barbra Streisand

Turtles

Frankie Valli

Diana Ross

Smokey Robinson

Mason Williams

John Wayne

Maria Muldaur

Brian Wilson

Johnny Mathis

Nancy Wilson

Junior Walker and the All Stars

Ray Charles

Twiggy

Petula Clark

Tina Turner

Ike and Tina Turner

Jim Nabors

Stanley Turrentine

Osmonds

Marketts

Ventures

Seals and Crofts

Loggins and Messina

Michael Parks

Peggy Lee

Barry White

Paul Williams

Harry Nilsson

Monkees

Byrds

Dean Martin

Chad and Jeremy

Frank Zappa

5th Dimension

Johnny Rivers

Elvis Presley

Routers

Jerry Lee Lewis

Dino, Desi & Billy

Jimmy Durante

Don Ho

Linda Ronstadt

John Davidson

Tiny Tim

Bob Keane

Darts

De-Fenders

Deuce coupes

José Feliciano

Bobby Darin

Everly Brothers

Bobby Vee

Carole Bayer Sager

Nitty Gritty Dirt Band

Jackie DeShannon

Renee Armand

Marjorie McCoy

Thelma Houston

Bobbie Gentry

Mark Lindsay

INDEX

Page numbers in *italics* indicate photographs.

The Fugitive (TV show), 63

Funny Girl (movie soundtrack), 175–177

G

the Gap Band, 228

Garrett, Snuff, 186

Gershwin, George, 14

Gilliland, Elsinore Machris, 20–21

"God Bless the Child," 183

Gold, Dave, 81

Golden, Milton, 137–138

Gold Star Recording Studios (Hollywood), 79–81, 91, 204

Gomer Pyle, U.S.M.C. (TV show), 163

Gordon, Jimmy, 58–61

Gordy, Berry, Jr., 218, 262–263

Gossett, Louis, Jr., 222

Grammy Awards, "Strangers in the Night" as Song of the Year, 96

Greene, Charlie, 82

Grofé, Ferde, 14

Gunsmoke (TV show), 63

H

Hallcom, Dale, 47, 204

Hamburg, Germany, 140–142

Hamm, Bill, 189

Hardin, Glen Dee, 173

harpsichord, 97–99, 142

Harris, Richard, 279

Harrison, George, 143

Hart, Bobby, 85–86

Hasegawa's General Store (Hana, Hawaii), 198

Haughn, Ray, 139, 141, 146, 147

Hawaii, 167, 198–200, 272–275

Hawkins, Jimmy, 63

S

U

United Recorders (Hollywood), 90, 92–96

V

Van Dyke, Dick, 70

the Ventures, 86

Viva Las Vegas (movie), 171

W

Waldorf Astoria Hotel (New York City), 83–84

Walker, Terry. *See* Rubini, Terry

Wallichs Music City (Hollywood), 44–45

Washburn, Donna, 229

Wasserman, Herman, 14–15

Welch, Raquel, 1–5, 269

West, Red, 170–171, 172

Western Recorders (Hollywood), 90

"Whole Lotta Shakin' Goin' On," 231–232

William Morris Agency, 28, 30

Williams, Roger, 225

Wilson, Nancy, *118*
    at Apollo Theatre, 161–162
    harpsichord on recordings of, 87
    horse riding accident, 156–158
    in Japan, 149–150, 156–158
    MR as musical director for, 89, 149, 182
    in Philippines, 158–161

Winters, David, 269–270

"With a Little Help from My Friends," 145

"Without You," 197

Wonder Woman (TV show), 208, 250

the Wrecking Crew, 80, 85, 90–92, *135,* 176, 190, 277–280

Y